RSF: The Russell Sage Foundation Journal of the Social Sciences

Using Administrative Data for Science and Policy

VOLUME 5, NUMBER 2, MARCH 2019

RSF: The Russell Sage Foundation Journal of the Social Sciences   ISSN 2377-8261

The Russell Sage Foundation

The Russell Sage Foundation, one of the oldest of America's general purpose foundations, was established in 1907 by Mrs. Margaret Olivia Sage for "the improvement of social and living conditions in the United States." The foundation seeks to fulfill this mandate by fostering the development and dissemination of knowledge about the country's political, social, and economic problems. While the foundation endeavors to assure the accuracy and objectivity of each book it publishes, the conclusions and interpretations in Russell Sage Foundation publications are those of the authors and not of the foundation, its trustees, or its staff. Publication by Russell Sage, therefore, does not imply foundation endorsement.

Board of Trustees

Claude M. Steele, *Chair*
Larry M. Bartels
Cathy J. Cohen
Karen S. Cook
Sheldon H. Danziger
Kathryn Edin
Jason Furman
Michael Jones-Correa
Lawrence F. Katz
David Laibson
Nicholas Lemann
Sara S. McLanahan
Martha Minow
Peter R. Orszag
Mario Luis Small
Hirokazu Yoshikawa

Mission Statement

RSF: The Russell Sage Foundation Journal of the Social Sciences is a peer-reviewed, open-access journal of original empirical research articles by both established and emerging scholars. It is designed to promote cross-disciplinary collaborations on timely issues of interest to academics, policymakers, and the public at large. Each issue is thematic in nature and focuses on a specific research question or area of interest. The introduction to each issue will include an accessible, broad, and synthetic overview of the research question under consideration and the current thinking from the various social sciences.

RSF Journal Editorial Board

Sheldon H. Danziger, Russell Sage Foundation
Mesmin Destin, Northwestern University
Shigeo Hirano, Columbia University
Maria Krysan, University of Illinois, Chicago
Michal Kurlaender, University of California, Davis
Helen Levy, University of Michigan
Cecilia Menjivar, University of California, Los Angeles
Martha Minow, Harvard University
Becky Pettit, University of Texas at Austin
Sandra Susan Smith, University of California, Berkeley
Miguel S. Urquiola, Columbia University

Copyright © 2019 by Russell Sage Foundation. All rights reserved. Printed in the United States of America. No part of this publication may be reproduced, stored in a retrieval system, or transmitted in any form or by any means, electronic, mechanical, photocopying, recording, or otherwise, without the prior written permission of the publisher. Reproduction by the United States Government in whole or in part is permitted for any purpose.

Opinions expressed in this journal are not necessarily those of the editors, editorial board, trustees, or the Russell Sage Foundation.

We invite scholars to submit proposals for potential issues through the *RSF* application portal: rsf.fluxx.io. Submissions should be addressed to Suzanne Nichols, Director of Publications.

To view the complete text and additional features online please go to **www.rsfjournal.org**.

Open Access Policy

RSF: The Russell Sage Foundation Journal of the Social Sciences is an open access journal. It is published under a Creative Commons Attribution-NonCommercial-No Derivs 3.0 Unported License.

Russell Sage Foundation
112 East 64th Street
New York, NY 10065

ISSN (print):   2377-8253
ISSN (electronic):   2377-8261
ISBN: 978-0-87154-759-0

The Bill & Melinda Gates Foundation

Guided by the belief that every life has equal value, the Bill & Melinda Gates Foundation works to help all people lead healthy, productive lives. In developing countries, we focus on improving people's health and giving them the chance to lift themselves out of hunger and extreme poverty. In the United States, we seek to ensure that all people—especially those with the fewest resources—have access to the opportunities they need to succeed in school and life.

The foundation's U.S. Economic Mobility and Opportunity Program seeks to ensure that there are more public, private, philanthropic, and academic actors working together over the next decade to dramatically increase economic mobility. We are working to increase access to better information and tools needed to tackle barriers to opportunity and develop mobility strategies at the community, state, and national levels. We are committed to partnership, innovation, research, and programmatic investments that will help more Americans to climb the economic ladder and lead fulfilling, dignified lives.

Using Administrative Data for Science and Policy

ISSUE EDITORS
Andrew M. Penner, University of California, Irvine
Kenneth A. Dodge, Duke University

CONTENTS

Using Administrative Data for Social Science and Policy **1**
Andrew M. Penner and Kenneth A. Dodge

Part I. Building Administrative Systems

The American Opportunity Study: A New Infrastructure for Monitoring Outcomes, Evaluating Policy, and Advancing Basic Science **20**
David B. Grusky, Michael Hout, Timothy M. Smeeding, and C. Matthew Snipp

Educational Opportunity in Early and Middle Childhood: Using Full Population Administrative Data to Study Variation by Place and Age **40**
Sean F. Reardon

Part II. Child Welfare

Building Connections: Using Integrated Administrative Data to Identify Issues and Solutions Spanning the Child Welfare and Child Support Systems **70**
Lanikque Howard, Lisa Klein Vogel, Maria Cancian, and Jennifer L. Noyes

Understanding Vulnerable Families in Multiple Service Systems **86**
Robert M. Goerge and Emily R. Wiegand

Part III. Neighborhoods and Housing

Poverty and Academic Achievement Across the Urban to Rural Landscape: Associations with Community Resources and Stressors **106**
Portia Miller, Elizabeth Votruba-Drzal, and Rebekah Levine Coley

Subprime Babies: The Foreclosure Crisis and Initial Health Endowments **123**
Janelle Downing and Tim Bruckner

School Climate and the Impact of Neighborhood Crime on Test Scores **141**
Agustina Laurito, Johanna Lacoe, Amy Ellen Schwartz, Patrick Sharkey, and Ingrid Gould Ellen

Using Administrative Data for Social Science and Policy

ANDREW M. PENNER AND KENNETH A. DODGE

Several years ago, the director of social services in Durham, North Carolina, came to our Durham Connects Program research team with a request for collaboration. He administered several dozen "pockets" of dollars allocated for families with young children for programs such as childcare subsidies, housing loans, and Early Head Start. His administrative data systems detailed which families received the dollars, but the files were not linked with each other and had not been used to improve accountability or impact. On our side, we had been collecting interview data from the entire population of families at birth and therefore knew what resources families needed to support their infants' healthy development. We teamed up with him, merged and analyzed the combined data files, and gained many insights (for example, some families were receiving many thousands of dollars in support but still living in poverty).

The findings were often translated into public policy. For example, the population's need for substance abuse treatment for mothers of infants far exceeded the capacity of the community's allocated resources in this domain, and so the juxtaposition of the need and the capacity was presented to the county commissioners, who then increased their allocation. In another example, a high no-show rate at the community health clinic was discovered and thought to impede delivery of health care and cost many dollars in inefficiency; interviews with mothers showed that they failed to show up because the bus did not stop in the housing project and was too expensive. So the City Council changed the bus route to be more accessible and passed an ordinance to allow anyone carrying a baby to ride the city bus for free. No-shows at the clinic declined. A bonus of this collaboration was that in return for providing useful research findings to the community, university scholars were allowed to use the data files for their research.

This case study illustrates the tremendous potential of a university-community collaboration using administrative data. In addition to the profound human service gains, administrative data infrastructure has important potential to improve cutting-edge social science research. Not only do administrative data facilitate the

Andrew M. Penner is professor of sociology at the University of California, Irvine. **Kenneth A. Dodge** is Pritzker Professor of Early Learning Policy Studies and professor of psychology and neuroscience at Duke University.

© 2019 Russell Sage Foundation. Penner, Andrew M., and Kenneth A. Dodge. 2019. "Using Administrative Data for Social Science and Policy." *RSF: The Russell Sage Foundation Journal of the Social Sciences* 5(2): 1–18. DOI: 10.7758/RSF.2019.5.2.01. We are grateful to Nicole Deterding, Thad Domina, David Grusky, Paul Hanselman, NaYoung Hwang, Ryan Lewis, Silvia Melzer, Matthew Snipp, and participants in the Russell Sage Foundation administrative data conference for useful comments and discussions. Direct correspondence to: Andrew M. Penner at penner@uci.edu, University of California, Irvine, 4181 Social Science Plaza, Irvine, CA 92697.

Open Access Policy: *RSF: The Russell Sage Foundation Journal of the Social Sciences* is an open access journal. This article is published under a Creative Commons Attribution-NonCommercial-NoDerivs 3.0 Unported License.

evaluation of policies and interventions, they also enable researchers to address novel questions. Administrative data in many countries are routinely collected and used to improve policy and contribute to science to a much greater degree than in the United States. In this double issue, we hope to improve collaborations between American communities and academic scholars.

The value of "big data" is becoming increasingly apparent. In the current data revolution, firms' profits are determined by their ability to capture and analyze data. The capacity to collect and analyze data determines not only the winners and losers in the economy, but also which societies can best educate their citizens, train their workforce, keep their population healthy, and promote the well-being and flourishing of their citizens. Schools, hospitals, and many other organizations now routinely collect data that allow them to serve their students, patients, and other stakeholders more effectively. Understanding the lessons contained in these data, and how best to extract them, plays an important role in helping practitioners, administrators, and policymakers understand the challenges that the American public faces and the effects of current practices and policies.

Recent federal initiatives such as the Murray-Ryan Evidence-Based Policymaking Commission Act of 2016 and the resulting Foundations for Evidence-Based Policymaking Act of 2018 suggest that administrative data will become increasingly central in U.S. social science and policy. However, efforts to leverage administrative data in the social sciences are uneven. In domains such as public health and demography, administrative data are used routinely, while they are less frequently used in mental health, social behavior, and other areas. But even where administrative data are commonly used, current capacity constraints hinder their utility. Data that could be used to inform decisions are often unavailable to those making the decisions, leaving them with incomplete information.

One clear example is in education. Despite their focus on preparing students who are "college- and career-ready," schools have historically struggled to obtain data on the practices that will prepare their students to be successful because widespread links between students in K–12 educational systems and higher education outcomes have become available only recently, and links between K–12 data systems and the labor market remain relatively rare. These data linkages are important to understand the efficacy of school-based vocational programs, dropout recovery interventions, college readiness programs, and advancement placement course policies. But schools, like other organizations, typically lack the capacity and expertise to build this infrastructure and analyze the resulting data.

This double issue opens with a section that includes an article by Sean Reardon showing the potential value of examining nationwide data on student achievement (2019). He amasses an unprecedented administrative data file and then breaks it down in many ways that are useful to policy decision making as well as scientific understanding of child development and the impact of education. This file, and others like it, can be used to address numerous important issues that were previously unavailable to rigorous empirical scrutiny. For example, Megan Austin, Joseph Waddington, and Mark Berends show how administrative data can inform the important policy question of the impact of school vouchers on student achievement (2019).

Administrative data research seeks to bring the data-driven approach increasingly used in fields such as micro-targeting (where commercial firms individualize advertising according to one's buying patterns) and precision medicine to help answer important societal questions, providing schools, clinics, and others serving the public good with the information they need to work more effectively. To the degree that public-sector institutions are unable to build the infrastructure needed to understand the effectiveness of their programs, it seems likely that this lack of data infrastructure will result in inefficiencies (particularly relative to private sector institutions with fewer restrictions regarding data).

In this article and the double issue that follows, we seek to highlight the promise of administrative data to answer pressing questions for both science and policy. Our goal is not to be comprehensive, but to provide an indication of the potential that is currently barely being tapped, offer suggestions for advancing this infrastructure, and highlight some of the challenges currently facing the field. Likewise, our goal is to spark future work by highlighting the promise of these data by showcasing a few exciting administrative data initiatives and research projects.

THE CASE FOR ADMINISTRATIVE DATA INFRASTRUCTURE

Administrative data have many benefits for research that seeks to advance science and inform policy. These data typically originate not for research purposes, but instead as client-level service records or from administrators who are accountable for documentation of implementation of services. In many cases, the information available in administrative datasets and the analyses of these data will be useful to policymakers precisely because these are the variables for which policymakers are accountable. Furthermore, these datasets often attempt to reach the entire population of relevant participants and suffer less from selection bias than many original research datasets. Thus, not only does administrative data infrastructure provide important opportunities to understand the social world better, but it does so in contexts where stakeholders are ready to act based on the results of research. As a result, the analysis of administrative data has the potential to bridge basic and applied research.

Appropriate data infrastructure allows broad and equitable access, lessens the burden on the organizations providing the data, standardizes expectations around availability and privacy, and allows for best practices in data security. A robust administrative data infrastructure also lowers the marginal cost of conducting additional research, allowing researchers to address important issues using existing data that do not incur the effort or pecuniary costs of new data collection. Although the startup cost of establishing this infrastructure is not cheap, once established, it raises the quality of the research it permits and allows for more research by changing the cost curve for high-quality additional research. Furthermore, accessible administrative data files enable replication of data analyses and findings across independent research teams using the same and different files, which improves the robustness of the field. In a world where data analytics and knowledge are increasingly central to society, strong administrative data infrastructure is therefore not only important for knowledge creation, but also efficient.

Administrative data systems operate at scale. This feature allows researchers to consider questions such as whether all individuals benefit equally from a particular policy. When combined with research designs that allow for causal inference, these population-level data files afford answers about whether any individuals or groups are negatively affected and other questions of treatment-effect heterogeneity that are often prohibitively expensive to consider without the scale that administrative data provide. Having data on the entire universe of relevant individuals also allows for comparisons of small groups that are otherwise extremely difficult to isolate, for example, comparing employees with people doing the same job in the same establishment (Petersen and Morgan 1995). Operating at scale means that one can consider treatment not just at the individual level, but also at the community level, examining how spillover effects, feedback loops, and other dynamics might cause policies to work differently when implemented broadly. Finally, of course, having the population of participants available for analysis minimizes (but certainly does not eliminate) problems that survey researchers confront, such as biased attrition and missing data.

We next highlight several useful features of administrative data that are instrumental to advancing science and policy.

A Long-Term Perspective

Recent research has highlighted the utility of administrative data for understanding the long-term outcomes associated with a variety of interventions. Whereas much policy is necessarily driven by research and evaluations examining relatively short-term outcomes, administrative data can provide a longer-term perspective on the effects of past policies and thus a more accurate account of a policy's costs and benefits. Beyond following individuals who were exposed to interventions over time, administrative data can provide an important tool for understanding multigenerational cycles of advantage and disadvantage, allowing researchers to trace the descendants of individuals from different backgrounds as well as the multigenerational effects of antipoverty policies and interventions. Administrative data also provide opportunities to connect researcher-collected data (for example, observations of student behavior) with future administrative records to help understand the long-term implications of researchers' observations (such as longer-term cost outcomes related to early school behavior problems).

Administrative data research has pushed the boundaries of what we know about longer-term temporal processes, highlighting the important implications of understanding longer-term policy effects, as well as the intergenerational transmission of advantage and disadvantage more broadly. Standard intervention research typically ends data collection at the end of the study and provides an evaluation at that point. In some large-scale studies, follow-ups track outcomes for multiple years post-intervention (see, for example, Ludwig et al. 2013). Insofar as participants in interventions continue to be captured in administrative records after the end of the study, administrative records provide opportunities for an efficient approach to understanding the benefits of interventions decades later. Given the importance of understanding the long-term impacts of policies aimed at ameliorating poverty (Bailey et al. 2017), and the goal of changing not just individuals' current circumstances but also their longer-term trajectories, one of the most exciting features of administrative data is their ability to turn any study into a de facto longitudinal study. Recent work in this vein, for example, has highlighted the adult income effects of having an experienced or effective kindergarten teacher and higher-achieving classmates (Chetty et al. 2011; Chetty, Friedman, and Rockoff 2014a, 2014b), the increases in adult civic participation arising from a psychosocial intervention in elementary school (Holbein 2017), and the benefits of cash transfers to poor families on their children's educational outcomes, mortality, and income (Aizer, Eli et al. 2016).

Administrative data research has also extended a long tradition of survey-based research highlighting the intergenerational transmission of advantage and disadvantage (Blau and Duncan 1967; Ganzeboom, Treiman, and Ultee 1991). Survey-based research has examined parent-child transmission processes (for example, Campbell et al. 2014; Poulton et al. 2002), and in some cases, grandparents (Wightman and Danziger 2014). Administrative data allow researchers to push back on the time horizon of these studies. Using Swedish registry data, for example, Martin Hällsten examines the effects of not only grandparents, but also great-grandparents (2014). Likewise, work by Hyunjoon Park uses Korean historical registry information to examine the outcomes of ethnically Korean slaves, showing substantial effects on their descendants many generations after the abolition of slavery (2014). Multigenerational data are somewhat more rare in the United States, the Utah Population Database being a notable exception (see, for example, Temby and Smith 2014). A more detailed discussion of the opportunities provided by administrative data for understanding multigenerational processes is available from Xi Song and Cameron Campbell (2017). These data provide not only exciting new opportunities to advance the science of the multigenerational transmission of advantage, but also the long-term costs of stigmatized identities, poverty, and disadvantage. As data infrastructure matures, we expect to see more studies examining how social policies aimed at one generation affect their children and grandchildren (for example, Meghir, Palme, and Schnabel 2012).

Key Sites and Populations in the Production of Inequality

Inequality in opportunities and outcomes across groups and persons is one of the most vexing problems facing contemporary society. These inequalities are often produced in spaces that are difficult to examine using surveys or experiments. In the hiring process, for example, correspondence studies can examine who receives responses from potential employers but cannot help us understand how applicant pools are created, which interviewees receive offers, or whether pay differences exist among those who receive offers. Research on inequality in other institutional spheres such as health care, housing, and higher education faces similar challenges. Inequality in institutions is often shaped by processes that determine who is included and excluded, and how individuals are ranked within an organization. Administrative data on hiring pipelines, performance ratings, promotion decisions, and decisions about termination can provide valuable insights into the decisions made by gatekeepers at key sites regarding entry and exit from organizations, as well as important processes governing intraorganizational inequality regimes. One useful feature of workplace administrative records is that they allow researchers to compare individuals with others who have the same occupation working in the same establishment. Research making such comparisons suggests that much of the wage inequality observed across gender and race is created by sorting processes, as individuals doing the same work for the same employer receive largely similar pay (Petersen and Morgan 1995; Tomaskovic-Devey 1993).

Building on this insight, a long tradition of case studies uses administrative records from company human resource departments to understand inequality in these sorting processes. Trond Petersen and Ishak Saporta argue that in the current institutional context the opportunity for firms to discriminate is greatest at the point of hire (as opposed to discrimination in promotion or termination practices) and show that hiring is where the largest differences between men and women are observed (2004). Roberto Fernandez and his collaborators use human resource data in a series of papers that provide important insights into race and gender inequality in the hiring process; they show, for example, the importance of referrals (Fernandez and Greenberg 2013) and the importance of supply-side adjustments to perceived demand-side constraints (Fernandez and Friedrich 2011; Fernandez and Campero 2017). Recent work in this vein highlights the perhaps surprising egalitarian influence of an executive search firm (Fernandez-Mateo and Fernandez 2016), and in the current double issue Fernandez and Brian Rubineau use their extraordinary hiring data to provide novel analysis of network recruitment efforts and their impact on the gender-based glass ceiling in the biopharma industry (2019).

Beyond the labor market, administrative data from other sources also provide important insights into key sites for generating inequality. Research on NIH funding decisions, for example, uses detailed records to document the existence of gender inequality in the NIH review process (Li 2012). Research examining the criminal justice system uses administrative records from juvenile courts to estimate the effects of juvenile incarceration on later criminal justice and school outcomes (Aizer and Doyle 2015). One of the supposed keys to combating inequality and reaching life success is, of course, education. Although we know that dropping out of high school breeds failure and college graduation brings success, much less clear is the value of post–high school associate degrees, vocational diplomas, certificates, and partial college. In this double issue, ChangHwan Kim and Christopher Tamborini merge school administrative data files with earnings files to examine the long-term earnings that accrue from these post–high school accomplishments (2019).

Janelle Downing and Tim Bruckner use housing foreclosure administrative records and birth records to highlight yet another source of inequality (2019). They show that housing foreclosures (and presumably the stress they cause) contribute to premature births and increase inequality in birth outcomes across race and ethnic groups.

Administrative data also allow us to understand small, often difficult to access, populations that are theoretically important. For example, research using large administrative datasets has shown that millionaire tax flight does not occur at levels that are socially meaningful (Young et al. 2016), and that top earners are increasing isolated from the rest of the population (Godechot 2013). Insofar as many large administrative datasets include information on the whole population, these data allow researchers to examine relatively small and theoretically important groups (for example, those that are hard to capture in a probability sample without an explicit oversample) without compromising representativeness (Liebler, Bhaskar, and Porter 2016). From a local policy perspective, the ability to identify small groups of people is helpful because it allows policymakers to ensure that the policies they implement are having their intended effects for all stakeholders, and to determine where adjustments to existing policies are needed (Howard et al. 2019).

Understanding Individuals in Their Social Contexts

The importance of context is a truism in social science research. From network influences to cultural factors to questions about positional goods, contextual considerations play a profound role in shaping an individual's outcomes. Despite this, interventions and policies have historically operated from a baseline that presupposes constant universal effects that operate at scale if implemented with fidelity (Dodge 2011). The density of information in administrative data is useful in providing opportunities to examine important sources of heterogeneity (particularly contextual sources, but also individual-level factors), as well as providing opportunities to investigate policies and interventions at scale. Durham Connects, for example, takes advantage of administrative data by assigning all newborns in Durham born on even days to receive a nurse home visit (Dodge et al. 2014). This design allows for children to be followed in administrative records throughout their lives in an ethical manner without the requirement of individual consent (because data can be de-identified before being analyzed but retain the essential characteristic of assignment to intervention) without necessitating additional data collection.

Further, thinking about changes to the social system more broadly (for example, moving bus stops to help mothers travel to local clinics) shifts research and policy discussions away from a methodological individualism that focuses on the effects of treatments on individuals, and toward considering how programs and policies affect social systems more broadly (see, for example, Denice and Gross 2016). These systems-level approaches are important for both science and policy, as they address an important shortcoming of much social science research. Research often asks what would happen if everything was held constant and only one consideration was changed. This can be instructive, but it fails to take into account the myriad of ways that people and their social worlds are interconnected. Analyses of how community-level policies and interventions shape not only individuals' outcomes, but also society more generally, allow researchers to capture the complicated feedback loops and spillover effects that occur when interventions and policies operate at scale, providing insight into how policies might change society more broadly (Dodge 2009; Penner et al. 2015). Although in theory such analyses are possible without using administrative data, in practice the existence of administrative records greatly facilitates them.

Research using administrative data can also provide a more complete account of certain aspects of context, including the government services context. For example, Robert Goerge and Emily Wiegand examine the overlap in families' access of government services across multiple agencies to show how some families are accessing many agencies whereas others seem to be underaccessing resources that might benefit them (2019). Goerge and Wiegand show that these differences vary across geographical locations within Illinois, suggesting that local practice might contribute to, and mitigate, any biases. Lanikque Howard and colleagues examine the relation between parents' payment of child support and children's involvement in the child welfare system (2019). Agustina Laurito and colleagues combine multiple administrative datasets to show how school climate and neighborhood crime levels affect student achievement (2019).

Administrative data can also afford studies that are simply not plausible through original data collection. For example, it is difficult to imagine survey data tracking all of the classmates that a student had or all of the co-workers over an employee's career, but educational administrative data and linked employer-employee datasets often include this information (Abowd, Haltiwanger, and Lane 2004). Administrative records can thus provide information not only about an individual research subject but also about the environment surrounding them. Christopher Candelaria exploits such data in education, where he disentangles the long-term effects of a third-grade teacher, the medium-term effects of middle-school teachers, and the short-term effects of an eighth-grade teacher (2015).

Linking administrative data files across levels also provides innovative opportunities to understand individual behavior in broader context. Elizabeth Ananat and her colleagues, for example, link county-year-level administrative data about community-level job loss with individual student educational administrative data files in order to discover the impact of local economic downturns on student academic progress (2017). Further, as noted previously, administrative data allow for individuals to be placed in a multigenerational familial context. In providing dense coverage of populations, these data allow researchers to examine whether policies had spillover effects (either positive or negative) on those around the targeted populations, and to examine questions around how context moderates the effectiveness of treatment. Heterogeneity in treatment effectiveness is important not only for contributing to scientific understanding regarding the mechanisms through which interventions work, but also because it has important implications for generalizability and scalability (Domina et al. 2016).

An Iterative Policy Design, Implementation, and Evaluation Cycle

A common goal of scientific research is to improve societal outcomes. Social scientists often seek to do this by evaluating and informing existing policies, and it is not uncommon to hear researchers bemoan the lack of policy responsiveness to research. Although obtaining access to administrative data can be time consuming in some contexts, a potential advantage of administrative data analysis in many contexts is that the institution generating the data is also making and implementing the policies being evaluated, so that there is an audience that is positioned to make decisions about practice and policy based on researchers' findings (Howard et al. 2019). This is particularly true in researcher-practitioner partnerships, where researchers partner with organizations to help them use their administrative data in better ways to answer questions of interest to decision makers and stakeholders.

The research-policy link in social science is often conceptualized as one in which research informs or evaluates policies, but in research-practitioner partnerships, policy implementation and research can have a bidirectional synergistic relationship. These partnerships provide data researchers could not otherwise access. This unusual opportunity holds not only for companies' human resource data, but also for educational data, where laws protecting the privacy of student data allow data to be shared with organizations conducting research on behalf of educational agencies to help improve instruction. Further, researchers not only have the opportunity to study important policies in real-world settings but can often inform the implementation process. This relationship not only allows for policies that draw on researchers' expertise, but can also lead to opportunities for better research because researchers can help implement policies in ways that facilitate high-quality evaluations (such as introducing lottery-based assignments for oversubscribed programs or thresholds in assignment scores that enable regression discontinuity-based designs). In contexts that facilitate the timely incorporation of feedback, data collected can be used to inform Bayesian adaptive designs to help improve interventions in real time (Finucane, Martinez, and Cody 2017).

By bringing researchers into the policymaking process, rigorous research becomes part of the iterative process of policy implementation and adjustment and the policy adjustments made in implementation are better captured by research (Howard et al. 2019). This approach can provide both better policy and better research and serves as a model for how to accumulate and incorporate knowledge beyond simply conducting a series of single-policy evaluations. Although shortening the feedback loop among implementation, research, and redesign is likely to be positive overall, one challenge of this linkage is that long-term outcomes by definition cannot be observed quickly, and many policies—particularly those aimed at implementing organizational changes—have effects that take time to emerge or vary across different stages of the implementation cycle (Mills and Wolf 2017; Sun, Penner, and Loeb 2017).

EXPANDING ADMINISTRATIVE DATA INSIGHTS

Existing administrative data have allowed researchers to address a variety of important questions, and in many contexts, administrative data provide the best opportunities to answer important policy questions (Austin, Waddington, and Berends 2019). Current infrastructure, however, constrains research and limits the ability to answer questions that are important for science and policy. In the section that follows, we highlight important frontiers for administrative data research, highlighting noteworthy exemplars of work in these areas. We frame the points as strengths, but they could also be conceptualized as ways to address the potential weaknesses of administrative data.

Combining Datasets Across Sources

Although current administrative data research focuses on contemporary data sources, there is a long tradition of using administrative records in archival and historical research (see, for example, Kessler-Harris 1982; Wilde 2004). Research using administrative data has much in common with history and archeology, insofar as it observes the tracks that individuals leave as they move through society and draws lessons from these glimpses into their lives. A key difference is that when records outlast people, opportunities for supplementing and triangulation through interviews, surveys, or ethnography decline, leaving scientists to reconstruct meaning from the traces people have left behind. Although administrative data researchers using contemporary data draw conclusions from the traces left behind in current records in a similar manner, research using contemporary records has the potential to incorporate information directly from individuals through surveys and observations to supplement the data in administrative records.

Given their origin in a particular institutional context, administrative records are typically fragmented, and these data are often not linked to other data that would be useful for research and policy. Hospitals, for example, collect detailed information about patients' health, schools regularly collect information about student development, and employers often keep records not only about the performance of employees, but also about applicants who were ultimately not offered positions. Although various combinations of these data can provide important insights, they are typically compartmentalized. Likewise, given their origin, administrative records often lack certain kinds of information that are less likely to be collected in these records. For example, information about attitudes, affinities, and motives are not often collected in administrative records. Combining administrative data with records from other sources—either by linking administrative records across sources or by making administrative records available to be linked to data collected via other means—is thus central to building administrative data infrastructure.

Linking Administrative Data Records Across Domains

By virtue of how they come into existence, administrative data are typically focused on one facet of an individual's life, and data and insights are often siloed. Given that the potential for insight grows exponentially as data are integrated, combining administrative data across domains is of vital importance, and enables researchers to trace connections between settings like schools, criminal justice institutions, health organizations, and employers, and see how inequalities compound across these domains. Our introduction describing Durham Connects highlights the power of these insights for understanding the needs of families across diverse domains, and others likewise underscore the utility of linking administrative records across domains to understand the challenges facing families in poverty (Goerge and Wiegand 2019). Research linking data across domains documents how inequality in one domain shapes outcomes in others, highlighting, for example, the health consequences of foreclosure (Downing and Bruckner 2019) and how air pollution shapes mortality risk (Di et al. 2017). Other research in this vein allows us to understand the broad effects of policies, showing how lead abatement efforts lower children's blood lead levels and improve student achievement (Aizer, Currie et al. 2016), and how Superfund site cleanup improves children's later educational outcomes (Persico, Figlio, and Roth 2016).

Beyond helping us understand disadvantage better at any given point in time, linking data across domains can also open opportunities to follow individuals as they move through different institutional settings. Administrative records from birth, education, criminal justice, labor market, and mortality often capture different points in an individual's life; combining data across these stages allows us to understand how inequalities unfold over the arc of an individual's life. For example, research linking educational records with IRS records highlights the long-term income benefits associated with high-quality teachers (Chetty, Friedman, and Rockoff 2014a, 2014b) as well as the link between college major choices and later life income (Kim and Tamborini 2019). Similarly, research on the school-to-prison pipeline in Texas links education and justice records to trace the juvenile justice involvement of students suspended from school (Fabelo et al. 2011).

Much of the attention in administrative data infrastructure has focused on large-scale population-level data. However, as noted earlier, one of the potential advantages of using administrative data is that they provide information about social processes that are otherwise very difficult to study (such as the hiring pipeline). Research using administrative records to study otherwise inaccessible processes typically does not focus on linking across domains to the same degree as population-level administrative data research, presumably because of the underlying logic of these projects, which focuses primarily on isolating a hard-to-identify set of processes. Further, the unique relationship between data owners (often private companies) and researchers, and the difficulty in linking with public administrative sources (for example, the Census Bureau must avoid doing research that would favor one company over another) make linkage particularly challenging. That said, linking administrative records from these contexts with other administrative records could provide important insights and would appear to be an important frontier for administrative records research. For example, such data could help us understand how graduates from job search and other training programs fare at different stages in the hiring process. To date, we are aware of only one project that has linked human resource records with other individual-level data: linking human resource data on the hiring pipeline at a school district with data at the Census Bureau (Brummet and Penner 2017). Among other things, such data linkages provide opportunities for understanding the labor market implications of unsuccessful applications. We suspect that as the importance of evidence-based practices grows—both generally and in the context of securing foundation funding—opportunities for linking data from local organizations with important domain-specific information will continue to increase.

Combining Survey Data with Existing Administrative Records

The narrow specificity of some administrative data files often limits the range of scientific research questions that analyses drawing solely on that file can examine. Although this has the benefit of focusing researchers' attention on the measures salient to practitioners and policymakers, researchers often supplement administrative records with other information. For example, by linking administrative records with surveys measuring constructs of interest, researchers have examined teacher effects on motivation (Ruzek et al. 2015), shown how school climate can mitigate the academic effects of neighborhood violence (Laurito et al. 2019), and demonstrated how a manager's human resource practices moderate the relation between manager gender and gender wage inequality among workers (Abendroth et al. 2017). Future research in this vein linking implicit bias measures with hiring managers' real-world decisions from human resource data would also help us greatly expand our understanding of how organizational context and policies might moderate the effects of these biases. Likewise, researchers who have information on particular individuals often supplement that information with administrative records. A number of studies, for example, have used administrative data to examine the long-term outcomes associated with interventions, linking researchers' information about who received the treatment with administrative records (Chetty et al. 2011; Holbein 2017).

Elsewhere in this double issue, David Grusky,

Michael Hout, Timothy Smeeding, and Matthew Snipp highlight an additional benefit of combining survey and administrative data, noting that a common data infrastructure would allow surveys to be overlaid on top of administrative data and alleviate respondent burden (2019). This would enhance what is possible using either the survey or the administrative data independently.

Qualitative Research with Administrative Data

Although much of the research using administrative data uses quantitative information, administrative records also contain vast amounts of qualitative information. Archival research using administrative records provides a strong indication of the considerable value of qualitative work using administrative records. Although qualitative social science research using contemporary administrative records is also just beginning to realize its potential, several examples evince the promise of such approaches. Recent qualitative research in medicine, for example, highlights gender differences in the feedback that medical school residents receive (Mueller et al. 2017), and research on online dating profiles underscores how racial boundaries are reinforced not just by racial homogamy, but also by those looking to date across racial lines (Rafalow, Feliciano, and Robnett 2017).

In many administrative contexts, given the scale of textual data, advances in machine coding offer a promising approach to turning rich qualitative data into quantitative data. In this double issue, Emily Penner and her colleagues provide one example of this approach, showcasing how essays submitted as part of teacher applications are correlated with a variety of policy-relevant considerations (2019). The promise of such approaches in researcher-practitioner partnerships is difficult to overstate, because when these organizations begin to leverage their data in the ways that large tech firms do, there would appear to be substantial benefits for both policy and science. With text mining becoming increasingly sophisticated and common, and the growth of software to aid in the transcription, storage, coding and sorting processes in qualitative research, the distinction between quantitative and qualitative research is one that could quickly fade in administrative data research.

TECHNICAL, LEGAL, ETHICAL, AND PERCEPTUAL CHALLENGES

In this last section, we highlight a few current challenges specific to working with administrative data. Many are extensions of challenges that exist in social science more broadly around balancing the privacy of research participants with making data widely accessible to lower the barriers to conducting research. In this respect, we see parallels between current efforts to democratize access to administrative records (see, for example, Grusky et al. 2019) and the advent of the General Social Survey, which made nationally representative survey data widely available to the scientific community. Prior to the General Social Survey, social scientists collected their own surveys and typically did not provide data access to outside researchers, so that access to survey data was typically restricted to prominent scholars and their students. More recently, calls for greater transparency and reproducibility have underscored the value of open science in experimental fields (see, for example, Ioannidis 2005; Open Science Collaboration 2015). Against this broader backdrop, thinking about what open science looks like in the context of administrative data research is critical.

Aggregation of individual data into group scores provides a partial solution to the challenge of privacy in many contexts. This double issue includes two studies that use aggregated data files. Brittany Murray and colleagues report the positive relation between strong parent-teacher associations and growth in student achievement (2019). Portia Miller, Elizabeth Votruba-Drzal, and Rebekah Coley find that community-level resources explain variation in student achievement (2019).

However, aggregated data cannot answer all questions, and in many cases answering research and policy questions requires individual-level data. To facilitate sharing of individual-level data, it is likely important to establish incentives for administrative data linking efforts so that more scholars contribute to this public good. One challenge here is that, due to the sensitivity of many administrative datasets, access is highly regulated, and it becomes prohibitively difficult and time consuming to navigate the multiple processes required to obtain access to data across different contexts. There are two broad models for addressing these challenges in international comparative research: the Comparative Organizational Inequality Network, which brings together researchers with access to the relevant data in different contexts around a set of common analyses that each researcher conducts on data from their home country; and the Luxembourg Income Study, which creates a largely harmonized set of data from across countries (currently nonadministrative survey data) and allows researchers to submit code to run on datasets from different countries without accessing the original data. Given their different costs and benefits, we suspect that both models have important roles to play in comparative research.

More broadly, the challenges in working with administrative data can be broken down into technical, legal, ethical, and perceptual challenges. We review each in turn.

Technical Challenges

Important technical challenges remain to constructing administrative data infrastructure. For example, address-based matches are difficult to implement in contexts that lack a well-defined address system (see, for example, Wynn, Reyes, and Caldwell 2011). Likewise, for computationally intensive analyses (for example, some social network analyses) it is currently not practical to conduct analyses that make use of the density of information available at the population level. These and other questions notwithstanding, in our estimation the largest challenges to administrative data are not technical per se but instead technical constraints imposed in response to legal or perceptual considerations.

For example, it is not clear that there is a strong rationale for why researchers need to be in Texas to analyze data from the state of Texas (except that it may be easier to arrest a misuser within state), or that data from Georgia should be allowed to be used on projects only with a collaborator from a university located in Georgia. Nevertheless, such arrangements remain relatively common. Although they are not insurmountable, they do create nontrivial barriers to access and hinder the democratization that researchers generally support in science. That said, given the level of trust required for companies to allow researchers to analyze key intellectual property (Fernandez-Mateo and Fernandez 2016) or for countries to allow outside researchers access to tax data (King et al. 2017), some restrictions to access beyond those governing survey data are warranted. These barriers highlight the point that the most important challenge to successful administrative data scholarship is not the technical nature of data storage or security, but rather, the human and institutional relationships that must be developed and maintained. The relational nature of data access in many cases—such as in long-term researcher-practitioner partnerships—does result in important constraints that are in tension with norms around data-sharing and open science.

One important challenge surrounding administrative data is the lack of consistency regarding which data are collected and how they are collected. Although national surveys typically use standardized measures and best practices for assessing various constructs, information contained in administrative data can be highly variable in terms of coverage and quality. One advantage of working in close partnership with the organizations generating administrative data is that they typically have a deep understanding of how the data are generated and areas where information may be inaccurate or have limited coverage, and can often adjust practices to generate data that are of mutual interest. Working closely with partners on the ground can also help avoid misattributing causal relations. As with most survey data, administrative data sources require that findings be disseminated only as aggregate statistics in order to protect privacy. As far as we are aware, very few cases of researchers infringing on the privacy of individuals using administrative records have been documented. At this point, then, the technical challenges involved in building data infrastructure are largely surmountable, and the larger remaining question is whether political will is strong enough to move forward.

Legal Challenges

Currently, legal constraints affecting administrative data infrastructure focus on balancing the privacy of individuals whose data are contained in the administrative records with the ability of institutions to find answers to their pressing policy questions, which in many cases will enable them to serve better those who are represented in their data. Allowing access to outside researchers working on behalf of the organization can greatly enhance the research capacity of institutions that generate administrative data and provide expertise in areas that might be otherwise difficult to obtain. In this context, analyses of administrative data should address questions of the data owner, presumably in service of either those represented in the data or the broader public. By contrast, scientists argue that science benefits from widespread, democratic access, and that this access can yield new insights that might be broadly beneficial to society, the institutions generating the data, and their stakeholders, even if these benefits might not have been anticipated. Although making administrative data more widely available is likely generally beneficial, it is currently difficult to know how to assess and weigh the benefits from broad access.

Many forms of administrative data are legally protected in ways that limit access. Under the Family Educational Rights and Privacy Act, identifiable educational data in the United States can only be shared with researchers in a limited number of contexts, including cases where the studies will help the schools improve instruction. Similar challenges apply to health information and Health Insurance Portability and Accountability Act regulations. The lack of a well-established administrative data infrastructure means that lawmakers often do not consider the impact of legislation on administrative records. For example, out of concerns regarding administrative records being used for enforcement purposes, California lawmakers sought to enact laws prohibiting data-sharing and initially did not recognize the limitations this would create for researchers and administrative data infrastructure. Presumably a more robust and salient administrative data infrastructure will help in avoiding such issues in the future.

In many ways, legal constraints are a question of political will. On this point, the bipartisan support for administrative data represented by the Murray-Ryan commission and the Foundations for Evidence-Based Policymaking Act is encouraging. One might imagine, for example, that evidence-based policies around education and workforce training programs might benefit from administrative records from schools, even if the resulting study might not help each school improve instruction. Although individual lawmakers may differ on policy priorities, it is encouraging that they agree on the need for better data and analysis to inform them.

Ethical Challenges

Beyond strictly legal questions, there are ethical questions as well. Typically, potential research participants have the choice to opt out of a study. But this is not possible in most research that uses administrative records. Although consideration of informed consent is routine when it comes to whether a participant's data are used in traditional research designs, administrative records research is often considered to be nonhuman subjects research. To be clear, questions around individuals' rights vis-à-vis their data are a feature of administrative data more generally and not particular to research. This is apparent when one considers medical records. In approximately half of the states in the United States, physicians or hospitals own patients' records, and only in New Hampshire do these data belong to patients (in the remaining states data ownership is not clearly defined). It seems unlikely that patients would take issue with research analyzing these records for patterns that might help save their life. Likewise, it seems probable that most people would not object to their records being analyzed for research that might help save the lives of others. Nevertheless, because this research is often not considered to involve human subjects, and these data (outside New Hampshire) do not belong to the individual, it is unclear what rights patients should have to restrict the use of their data in administrative records research.

Historically, the argument has been that the primary potential harm in this research is that of disclosure, or harm to the individual due to a breach of privacy. Some legal scholars suggest that this individualistic perspective may be problematic. In a high-profile example, the Havasupai sued Arizona State University for using existing blood samples in ways not covered by agreements. In discussing this case, Katherine Drabiak-Syed notes that our current legal system is ill equipped to consider issues beyond an individualistic framework, so that harm to a collective group may not be recognized (2010). These questions are perhaps especially salient in the context of Native Americans, where issues over the right to opt out are laden with colonial legacies of ignoring indigenous perspectives and also raise questions of tribal sovereignty. These concerns are likely heightened where blood (or other physical samples) are involved, where research focuses on historically marginalized populations, or when researchers are partnering with data-collecting organizations. The concerns are perhaps somewhat attenuated when looking at historical data (for example, the Dutch Hunger Winter), but the larger point remains relevant for administrative records research.

More broadly, the issue could be conceptualized as whether individuals should have the right to ensure that their data are not used in systems against their wishes. One might imagine, for example, critics of structural racism not wanting their data to be used by companies that might perpetuate racial differences in homeownership through credit scores. But it is difficult not to be complicit when almost everyone is part of the administrative data ecosystem that creates and reproduces these inequalities. This is a feature of our societal data infrastructure and is not specific to research using this infrastructure. Nonetheless, administrative data researchers should be cognizant of these issues, particularly in contexts like researcher-practitioner partnerships where they might influence the kinds of data collected, and where the research being conducted might be used to justify or rationalize practices that may otherwise be seen as problematic.

Perceptual Challenges

Perceptual challenges relevant to administrative data research can be divided into those within the academy and those in the public domain. Within the academy, in many social science disciplines there is a bias against work that is viewed as overly applied. The term *evaluation research* for example, is sometimes used pejoratively in contrast with *pure* science, implying that scientific work is somehow contaminated by being useful to society. We argue that whatever the origins of this bias, it is a distinction that has outlived its usefulness, and that supporting human flourishing—both through better understanding the social world in the broadest and most abstract sense, as well as through understanding the implications of the concrete choices that we as a society make—ought to be one of the aims of science. The degree to which these biases are held in any given scientific field varies, suggesting that social science disciplines can learn much from those more engaged in policy. These disciplinary biases are perhaps a space that academics are well positioned to change. Although these norms may be deeply entrenched, they are nonetheless created and maintained by academics, suggesting that we as a community can change them by changing our hiring criteria, tenure and promotion letters, award nominations, and graduate training. We suspect that these perceptual challenges within the academy are decreasing, in part because administrative data allow researchers to address questions that are not only important for real-world applications, but also make fundamental contributions to discipline-specific and transdisciplinary research goals. We believe the proliferation of administrative data research suggests that over the long term, perceptual issues within the academy are likely to become less pronounced.

Beyond the academy, public skepticism about the limits of confidentiality and data protection threaten public support for the use of administrative data. Recent hacking events and misuse of large private data files at Facebook and Cambridge Analytica have shaken public faith in keepers of supposedly private data. The threat goes beyond misuse to include possible political obstruction by groups such as ALEC (American Legislative Exchange Council), which has taken the position that all governmental action should be minimal. The possibilities of misuse by insiders, hacking by outsiders, and opposition by politics will always be present, but we believe the marginal extra risk imposed by bringing researchers into this circle is very low. Researchers are required to be trained and credentialed in the use of sensitive data files, and universities tend to implement cutting-edge technologies in data security. Because of these threats and the public's vigilance, however, researchers would be wise to understand the treasure that they behold and to be extremely careful in their use of administrative data files.

At the same time that the public is skeptical, bipartisan support is also strong for administrative data science to improve our capacity to maximize the potential of our human resources. Data-sharing can be difficult in contexts marked by suspicion and mistrust, and larger conversations around privacy remain important. Legal protections governing administrative data use thus play central perceptual and scientific roles, as well as being important for ethical reasons (Anderson and Seltzer 2007). We believe that it is incumbent on scientists to help make the case for administrative data research by ensuring that the public benefits from the use of their data. Although in some cases this might mean working closely with policymakers and practitioners generating and using the data, press coverage of novel findings using engaging data visualizations that reach the public more broadly also play an important role in highlighting the utility of these data to the broader public. Wide dissemination of research findings not only helps inform public discourse around important social questions, but also plays an educational role by engaging people's curiosity and helping them understand how the social world works.

CONCLUSION

As a society, we have the data and expertise to address questions that are vital to our communal life, but we currently do not have the infrastructure to bring data from disparate sources together and provide access to researchers with high-impact projects. U.S. administrative data infrastructure has lagged behind that of its peers, leading to policies that are not as well tuned as they might be, and in many cases leading American social scientists to work with better data from other countries. Important policy-relevant scientific questions go unanswered, and scholars and policymakers are left to infer how things might work in the United States based on evidence from elsewhere. The lack of data infrastructure has human costs for our students, patients, and their families; has pecuniary costs for taxpayers; and puts American science at a disadvantage. Recent efforts to create administrative data infrastructure have great promise to rectify the situation, making it an exciting time to be an administrative data researcher.

One final word of caution is perhaps in order: in America, the logic of competition drives many of our collective efforts. When building infrastructure, however, coordination is important. To use a metaphor from physical infrastructure, having five sets of highway systems that do not connect with each other is considerably less useful than having a single, well-planned system. We have an opportunity to create world-class data infrastructure that will enable policymakers to make better policies, scientists to understand society better, teachers to instruct students better, and physicians to treat patients better. In moving forward, coordinating efforts to ensure that we build the best data infrastructure possible, and that our data can benefit the public as much as possible, is paramount.

REFERENCES

Abendroth, Anja-Kristin, Silvia Melzer, Alexandra Kalev, and Donald Tomaskovic-Devey. 2017. "Women at Work: Women's Access to Power and the Gender Earnings Gap." *ILR Review* 70(1): 190–222.

Abowd, John M., John Haltiwanger, and Julia Lane. 2004. "Integrated Longitudinal Employer-Employee Data for the United States." *American Economic Review* 94(2): 224–29.

Aizer, Anna, Janet Currie, Peter Simon, and Patrick Vivier. 2016. Do Low Levels of Blood Lead Reduce Children's Future Test Scores? No. w22558. National Bureau of Economic Research.

Aizer, Anna, and Joseph J. Doyle Jr. 2015. "Juvenile Incarceration, Human Capital, and Future Crime: Evidence from Randomly Assigned Judges." *Quarterly Journal of Economics* 130(2): 759–803.

Aizer, Anna, Shari Eli, Joseph Ferrie, and Adriana Lleras-Muney. 2016. "The Long-Run Impact of Cash Transfers to Poor Families." *American Economic Review* 106(4): 935–71.

Ananat, Elizabeth O., Anna Gassman-Pines, Dania V. Francis, and Christina M. Gibson-Davis. 2017. "Linking Job Loss, Inequality, Mental Health, and Education." *Science* 356(6343): 1127–28.

Anderson, Margo, and William Seltzer. 2007. "Challenges to the Confidentiality of U.S. Federal Statistics, 1910–1965." *Journal of Official Statistics* 23(1): 1–34.

Austin, Megan, R. Joseph Waddington, and Mark Berends. 2019. "Voucher Pathways and Student Achievement in Indiana's Choice Scholarship Program." *RSF: The Russell Sage Foundation Journal of the Social Sciences* 5(3): 20–40. DOI: 10.7758/RSF.2019.5.3.02.

Bailey, Drew, Greg J. Duncan, Candice L. Odgers, and Winnie Yu. 2017. "Persistence and Fadeout in the Impacts of Child and Adolescent Interventions." *Journal of Research on Educational Effectiveness* 10(1): 7–39.

Blau, Peter, and Otis Dudley Duncan. 1967. *The American Occupational Structure*. New York: John Wiley & Sons.

Brummet, Quentin, and Emily Penner. 2017. "After School: An Examination of the Career Paths and Earnings of Former Teachers." Paper presented at APPAM 2017. Chicago (November 2–4, 2017).

Campbell, Frances, Gabriella Conti, James J. Heckman, Seong Hyeok Moon, Rodrigo Pinto, Elizabeth Pungello, and Yi Pan. 2014. "Early Childhood Investments Substantially Boost Adult Health." *Science* 343(6178): 1478–85.

Candelaria, Christopher A. 2015. "Rethinking Teacher Effects on Student Achievement." Paper presented at the Association for Education Finance and Policy. Washington, D.C. (February 26–28, 2015).

Chetty, Raj, John N. Friedman, Nathaniel Hilger, Emmanuel Saez, Diane Whitmore Schanzenbach, and Danny Yagan. 2011. "How Does Your Kindergarten Classroom Affect Your Earnings? Evidence from Project STAR." *Quarterly Journal of Economics* 126(4): 1593–660.

Chetty, Raj, John N. Friedman, and Jonah E. Rockoff. 2014a. "Measuring the Impacts of Teachers I: Evaluating Bias in Teacher Value-Added Estimates." *American Economic Review* 104(9): 2593–632.

———. 2014b. "Measuring the Impacts of Teachers II: Teacher Value-Added and Student Outcomes in Adulthood." *American Economic Review* 104(9): 2633–79.

Denice, Patrick, and Betheny Gross. 2016. "Choice, Preferences, and Constraints: Evidence from Public School Applications in Denver." *Sociology of Education* 89(4): 300–20.

Di, Qian, Yan Wang, Antonella Zanobetti, Yun Wang, Petros Koutrakis, Christine Choirat, Francesca Dominici, and Joel D. Schwartz. 2017. "Air Pollution and Mortality in the Medicare Population." *New England Journal of Medicine* 376(26): 2513–22.

Dodge, Kenneth A. 2009. "Community Intervention and Public Policy in the Prevention of Antisocial Behavior." *Journal of Child Psychology and Psychiatry* 50(1-2): 194–200.

———. 2011. "Context Matters in Child and Family Policy." *Child Development* 82(1): 433–42.

Dodge, Kenneth A., W. Benjamin Goodman, Robert A. Murphy, Karen O'Donnell, Jeannine Sato, and Susan Guptill. 2014. "Implementation and Randomized Controlled Trial Evaluation of Universal Postnatal Nurse Home Visiting." *American Journal of Public Health* 104(S1): S136–43.

Domina, Thurston, Andrew McEachin, Paul Hanselman, Priyanka Agarwal, NaYoung Hwang, and Ryan Lewis. 2016. "Beyond Tracking and Detracking: The Dimensions of Organizational Differentiation in Schools." RAND Labor & Population working paper no. WR1155. Santa Monica, Calif.: RAND Corporation.

Downing, Janelle, and Tim Bruckner. 2019. "Subprime Babies: The Foreclosure Crisis and Initial Health Endowments." *RSF: The Russell Sage Foundation Journal of the Social Sciences* 5(2): 123–40. DOI: 10.7758/RSF.2019.5.2.07.

Drabiak-Syed, Katherine. 2010. "Lessons from *Havasupai Tribe v. Arizona State University Board of Regents*: Recognizing Group, Cultural, and Dignity Harms as Legitimate Risks Warranting Integration into Research Practice." *Journal of Health and Biomedical Law* 6(2): 175–226.

Fabelo, Tony, Michael D. Thompson, Martha Plotkin, Dottie Carmichael, Miner P. Marchbanks, and Eric A. Booth. 2011. "Breaking Schools' Rules: A Statewide Study of How School Discipline Relates to Students' Success and Juvenile Justice Involvement." New York: Council of State Governments Justice Center.

Fernandez, Roberto M., and Santiago Campero. 2017. "Gender Sorting and the Glass Ceiling in High-Tech Firms." *ILR Review* 70(1): 73–104.

Fernandez, Roberto M., and Colette Friedrich. 2011. "Gender Sorting at the Application Interface." *Industrial Relations: A Journal of Economy and Society* 50(4): 591–609.

Fernandez, Roberto M., and Jason Greenberg. 2013. "Race, Network Hiring, and Statistical Discrimination." In *Networks, Work and Inequality*, edited by Steve McDonald. Bingley, UK: Emerald Group Publishing.

Fernandez, Roberto M., and Brian Rubineau. 2019. "Network Recruitment and the Glass Ceiling: Evidence from Two Firms." *RSF: The Russell Sage Foundation Journal of the Social Sciences* 5(3): 88–102. DOI: 10.7758/RSF.2019.5.3.05.

Fernandez-Mateo, Isabel, and Roberto M. Fernandez. 2016. "Bending the Pipeline? Executive Search and Gender Inequality in Hiring for Top Management Jobs." *Management Science* 62(12): 3636–55.

Finucane, Mariel McKenzie, Ignacio Martinez, and Scott Cody. 2017. "What Works for Whom? A Bayesian Approach to Channeling Big Data Streams for Public Program Evaluation." *American Journal of Evaluation* 39(1): 109–22.

Ganzeboom, Harry B. G., Donald J. Treiman, and Wout C. Ultee. 1991. "Comparative Intergenerational Stratification Research: Three Generations and Beyond." *Annual Review of Sociology* 17(1): 277–302.

Godechot, Olivier. 2013. "Financialization and Sociospatial Divides." *L'Année Sociologique* 63(1): 17–50.

Goerge, Robert M., and Emily R. Wiegand. 2019. "Understanding Vulnerable Families in Multiple Service Systems." *RSF: The Russell Sage Foundation Journal of the Social Sciences* 5(2): 86–104. DOI: 10.7758/RSF.2019.5.2.05.

Grusky, David B., Michael Hout, Timothy M. Smeeding, and C. Matthew Snipp. 2019. "The American Opportunity Study: A New Infrastructure for Monitoring Outcomes, Evaluating Policy, and Advancing Basic Science." *RSF: The Russell Sage Foundation Journal of the Social Sciences* 5(2): 20–39. DOI: 10.7758/RSF.2019.5.2.02.

Hällsten, Martin. 2014. "Inequality Across Three and Four Generations in Egalitarian Sweden: 1st and 2nd Cousin Correlations in Socio-Economic Outcomes." *Research in Social Stratification and Mobility* 35(1): 19–33.

Holbein, John B. 2017. "Childhood Skill Development and Adult Political Participation." *American Political Science Review* 111(3): 572–83.

Howard, Lanikque, Lisa Klein Vogel, Maria Cancian, and Jennifer L. Noyes. 2019. "Building Connections: Using Integrated Administrative Data to Identify Issues and Solutions Spanning the Child Welfare and Child Support Systems." *RSF: The Russell Sage Foundation Journal of the Social Sciences* 5(2): 70–85. DOI: 10.7758/RSF.2019.5.2.04.

Ioannidis, John P. A. 2015. "Why Most Published Research Findings Are False." *PLoS Medicine* 2(8): e124.

Kessler-Harris, Alice. 1982. *Out to Work: A History of Wage-Earning Women in the United States*. Oxford: Oxford University Press.

Kim, ChangHwan, and Christopher R. Tamborini. 2019. "Are They Still Worth It? The Long-Run Earnings Benefits of an Associate Degree, Vocational Diploma or Certificate, and Some College." *RSF: The Russell Sage Foundation Journal of the Social Sciences* 5(3): 64–85. DOI: 10.7758/RSF.2019.5.3.04.

King, Joseph, Andrew M. Penner, Nina Bandelj, and Aleksandra Kanjuo-Mrčela. 2017. "Market Transformation and the Opportunity Structure for Gender Inequality: A Cohort Analysis Using Linked Employer-Employee Data from Slovenia." *Social Science Research* 67 (September): 14–33.

Laurito, Agustina, Johanna Lacoe, Amy Ellen Schwartz, Patrick Sharkey, and Ingrid Gould Ellen. 2019. "School Climate and the Impact of Neighborhood Crime on Test Scores." *RSF: The Russell Sage Foundation Journal of the Social Sciences* 5(2): 141–66. DOI: 10.7758/RSF.2019.5.2.08.

Li, Danielle. 2012. "Essays on the Organization of Science and Education." Ph.D. diss., Massachusetts Institute of Technology.

Liebler, Carolyn A., Renuka Bhaskar, and Sonya R. Porter. 2016. "Joining, Leaving, and Staying in the American Indian/Alaska Native Race Category Between 2000 and 2010." *Demography* 53(2): 507–40.

Ludwig, Jens, Greg J. Duncan, Lisa A. Gennetian, Lawrence F. Katz, Ronald C. Kessler, Jeffrey R. Kling, and Lisa Sanbonmatsu. 2013. "Long-Term

Neighborhood Effects on Low-Income Families: Evidence from Moving to Opportunity." *American Economic Review* 103(3): 226–31.

Meghir, Costas, Mårten Palme, and Marieke Schnabel. 2012. "The Effect of Education Policy on Crime: An Intergenerational Perspective." NBER working paper no. w18145. Cambridge, Mass.: National Bureau of Economic Research.

Miller, Portia, Elizabeth Votruba-Drzal, and Rebekah Levine Coley. 2019. "Poverty and Academic Achievement Across the Urban to Rural Landscape: Associations with Community Resources and Stressors." *RSF: The Russell Sage Foundation Journal of the Social Sciences* 5(2): 106–22. DOI: 10.7758/RSF.2019.5.2.06.

Mills, Jonathan N., and Patrick J. Wolf. 2017. "Vouchers in the Bayou: The Effects of the Louisiana Scholarship Program on Student Achievement After 2 Years." *Educational Evaluation and Policy Analysis* 39(3): 464–84.

Mueller, Anna S., Tania M. Jenkins, Melissa Osborne, Arjun Dayal, Daniel M. O'Connor, and Vineet M. Arora. 2017. "Gender Differences in Attending Physicians' Feedback to Residents: A Qualitative Analysis." *Journal of Graduate Medical Education* 9(5): 577–85.

Murray, Brittany, Thurston Domina, Linda Renzulli, and Rebecca Boylan. 2019. "Civil Society Goes to School: Parent-Teacher Associations and the Equality of Educational Opportunity." *RSF: The Russell Sage Foundation Journal of the Social Sciences* 5(3): 41–63. DOI: 10.7758/RSF.2019.5.3.03.

Open Science Collaboration. 2015. "Estimating the Reproducibility of Psychological Science." *Science* 349(6251): aac4716.

Park, Hyunjoon. 2014. "The Legacy of Disadvantaged Origins: Blocked Social Mobility of Descendants of Nobis in Late Joseon (Korea)." Ann Arbor: Nam Center for Korean Studies, University of Michigan.

Penner, Andrew M., Thurston Domina, Emily K. Penner, and AnneMarie Conley. 2015. "Curricular Policy as a Collective Effects Problem: A Distributional Approach." *Social Science Research* 52 (July): 627–41.

Penner, Emily K., Jane Rochmes, Jing Liu, Sabrina Solanki, and Susanna Loeb. 2019. "Differing Views of Equity: How Prospective Educators Perceive Their Role in Closing Achievement Gaps." *RSF: The Russell Sage Foundation Journal of the Social Sciences* 5(3): 103–27. DOI: 10.7758/RSF.2019.5.3.06.

Persico, Claudia, David Figlio, and Jeffrey Roth. 2016. "Inequality Before Birth: The Developmental Consequences of Environmental Toxicants." NBER working paper no. w22263. Cambridge, Mass.: National Bureau of Economic Research.

Petersen, Trond, and Laurie A. Morgan. 1995. "Separate and Unequal: Occupation-Establishment Sex Segregation and the Gender Wage Gap." *American Journal of Sociology* 101(2): 329–65.

Petersen, Trond, and Ishak Saporta. 2004. "The Opportunity Structure for Discrimination." *American Journal of Sociology* 109(4): 852–901.

Poulton, Richie, Avshalom Caspi, Barry J. Milne, W. Murray Thomson, Alan Taylor, Malcolm R. Sears, and Terrie E. Moffitt. 2002. "Association Between Children's Experience of Socioeconomic Disadvantage and Adult Health: A Life-Course Study." *The Lancet* 360(9346): 1640–45.

Rafalow, Matthew H., Cynthia Feliciano, and Belinda Robnett. 2017. "Racialized Femininity and Masculinity in the Preferences of Online Same-Sex Daters." *Social Currents* 4(4): 306–21.

Reardon, Sean F. 2019. "Educational Opportunity in Early and Middle Childhood: Using Full Population Administrative Data to Study Variation by Place and Age." *RSF: The Russell Sage Foundation Journal of the Social Sciences* 5(2): 40–68. DOI: 10.7758/RSF.2019.5.2.03.

Ruzek, Erik A., Thurston Domina, AnneMarie M. Conley, Greg J. Duncan, and Stuart A. Karabenick. 2015. "Using Value-Added Models to Measure Teacher Effects on Students' Motivation and Achievement." *Journal of Early Adolescence* 35(5–6): 852–82.

Song, Xi, and Cameron D. Campbell. 2017. "Genealogical Microdata and Their Significance for Social Science." *Annual Review of Sociology* 43(1): 75–99.

Sun, Min, Emily K. Penner, and Susanna Loeb. 2017. "Resource- and Approach-Driven Multidimensional Change: Three-Year Effects of School Improvement Grants." *American Educational Research Journal* 54(4): 607–43.

Temby, Owen F., and Ken R. Smith. 2014. "The Association Between Adult Mortality Risk and Family History of Longevity: The Moderating Effects of Socioeconomic Status." *Journal of Biosocial Science* 46(6): 703–16.

Tomaskovic-Devey, Donald. 1993. *Gender & Racial*

Inequality at Work: The Sources and Consequences of Job Segregation. Ithaca, N.Y.: Cornell University Press.

U.S. Census Bureau. 1996. "Puerto Rico, Virgin Islands, and the Pacific Island Territories." In *1990 Census of Population and Housing, History*, chapter 13. Washington: Government Printing Office.

Wightman, Patrick, and Sheldon Danziger. 2014. "Multi-Generational Income Disadvantage and the Educational Attainment of Young Adults." *Research in Social Stratification and Mobility* 35(1): 53–69.

Wilde, Melissa J. 2004. "How Culture Mattered at Vatican II: Collegiality Trumps Authority in the Council's Social Movement Organizations." *American Sociological Review* 69(4): 576–602.

Wynn, John D., Daniel A. Reyes, and Willard E. Caldwell. 2011. "United States Census 2010: A Description of the 2010 Census Operations and Data Products of the Island Areas, and How They Compare to the 50 States and the District of Columbia." Washington: U.S. Census Bureau.

Young, Cristobal, Charles Varner, Ithai Z. Lurie, and Richard Prisinzano. 2016. "Millionaire Migration and Taxation of the Elite: Evidence from Administrative Data." *American Sociological Review* 81(3): 421–46.

PART I
Building Administrative Systems

The American Opportunity Study: A New Infrastructure for Monitoring Outcomes, Evaluating Policy, and Advancing Basic Science

DAVID B. GRUSKY, MICHAEL HOUT, TIMOTHY M. SMEEDING, AND C. MATTHEW SNIPP

The American Opportunity Study is an ongoing initiative to build the country's capacity to access and analyze linked administrative data. It is best viewed as a population-level scaffolding on which other administrative data can then be hung. This scaffolding, if used as a stand-alone resource, will allow for long-run analyses of fundamental population and labor market processes. If combined with data from other sources, it will allow for long-run program evaluation and other experimental and quasi-experimental analyses. We discuss the current status of the American Opportunity Study, its potential to advance the field, remaining obstacles that must be overcome to build it, and how it can work within the guidelines suggested by the Commission on Evidence-Based Policymaking.

Keywords: administrative data, data linkage, social mobility, program evaluation

The administrative data revolution is in full blossom (Reamer and Lane 2018). Until recently, this revolution was pitched largely in terms of its promise and represented as our future (see, for example, Decker 2014). But that future has clearly arrived.

A broad consensus about the value of administrative data has been reached among policymakers, elected officials, data administrators, and researchers at the federal and state levels. This consensus arose when federal statistical agencies began sharing special-purpose linked administrative files with researchers in universities, think tanks, and program-evaluation

David B. Grusky is Barbara Kimball Browning Professor in the School of Humanities and Sciences at Stanford University. **Michael Hout** is professor of sociology at New York University. **Timothy M. Smeeding** is Lee Rainwater Distinguished Professor of Public Affairs and Economics at the La Follette School of Public Affairs, University of Wisconsin–Madison. **C. Matthew Snipp** is Burnet C. and Mildred Finley Wohlford Professor of Humanities and Sciences in the Department of Sociology at Stanford University.

© 2019 Russell Sage Foundation. Grusky, David B., Michael Hout, Timothy M. Smeeding, and C. Matthew Snipp. 2019. "The American Opportunity Study: A New Infrastructure for Monitoring Outcomes, Evaluating Policy, and Advancing Basic Science." *RSF: The Russell Sage Foundation Journal of the Social Sciences* 5(2): 20–39. DOI: 10.7758/RSF.2019.5.2.02. The authors thank all of those who have inspired and advanced the ideas, concepts, and moving parts of the American Opportunity Study. We also thank the reviewers for their careful reading and excellent comments, David Chancellor for graphing assistance, and the Carnegie Corporation, the National Research Council, and Stanford University for their support of the AOS. The authors alone assume responsibility for all errors of omission and commission. Direct correspondence to: Timothy M. Smeeding at smeeding @wisc.edu, Department of Economics, 3464 Social Science Building, 1180 Observatory Dr., University of Wisconsin, Madison, WI 53706.

Open Access Policy: *RSF: The Russell Sage Foundation Journal of the Social Sciences* is an open access journal. This article is published under a Creative Commons Attribution-NonCommercial-NoDerivs 3.0 Unported License.

companies (Kille 2015). These partnerships demonstrated the research value of data that governments collected for administrative purposes. Likewise, former President Obama and his Council of Economic Advisers stressed the need for better access to public administrative data to examine program effectiveness (see Council of Economic Advisers 2015). Meanwhile, and relatedly, Congress passed the Evidence-Based Policymaking Commission Act of 2016 (P.L. 114–140) that created the Commission on Evidence-Based Policymaking (CEP). The commission's final report advocated for a "national secure data program" that would facilitate access to administrative data (CEP 2017). Within the policy world, many of the most important findings on the effects of poverty, inequality, education policy, and social programs now rest on public administrative data.

It is useful to consider the next steps that should be taken in this "new era of administrative data and evidence-based policy" (Haskins and Margolis 2014, 238). In any era of innovation, the early days in retrospect look chaotic. That applies here as well. Access to administrative data has frequently depended on personal networks and relationships with personnel in federal or state agencies. Datasets were built for one-time analyses. Documentation served agency insiders but was inadequate for new users. Given this state of affairs, some routinization is essential but, to be productive, we need to take a long view. The nation needs to develop—as swiftly as possible—an administrative data infrastructure that guarantees high-quality linkages, common standards for documentation, security and confidentiality, and fair access to researchers with good ideas and the requisite skills.

How might these goals be realized? The first step entails building an on-demand administrative database of the sort proposed by the Commission on Evidence-Based Policymaking in the form of a National Secure Data Service (NSDS) (CEP 2017). The second step is to set up institutions for ensuring both full access for qualified users and the confidentiality of the data for the public whose data are encoded.

The American Opportunity Study (AOS), which is being developed in collaboration with the Census Bureau, can assist in realizing these goals and thus achieving better access with confidentiality. The AOS is an ongoing effort to link the censuses of 1960 through 2010 and the American Community Surveys (ACS) and thereby convert cross-sectional decennial census data into a bona fide panel that will represent the full U.S. population over the last seventy years. Because this panel will be continuously refreshed as additional census and ACS data become available, it can serve as a population-level scaffolding on which other administrative data (such as tax records, earnings reports, program data) are then hung. The National Research Council (NRC) established the Standing Committee on Creating the American Opportunity Study and charged it with facilitating the digitizing of census data, examining matching and record linkage methodology, building a user committee for the AOS (NRC 2016), and examining governance options based on the 2017 CEP report.[1]

The AOS capitalizes on the importance of long-run analyses for both evaluating programs and monitoring trends. It promises not only to upgrade the country's capacity to study economic and social mobility but also to assist with a broader range of analyses oriented to monitoring long-term trends in poverty, inequality, and labor market outcomes and assessing the long-term effects of policy treatments and experiments. The AOS initiative is thus part of the broader goal to democratize access to administrative data, make that access safe and secure, and thereby realize the potential of linked administrative data (Mervis 2014). In other countries that have linked data, such as Wales and New Zealand, a well-developed infrastructure allows access to carefully vetted scholars, with the result that high-quality evidence is more frequently brought to bear on policy decisions. The payoff to developing this capacity is clear. In collaboration with the Cen-

---

1. See "Standing Committee on Creating the American Opportunity Study: First Phase," National Academies of Sciences, Engineering, and Medicine, http://sites.nationalacademies.org/DBASSE/CNSTAT/DBASSE_172151 (accessed October 5, 2018). The authors are members of the committee.

sus Bureau, we have thus begun to build the AOS and close the gap between the United States and other countries in this capacity for authentic evidence-informed policy. The cost of failing to do so is substantial and puts the United States at a competitive disadvantage relative to other countries.

Although many other countries are well ahead of the United States in developing administrative data resources, evidence of its payoff within the United States is already ample. This payoff takes the form of administrative data research on policy and program impacts on health, longevity, well-being, poverty, and socioeconomic mobility (Chetty et al. 2017; Figlio et al. 2014; Almond, Hoynes, and Schanzenbach 2011; Almond, Currie, and Duque 2018; Chetty, Hendren, and Katz 2015; see also CEP 2017). By virtue of these analyses, we now know that absolute economic mobility has fallen steadily since the 1940 birth cohort; that government efforts to support low-income and at-risk families yield health, educational, and economic benefits far in excess of their costs; that public investments in preschool, income support, housing, health care, and nutrition bring about substantial gains for children; and that long-term exposure to poor neighborhoods and polluted areas have lasting effects on social outcomes, health, and life expectancy. We review these and other studies to make it clear that the country's capacity to deliver authentic evidence-based policy will depend in no small part on successfully institutionalizing the administrative data revolution. Throughout this review, we focus on those types of analyses that, by virtue of requiring long-run assessments, reveal the payoff to building the AOS.

This payoff has been substantial because linking administrative data solves a host of problems that have long plagued conventional survey-based analyses of long-run processes. If the AOS is built, it can deliver enough cases to examine long-run effects on smaller populations; provide the power needed to carry out nonparametric analyses; enable intergenerational linkages that allow us to examine social mobility, intergenerational transfers, and sibling effects; provide new opportunities for quasi-experimental analysis over the long run (via, for example, state and local variability in the timing of program delivery); combine sources that allow for more comprehensive studies of program use and labor market processes; and both reduce and better understand the attrition that has long been the bane of survey-based panels.

In this article, we review these potential payoffs in more detail, focusing on what needs to happen to ensure that they are fully realized. The theme throughout is that the AOS should attract widespread support. It should appeal at once to those who believe that better data will demonstrate that existing programs and policies are typically effective and those who are skeptical and expect that many existing programs will be shown to be inefficient. The AOS is, in short, a critical vehicle for shifting the terms of debate about social programs into a straightforward discussion of the evidence. Although we are not so naive as to believe that this transformation will be absolute or uncomplicated, the AOS will bring us closer to realizing the vision of authentic evidence-based policymaking.

THE PAYOFF TO ANALYZING PROGRAMS AND POLICIES WITH BIG PUBLIC DATA

The administrative data revolution is not a recent development. Most notably, public administrative data has been the basis of social science research for many decades in Scandinavia, where data registers provide family records for economic and social outcomes for the entire population of a country. These data, along with more recently available administrative data in the United States, have improved causal analyses within economics and, to a lesser extent, other social sciences (Einav and Levin 2014). The turn to administrative data has accelerated over the last three decades: only 20 percent of microdata-based articles in the "top four" economics journals used administrative data in 1980, whereas 60 percent did so by 2010 (Chetty 2012).[2] This explosion in administrative data analysis is also clearly in play in the major social

---

2. The ACS, an extension of the decennial census, counts as administrative in this reckoning, despite including the word *survey* in its title.

science policy journals, such as the *American Economic Journal, Economic Policy*, and *Journal of Policy Analysis and Management*.

Although U.S. administrative data are becoming increasingly available, this revolution has relied disproportionately on non-U.S. data, especially from Scandinavia. The research based on Scandinavian population registries has straightforwardly informed policy in the countries from which the data are drawn. It is less clear that we can safely generalize these results to other countries. This reluctance to base policy or social science around results from countries with very different institutions, populations, and cultures is one of the driving forces behind the move to develop Scandinavian-inspired data resources in the United Kingdom (Yiu 2012), Australia (Tam and Clarke 2015), Canada (Trépanier, Pignal, and Royce 2014), and many other countries.

Because the United States is arguably more decentralized than any of these countries, it faces special challenges in harmonizing data across jurisdictions, but also has the potential advantage of leveraging policy variations across those jurisdictions to develop quasi-experimental evidence. It also already has a relatively long and distinguished history of administrative data analysis within many states. For example, Wisconsin state agencies have partnered with researchers to study child support records to evaluate the effectiveness of programs, an arrangement that has become an important model for many other states (see Cancian, Heinrich, and Chung 2013). This partnership involved mutual learning, trust, and understanding, and ultimately led to the development of a larger linked database, the multi-sample person file. The Wisconsin multisample person file links administrative records on more than twenty programs to individual and family beneficiaries (Noyes 2015). Because it is one of the earlier state efforts, it now allows for relatively long-run analyses, though it does not of course have the reach that the AOS promises.

This is but one example of state-level partnerships. In many other states, researchers have effectively exploited administrative data, most notably in Florida, Tennessee, North Carolina, Washington, and California. These data have allowed researchers to examine the long-term effects of birth conditions (Figlio et al. 2014), government preschool programs (Chetty et al. 2011), community college programs (Stevens, Kurlaender, and Grosz 2015), mandatory college preparation curricula in high schools (Jacob et al. 2016), prison release programs (Harding, Siegel, and Morenoff 2017; Lee, Harding, and Morenoff 2017), and even economic downturns (Ananat et al. 2011; Ananat, Gassman-Pines, and Gibson-Davis 2013). But state-level administrative data have limits because of interstate geographic mobility and because some of the key variables of interest are unavailable with state data. The AOS, by contrast, will allow us to overcome the problem of geographic mobility, provide additional variables of interest, and allow for longer-run analyses of social and economic program effects.

In the following section, we review three signal achievements coming out of these analyses of state and federal administrative data. In doing so, our intent is not just to illustrate the potential of linked administrative data, but also to focus on how the AOS, in particular, could advance the administrative data revolution.

Poverty and the Safety Net

The payoff to administrative data has been especially obvious in the fields of poverty measurement and antipoverty program evaluation. For example, Wisconsin has combined state-level administrative data with the ACS to build a Supplemental Poverty Measure (SPM), thus improving on traditional poverty measures that do not take program income and benefits into account (NRC 2005). With the SPM, Wisconsin policymakers can monitor trends in poverty, assess the effects of social programs on poverty without underreporting key program receipt and benefit levels, and gauge how possible changes in policy will affect poverty (Smeeding and Thornton 2017). The California Poverty Measure (CPM), which is likewise based on administrative data, has been used in similar ways (Wimer et al. 2013, 2014). The California government used the CPM, for example, to understand the likely costs and benefits of a state earned income tax credit supplement before it was enacted (Wimer et al. 2016). This measure will soon be upgraded by combining California Franchise Tax Board data and program data.

Similar administrative data initiatives are under way in New York City (Office of the Mayor 2014) and several other states, such as Oregon. In a related effort, Bruce Meyer, Wallace Mok, and James Sullivan have also assessed antipoverty program effects across many states using program data, leading to the key finding that income support benefits are underreported in survey data (2015).

The AOS, when it becomes available, will make it possible for other states to more easily calculate SPM-style measures. By providing a population-level panel, it will allow states to calculate poverty rates at more detailed geographic levels (by supplementing the ACS with population earnings and tax data), at more frequent intervals (by exploiting tax data, earnings reports, and other frequently released data), and with direct evidence on program use (via administrative program data).

Early Childhood Interventions

A decade ago, James Heckman argued that programs and policies that entail intervening prenatally or in early childhood show an especially attractive return on investment (Cunha and Heckman 2008; Heckman and Mosso 2014; see also Barker 1995; Council of Economic Advisers 2015). Although some of the evidence on behalf of early intervention is survey based, much of it has also turned on administrative analysis (Almond and Currie 2011; Cascio and Schanzenbach 2013; Aizer and Currie 2014).

Administrative data have been important, for example, in reassessing the claim that early childhood education programs may initially stimulate learning but that, over time, the benefit of this early participation tends to diminish. Although the Head Start Evaluation suggested, for example, that learning gains from that program faded by the third grade, analyses of administrative data revealed other compensating long-run benefits (Duncan and Magnuson 2013). When high-quality administrative data were used to reexamine the long-term effects of nutrition interventions, parenting programs, and various high-quality and "moderate-quality" preschool programs (Head Start, for example), they revealed persisting later-life effects on graduation rates, earnings, and crime (Hoynes, Page, and Stevens 2011; Chetty et al. 2011; Council of Economic Advisers 2015). The AOS, when available, will allow us to build an even richer evidence base on the long-term effects of home visiting programs, childcare and preschool, and early childhood education.

Administrative data have also been important in establishing the long-run effects of tax credits, cash transfers, and near-cash programs (for recent important reviews of this literature, see Shaefer et al. 2018; Almond, Currie, and Duque 2018). We now know, for example, that the earned income tax credit, one of the government's most important child-poverty programs, reduces the incidence of low birth weight, raises math and reading scores, and boosts college enrollment rates (Dahl and Lochner 2012; Evans and Garthwaite 2014). The Supplemental Nutrition Assistance Program (food stamps) has similarly long-lasting benefits for child recipients as well as positive effects on pregnancy outcomes (Almond, Hoynes, and Schanzenbach 2011) and adult obesity (Hoynes, Schanzenbach, and Almond 2016). Likewise, evidence from the United States and Canada indicates that many types of tax-based refundable cash transfers, such as the Canadian Child Tax Benefit, increase child cognitive achievement and health (Dahl and Lochner 2012; Milligan and Stabile 2009; Evans and Garthwaite 2014). Children who receive Medicaid are more likely to graduate from high school, more likely to complete college, and less likely (at least if they are African American) to die in their late teens or be hospitalized by age twenty-five (Wherry et al. 2015).[3]

Long-Run Effects of Cash Support

Our third illustrative example pertains to administrative data analyses of direct cash support, for both those who can and cannot work. Much research has been completed on the effects of cash income support and "negative income taxes," often called basic income, on such short-term outcomes as work effort or childbearing. But until recently we knew less about

---

3. Research using administrative data from Medicaid and tax records reveals that the public recoup their Medicaid investment via increased tax revenues (Brown, Kowalski, and Lurie 2015).

their long-term effects.[4] Using administrative records from the Mothers' Pension program (1911–1935), a precursor to the AFDC program, researchers have now assessed the impact of cash transfers across the entire life course by matching program participants to World War II enlistment records and 1940 census records (Aizer et al. 2014). By using Social Security data to follow program beneficiaries, it was shown that children who receive benefits, even for just a few years, are affected for as long as eighty years or more. Most notably, the poorest children in this sample experienced a 1.5-year increase in longevity by virtue of receiving cash transfers; better-off children saw smaller increases. It was further shown that cash transfers reduced the probability of being underweight by half, increased educational attainment by 0.4 years, and increased income by 14 percent during adulthood (Aizer et al. 2014; Furman 2015). This benefit, which comes mainly from helping low-income families pay for basic needs (such as food, housing, health care), has been shown to have effects on child well-being over and above those of direct service programs, like preschool education and health care (Shaefer et al. 2018; Duncan, Magnuson, and Votruba-Drzal 2014; Furman 2015).

This short review, which is more illustrative than exhaustive, shows that the frontier of research on the effectiveness of social policy has relied on—and will likely continue to rely on—linkages to census and administrative data. This approach has improved the accuracy of our data, reduced the need to field costly surveys, allowed for better monitoring of labor market outcomes, and provided high-quality evidence on the long-term consequences of policies, interventions, and economic and social change.

For all the successes to date, administrative data have yet to be fully exploited because access has been granted idiosyncratically to a few well-connected researchers, and because studies have relied on a small number of administrative data sources and thus been able to address only a limited subset of questions. These problems can be overcome with the AOS. It will serve as a standing resource that regularizes and expands access to administrative data, that links a more comprehensive constellation of census and administrative data, and that makes a wider range of long-run analyses possible.

A SHORT HISTORY OF THE AMERICAN OPPORTUNITY STUDY

The payoff to building this more comprehensive resource is wide ranging, but in the early history of the AOS most of the protagonists were motivated by a rather narrow interest in monitoring recent trends in social mobility. We briefly review this impetus because of its relevance to how the larger AOS initiative developed.

The initial animating interest in the AOS rested on assessing the long-standing American Dream that hard work and ingenuity will be rewarded with material success even for children born into poor families. The American Dream narrative is deeply embedded within American culture, has attracted generations of immigrants seeking a better life in this nation, and continues to be widely embraced and celebrated among Americans (Manza and Brooks 2016; Mitnik et al. 2015).

It is nonetheless striking that the empirical evidence on recent trends in social mobility is relatively scarce. Although many commentators have openly worried that both relative and absolute mobility are declining across generations, the evidence bearing on these worries is limited. Because the necessary data are unavailable, our evidence on long-term trends in absolute mobility has been pieced together from cross-sectional data and strong assumptions about the trend in relative mobility (see Chetty et al. 2017; also see Hout 2018 for a study of more recent trends in absolute mobility based on the General Social Survey). A handful of studies further suggest a possible decline in relative mobility (Aaronson and Mazumder 2008; Mitnik, Cumberworth, and Grusky 2016). But other studies suggest otherwise (Chetty et al. 2014; Lee and Solon 2009; Hout 2015).

---

4. The data collected by the various negative income tax studies of the 1960s and 1970s, which mainly examined effects on labor supply, have not been preserved and thus cannot be used to address long-term effects (but see Price and Song 2018).

It is also problematic that most of the current research on mobility is limited to economic (earnings or income) mobility alone. Income offers an important but incomplete view of social mobility. The case for a more complete assessment rests on evidence that occupations and related measures of social class can affect behaviors, attitudes, and political participation in ways not understandable in wholly economic terms (Weeden and Grusky 2005, 2012). It also rests on the understanding that economic mobility is endogenous to the underlying structure of occupational opportunities that give rise to earnings and income. The occupational structure represents this larger organization of opportunities that may be facilitated or limited by various types of social closure that operate partly at the occupation level (such as unions or occupational licenses). Even more important, it is likely that some individuals trade off earnings for other occupational rewards (autonomy, prestige), the implication being that analyses based on economic standing alone may misrepresent the true amount of opportunity. In short, data on occupational mobility are fundamental in themselves and would be important to collect even if it were possible to fully describe income and earnings mobility.

Nearly a half-century has passed since the last multidimensional assessment of social mobility in the United States (Featherman and Hauser 1978; see also Blau and Duncan 1967), a state of affairs that contrasts sharply with practices in other countries (Breen, Mood, and Jonsson 2016). This is a striking lapse considering the profound changes that have taken place in U.S. society over the past four decades. These changes include, for example, the historic increase in women's labor force participation, the decline in manufacturing jobs, the rise of service employment, rising immigration and the associated ethnic diversification of the population, the decline in white men's labor force participation, the ongoing changes in family and household structure, and the increase in economic inequality (Fischer and Hout 2006). How have these changes affected opportunities within American society? We cannot know until a full multidimensional assessment of mobility is undertaken.

This state of affairs led David Grusky and Matthew Snipp to meet with officials at the Census Bureau, the Office of Management and Budget (OMB), and the National Science Foundation in 2012 to begin a conversation about how to collect the requisite data. These conversations made it clear that a follow-up study of social mobility comparable to the two previous studies (Blau and Duncan 1967; Featherman and Hauser 1978) would be an expensive undertaking. The 1973 study, based largely on a monthly supplement to the Current Population Survey (CPS), cost approximately $2.0 million, which is nearly $12.0 million in 2018 dollars.[5] Worse yet, a new study that does not take the form of a CPS supplement likely would cost many times this amount, possibly exceeding the entire annual budget that the National Science Foundation allocates for sociological research.

With support from the National Science Foundation and the National Research Council, work commenced in 2013 to develop a plan for launching a new study of social mobility.[6] The core task at that point was to identify a survey vehicle for the study, with the main possibilities being the CPS, the Survey of Income and Program Participation (SIPP), and the ACS. The second task was to identify the most important content domains to be included in this new study. To accomplish these tasks, the group sought the assistance of a wide range of social scientists, mainly sociologists, political scientists, and economists who were experts in social mobility, education, immigration, and demography. These individuals were invited to prepare papers on possible content domains for presentation at a workshop held in June 2013 at the National Academy of Science's Keck Center in Washington, D.C. The resulting papers were subsequently published as a volume in the *Annals of the American Academy of Political and Social Science* (Grusky, Smeeding, and Snipp 2015).

---

5. Robert M. Hauser, personal communication with the authors.

6. The initial meeting and founding group included the authors and a few additional social and behavioral scientists.

This workshop was followed by a series of meetings of a smaller executive committee. The final meeting was held in August 2014. In the interim, Grusky, Timothy Smeeding, and Snipp met with the Census Bureau, OMB, the Department of Commerce, and other agencies to discuss the development of plans for the AOS. In addition to the original group, representatives of the Census Bureau, the Internal Revenue Service (IRS), and other federal government organizations were included in the meetings and deliberations.

Throughout these deliberations, the choice of the survey vehicle became clouded by various external considerations, especially the viability of securing space on the CPS or ACS instruments. Holding such external considerations aside, one of the workshop papers expertly reviewed the costs and benefits of different survey vehicles, with the conclusion that the ACS might be the best option (Warren 2015). The SIPP, although rich in content, was rejected because its sample was not large enough to capture small immigrant groups and less common family structures. The CPS, although larger than the SIPP, was less rich in content and still too small to analyze certain immigrant groups and areas smaller than states. The ACS was even more circumscribed in content but delivered the most statistical power by virtue of its sample size. Ultimately, the group concluded that neither the CPS nor the ACS would be suitable, whereas the smaller SIPP panel with its "gold standard" linkages to administrative data contained the all-important hint that administrative data might be a way forward.[7]

Given these constraints, the committee explored the possibility of a "linkage solution" in which parent-child linkages were identified (via co-residency) in, for example, the 1990 census, and the subsequent occupation of the child was secured by linking to the 2000 census and the ACS. This approach was congruent with Census Bureau's research program in the Center for Administrative Records Research and Analysis (CARRA). The CARRA staff had successfully linked records in the 2000 and 2010 censuses to data from the Social Security Administration and the Internal Revenue Service. These data were further linked to the 2004 and 2008 SIPP panels to form the SIPP gold standard file (Johnson, Massey, and O'Hara 2015). Based on these and other linkage projects, the committee developed a more robust and lasting project that entailed first adding links to the 1990 census, then turning to those from 1950 to 1980. The committee christened it the American Opportunity Study.

THE STRUCTURE OF THE AMERICAN OPPORTUNITY STUDY

Because the data making up the AOS already exist, the initiative adds value solely by finding low-cost ways to digitize existing data, link them, and deliver them widely and safely (see Warren 2015; Johnson, Massey, and O'Hara 2015). The AOS will rest on two types of links: intergenerational links to parents and other ancestors and intragenerational links across all censuses. The panel that results from linking censuses will be very useful in and of itself, but the research value will be even greater if it becomes possible to link them to other administrative databases and surveys. The resulting full panel is represented in figure 1. Although this figure represents the AOS as a single massive panel tracing many generations of American families from their arrival in the United States to the present, in practice it will be a *potential* dataset, in which only parts are assembled for any given research project. It is highly unlikely that any researcher would be given access to the AOS in its entirety.

The payoff to building out a full AOS, as represented in figure 1, would be substantial. If, for instance, approval to link to IRS 1040 and Social Security Administration (SSA) earnings records were secured, additional high-quality reports of income, earnings, and other variables would become available on an annual basis. Although IRS 1040 and SSA earnings reports are perhaps the most valuable linkages for the purposes of mobility research, other administrative records could be usefully incorporated

---

7. Indeed, a new version of the SIPP might follow the path of omitting detailed questions on income and earnings, instead asking respondents for permission to access IRS, SSA, and other administrative data to measure income, earnings, and other variables more accurately assessed by administrative data.

Figure 1. Schematic of the American Opportunity Study

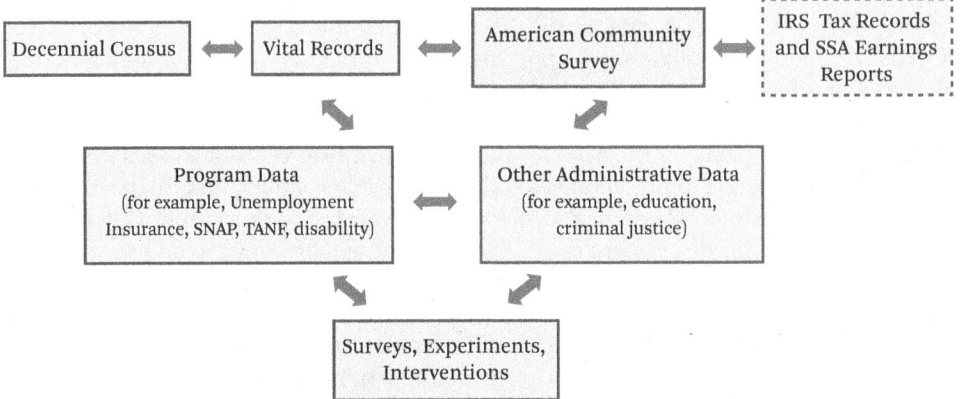

Source: Authors' schematics.

as well (program participation records, incarceration records, veterans' records). The practical and legal obstacles to including additional types of administrative data are not trivial (for discussion, see Johnson, Massey, and O'Hara 2015; CEP 2017).

How will the links be made? Researchers at the Census Bureau have developed a crosswalk from the universe of all social security numbers (SSNs) ever assigned to a new set of identifiers known as the protected identification keys (PIKs). Using the names, addresses, and birthdates in the 2000 and 2010 censuses and then comparing them with the names, birthplaces, and birthdates associated with SSNs, the researchers have assigned PIKs to nearly every person record in the 2000 and 2010 censuses and the 2008 through 2016 ACS. The 1990 and earlier censuses, by contrast, have not yet been PIKed. Assembly of the AOS thus requires four more steps:

Assign PIKs to the person records in the 1990 census (and ultimately all censuses from 1950 to 1980 as well).

Use these identifiers to then link to the same individuals in the 2000 through 2010 decennial censuses, the 2008 through 2016 ACS, and ultimately future decennial censuses and ACS.

Add variables by using the same identifiers to link to data from other administrative sources (such as Social Security, Medicare and Medicaid, Veterans Administration, Bureau of Justice Statistics, Department of Education, and Internal Revenue Service data).

Link parents to co-resident children within censuses. Verify and extend these intergenerational links by drawing on existing databases that match the SSNs of parents to those of their children.

In all likelihood, two versions of the AOS will have to be created, one that omits sensitive administrative data and other information to prevent deductive disclosure, and another highly "secure version" that could only be analyzed in federal statistical research data centers (FSRDCs). The latter highly controlled version would include administrative data and would be accessible only under stringent restrictions and protocols, such as those outlined by the Commission on Evidence-Based Policymaking. In the balance of this section, we elaborate on each of the four steps, paying special attention to the various obstacles likely to be encountered in the course of doing so.

It is useful to begin by discussing how PIKs can be assigned to each individual in the 1990 census. This procedure is carried out by using a set of variables (first name, last name, date of birth, address, sex) that, when taken together, make it possible to find an individual's SSN in the Social Security Administration's Numident file. The current PIKing procedures can likely be improved (see Warren 2015; Johnson, Massey, and O'Hara 2015). It is possible, for example, that direct census-to-census linkages will yield results that are superior to approaches that involve "going up" to the Numident and assigning PIKs. When an optimal procedure is settled upon, it can be used to redo the existing PIKs for the 2000 through 2010 censuses and the 2008 through 2016 ACS, and then to PIK, for the first time, the 1950 through 1990 censuses. The latter step will allow us to go back further in time to monitor long-term trends or carry out long-run analyses of programs.

The AOS panel will thus provide observations on individual income, education, or occupation for individuals appearing in the 1990 and earlier censuses, the relevant administrative sources (IRS 1040, SSA earnings reports), and the ACS. The final step is to match parents and children by exploiting relationship pointers in the 1990 census and by drawing on databases that link parents' SSNs to those of their children. The "Kidlink" files currently used by the IRS to determine whether tax filers are making legitimate claims to dependent children could be used, for example, for intergenerational matching in the AOS (for details and limitations, see Johnson, Massey, and O'Hara 2015). Additionally, IRS 1040 forms can be used to improve the quality and scope of parent-child matches, given that parents claiming children as dependents have been required, since 1987, to list the SSNs of the children they claim, whether the children live with the parent or not. Finally, the ACS and decennial censuses also identify children of the household head, thus providing a further source of parent-child matches (see Johnson, Massey, and O'Hara 2015).

The AOS, as designed, will provide a high-quality scaffold for monitoring mobility without the cost of mounting a new mobility survey, without further burdening existing surveys with intergenerational modules, and without troubling people by repeating questions they have already answered. It thus provides a partial solution to the problems arising from low response rates and measurement errors for many survey-based reports, particularly earnings and income (Meyer, Mok, and Sullivan 2015). It is unlikely, however, that surveys will disappear altogether from this post-AOS world (NASEM 2017). To the contrary, the AOS would allow surveys to become more efficient because they could be used exclusively to ascertain variables that are not available in the AOS. Given the AOS's architecture, any sufficiently large survey with individual identifiers could be linked to it, which means that additional variables collected as part of that linked survey could be appended to the AOS variables.[8] Although an analysis based on the AOS alone would suffice for a wide range of descriptive studies, a survey supplement to the AOS might be useful for studies of the causes, consequences, and social correlates of mobility and of other program and policy effects.

The AOS will also provide multiple reports on many outcomes. We know, for example, that the detailed earnings records (DER) do not accurately measure earned income, given that respondents at the bottom ranges of the income and earnings distribution often overreport DER-based earnings because of wages earned outside the Social Security system (Bollinger et al. 2015; Hokayem, Bollinger, and Ziliak 2015). Even for higher-income earners, both the DER and IRS tax data help fill in unreported and underreported earned incomes, which again speaks to the value of repeated measures of the sort that the AOS will provide.[9]

BENEFITS OF THE AMERICAN OPPORTUNITY STUDY

Will the benefits of building the AOS outweigh the costs? We address this question by describing how the AOS will assist with census operations and how it will support basic, applied, and policy-relevant research. We suspect that, re-

---

8. For voluntary surveys, respondent consent is required before any links can be made to administrative records, to the ACS, or to decennial censuses.

9. The AOS panel will be compromised insofar as many individuals are incorrectly linked (either intergenerationally or intragenerationally), or many individuals cannot be linked at all. The available evidence suggests that these problems will be relatively minor and can be successfully remediated with sample weights and other approaches (only some of which assume that the data are missing at random).

gardless of whether the AOS is built out in the near term, the country will eventually turn to an infrastructure of the AOS sort. This outcome is likely given the dividends to fully exploiting the country's capacity to assemble a high-quality panel. These dividends include the following:

the substantial cost savings and efficiencies that arise from reusing information that has already been collected for other purposes (rather than mounting a new and replicative data collection effort);

the capacity to base multigenerational comparisons on contemporary reports rather than recollections;

the relatively high quality of administrative data (relative to survey-based measures);

the spinoffs and cost savings to various census products that become possible by advancing methods for PIKing and intergenerational matching (see Johnson, Massey, and O'Hara 2015);

the development of a monitoring infrastructure that, by virtue of being automatically "refreshing," sidesteps the problems with unrepresentativeness that plague other long-running panels, such as the Panel Study of Income Dynamics (PSID) and the National Longitudinal Surveys (NLS);

the capacity to examine patterns of nonresponse and attrition in surveys, such as the PSID and NLS, when they are linked to the AOS;[10]

the opportunity to gradually grow the AOS and extend its research uses by adding new administrative records (health data, program use data);

the capacity to field leaner and more efficient surveys by using the AOS as a sampling frame and filling in core economic and demographic items before contacting survey respondents; and

the spinoff of an automatically refreshing sampling frame that, by virtue of combining census, ACS, tax, earnings, and other sources, may be superior to any competing frames.

This formidable list of infrastructural benefits justifies in itself a move to an AOS-style panel. The policy and research benefits add further weight to the case for an AOS. The analysis of social mobility, which was the main impetus for developing the AOS, will of course benefit. It will be possible to carry out trend analyses of mobility, sibling analyses of shared family effects, multidimensional analyses of mobility (combining income, education, occupation, and other dimensions), and even twin analyses of mobility (given the large sample size and hence large twin population). It will also be possible to exploit the replicate measurements embedded in the AOS to complete better analyses of economic, socioeconomic, and labor market outcomes.

When additional administrative or survey data are linked to the infrastructure, even more research payoffs open up (see figure 2). It will be possible, for example, to examine the long-run effects of earlier life circumstances on any of the additional dependent variables that then become available (health, political attitudes, social attitudes, retirement behavior). There would likely be substantial payoff, for example, to linking to the National Health and Nutrition Examining Survey, Add Health, the National Election Survey, the General Social Survey, Fragile Families, the Health and Retirement Study, the Panel Study of Income Dynamics, and the National Longitudinal Surveys.

The AOS could also be used to examine the long-run effects of key independent variables that take the form of experimental treatments, nonexperimental exposure, or other types of life-cycle spells. The main payoff to the AOS is precisely this new capacity to examine the long-run effects of social programs or policies (such as the GI Bill), individual-level institutional participation (such as military service), tax policy (such as the earned income tax credit), or various types of cohort or period effects (such as the Vietnam War). This capacity is represented at the bottom of figure 2.

---

10. Existing surveys, such as the PSID, can be used to test the accuracy of intergenerational linkages in the AOS (by PIKing the PSID and linking it to the AOS).

Figure 2. Expanded Schematic of the American Opportunity Study

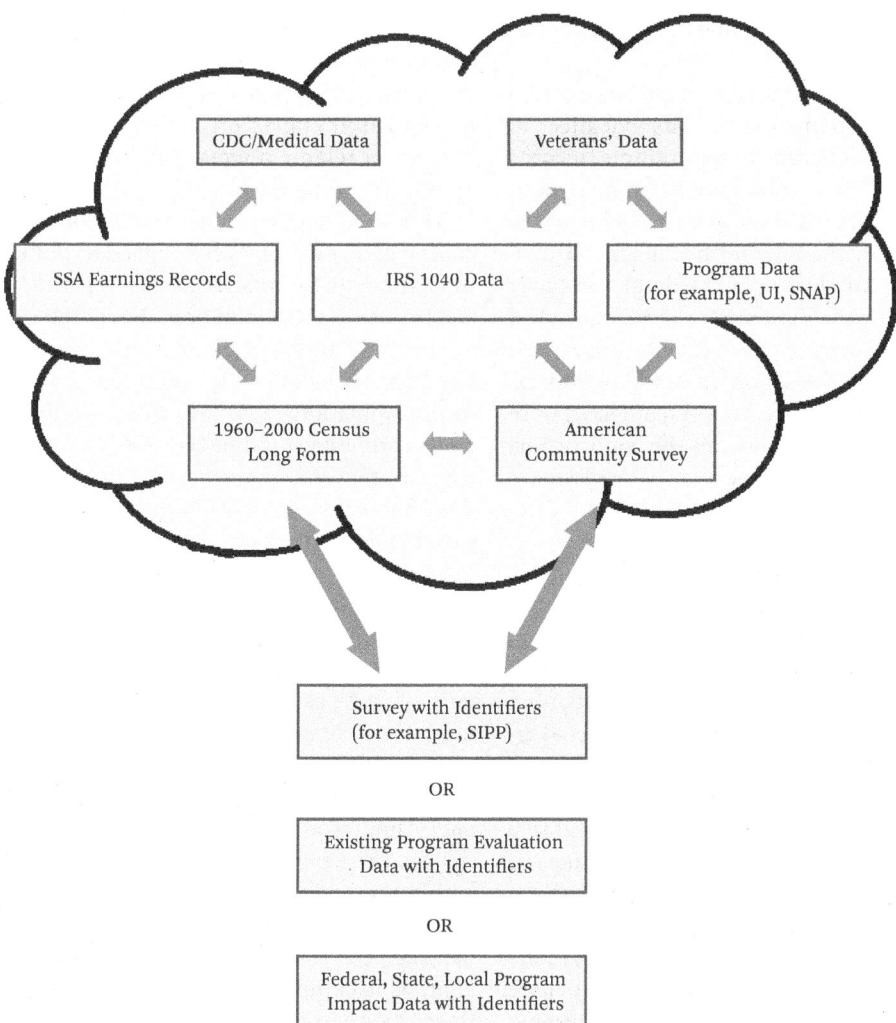

Source: Authors' schematics.

The effects of many different types of institutional experiences could also be examined. We could, for example, link to Bureau of Justice data (or state and local data), making it possible to assess the long-term effects of incarceration on earnings, recidivism, and much more (see Looney and Turner 2018). We could likewise assess the effects of training programs during and after incarceration as well as various post-incarceration conditions (such as reception programs) on the life course of those experiencing incarceration. If we linked to Veterans Administration data on military service, we could examine the long-term effects of service on various economic and non-economic outcomes (see Autor et al. 2015).[11] By linking to state data on schooling, we could better estimate the economic and non-economic payoffs to various types of education. The same approach could be used to examine the effects of nurse home

---

11. This study combines administrative data from the U.S. Army, Department of Veterans Affairs (VA), and the Social Security Administration to analyze the effect of the VA's Disability Compensation (DC) program on veterans' labor force participation and earnings.

visiting programs, job training programs, childcare and early childhood education, school experiments, tax credits, and much more (Berlin 2016).

The independent variable of interest can also take the form of historical events that affect all or some birth cohorts. If, for example, records from the Federal Emergency Management Agency were linked to the AOS, it would be possible to study the long-term impact of Hurricane Katrina and the role of federal assistance in mitigating the disruption the storm caused to those who were exposed to it. In this case, a standard one-off assessment would be very expensive because those who were affected were relocated to sites throughout the country. The AOS would allow for an inexpensive assessment that exploited powerful quasi-experimental designs. We could likewise use the AOS to assess the long-run effects of various wars, the effects of economic recessions and crises on those living in hard-hit areas, and the effects of school shootings, terrorist attacks, and other traumatic events (such as the attacks of September 11, 2001) on those living within the affected areas (even if they moved thereafter).

For all of these examples, the analysis becomes possible insofar as those exposed to a treatment can be identified via the census or administrative data already in the AOS, new surveys that are linked to the AOS, or new administrative data that are linked to the AOS. In the limiting case, a simple list of those participating in the treatment would also suffice, assuming that approval to use that list is secured.

How would treatment effects then be assessed? If a bona fide experiment has been carried out (such as a basic income experiment), we could observe the long-run outcomes of the treatment and control groups within the AOS architecture without incurring the usual high costs of tracking participants and repeatedly administering survey protocols.[12] Although the country's main social science experiments have of course already been assessed in some fashion, these assessments frequently have not been able to fully examine long-run effects. The AOS would also provide for high-quality assessments in the absence of an explicit control group. In this case, the AOS would have the reach and sample size to allow for matched within-community comparisons, various types of regression discontinuities, fixed effects on individuals, and all manner of related nonexperimental or quasi-experimental approaches.

This suggests that policy evaluation in the context of an existing AOS would be revolutionized. Although the analysis of past experiments and treatments will sometimes be complicated by this need to find a list of participants, the same requirement can be met more easily for future evaluations. It follows that experiments and treatments could be assessed at very low cost. Whenever a new experiment or program was established, it could automatically be evaluated—with only relatively small investments in planning—within the context of the AOS architecture.

Could research of this sort be completed without the AOS? Could the current state of affairs—relying as it does on one-off analyses of tax and other administrative data—get the same work done? The existing approach is problematic because access to administrative data is limited and meted out idiosyncratically; the analyses typically have to be completed within the context of a single administrative dataset or a relatively small number of linked datasets; the total cost is high because each analysis is completed as a one-off study; and the capacity to carry out long-run analyses is compromised (given that the pre-2000 censuses have not been PIKed and converted into a panel). If the AOS were built, all of these problems would be solved at once.

THE AMERICAN OPPORTUNITY STUDY AND THE COMMISSION ON EVIDENCE-BASED POLICYMAKING

Two critical questions affect prospects for further developing the AOS. First, how does the AOS fit within the recommendations recently issued by the Commission on Evidence-Based Policymaking? Second, how does the National

---

12. The basic income experiment conducted by Y Combinator Research will rely, for example, on administrative data to unobtrusively monitor key economic and non-economic outcomes.

Secure Data Service, as laid out by the CEP, relate to the AOS?

The CEP provides a principled approach to ensuring privacy and confidentiality, addressing key research questions, providing channels for public comment, and ensuring public availability of evidence. The NSDS further ensures that the capacity to generate, access, and use data and evidence can be integrated within government institutions that are adequately funded and staffed. The NSDS may be understood in this context as the "cloud" in figure 2 surrounding the top two levels of the AOS in figure 1.

The NSDS sub-agency charged with data access will receive projects, surveys, and evaluations from qualified and approved researchers. These newly received data will then be linked to existing data within the cloud (when permission to link has been granted). Without directly assembling a master file in the cloud, the NSDS will make the required linkages, prepare a secure dataset for analysis, and provide the qualified research team with a report on the quality of the matched data and data edits. The NSDS will eventually be charged with producing reports on data sensitivity and risk assessments for public release of de-identified confidential data. At the same time, each agency producing administrative data will have an office charged with producing cleaned administrative data, with these data then made available to the NSDS to link with other data for qualified and approved research.

This vision will require streamlining and modernizing standards for accessing data for research purposes. The NSDS will be guided by data-sharing agreements, data use agreements, and memorandums of understanding. As it stands, a standard template for these legal documents does not exist; instead, a patchwork quilt of laws governs data access and security. These must be updated with a uniform standard that works for the wide range of data that might be made available under the NSDS. This new standard might, for example, reconcile United States Code (USC) Title XIII (covering access to data collected by the Census Bureau), USC Title XXVI (governing data produced by the Internal Revenue Service), and the Confidential Information Protection and Statistical Efficiency Act (governing data produced by the National Center for Health Statistics and other federal statistical agencies).

These CEP recommendations are in the process of being implemented. In late 2017, the U.S. House of Representatives passed the Foundations for Evidence-Based Policymaking Act of 2017 (H.R. 4174), which implements ten of the recommendations in the CEP report. It lays out the fundamental responsibilities of federal statistical agencies and the proactive duty of parent departments and agencies to support their statistical agency or agencies; it stipulates that each cabinet department and independent agency should designate a chief evaluation officer, a chief data officer, and a statistical official; it declares that agencies are to make their data assets publicly available except where the data are restricted (such as for confidentiality considerations); and it declares that agencies are to make their data assets available to statistical agencies for purposes of developing evidence (unless data-sharing is clearly prohibited by law).

However, twelve of the CEP's recommendations were not included in H.R. 4174, and the creation of the NSDS was conspicuously among those that were absent. Because the legislation does call for the creation of an advisory board to set policies for the NSDS, it suggests that the NSDS might be established in a subsequent piece of legislation. The Bipartisan Policy Center, a Washington, D.C., think tank and a leading advocate behind H.R. 4174, indicated that this was indeed their strategy. Responding to a query about why all twenty-two recommendations made by the CEP do not appear in H.R. 4174, Bipartisan Policy Center staff reply that "the ten CEP recommendations included in the bill reflect those prioritized to build basic capacity while prioritizing important privacy protections at the outset. Future authorizing and appropriations legislation will incorporate additional CEP recommendations" (Hart and Davis 2017).

Nonetheless, because the organizational foundation for an NSDS has been in place for more than twenty years, it is hardly a radical step to formalize it. In 1994, the Census Bureau opened its first research data center (RDC) at the National Bureau of Economic Research in

Cambridge, Massachusetts. The objective was to create a secure enclave where researchers could access confidential census data in a highly controlled environment. Before any analyses could be carried out in an RDC, all researchers were carefully vetted, and their projects were likewise carefully reviewed. The output from the resulting data analyses were also reviewed by a Census Bureau employee trained in disclosure review before it was allowed to leave the facility.

Some twenty years later, twenty-nine RDCs operate around the country, and plans are to open more in the coming years. Although the early RDCs contained only data produced by the Census Bureau, the National Center for Health Statistics subsequently decided to make its confidential data available through the RDC network. Encouraged by the White House Office of Management and Budget, other agencies also began to make their data available through the RDC network. Currently, data from eleven federal agencies can be accessed through the RDC network, and more agencies are expected to become part of this system. To reflect this growth, the name of the Census Bureau RDC network was changed to the Federal Statistical Research Data Center system in 2014. It is, then, only a short step from the FSRDC system to the more ambitious NSDS. If the NSDS were to be formed, it would entail building up the capacity of the FSRDC system, broadening access to new data, and adding staff to support the new work.

It follows that the AOS aligns well with the CEP's vision for the future. When census, ACS, and tax data are PIKed and thus linkable from 1950 to the present day, the country will have an exhaustive panel that represents the country's population at any point in time, builds links across generations, and provides the rudimentary scaffolding on which a vast array of administrative data might be added. The NSDS, as outlined by the CEP, thus becomes the organizational mechanism through which administrative data are accessed and successfully linked to this scaffolding.

CONCLUSION

The growing availability of administrative data will continue to transform how public policy is evaluated at all levels of government. The CEP, along with earlier initiatives undertaken at the OMB by the Obama administration, should be understood as important steps in expanding access to government data in policymaking. The AOS initiative should be understood, in turn, as providing the population-level scaffolding for this administrative data revolution.

These efforts to link and deploy administrative data still face many legal, bureaucratic, and political hurdles. The most commonly voiced concerns pertain, of course, to issues of confidentiality. It is important in this regard to distinguish between first-order concerns about actual compromises to identifiable data and second-order concerns about the fallout from unwarranted public worries about such compromises.

The first-order concerns are arguably the less formidable ones. This is because, as legitimate as first-order concerns are in other contexts, no special or troubling confidentiality issues arise with the AOS. In assembling the AOS, the NSDS would indeed rely on various identifiers, but these are only interim "production tools" that will ultimately be stripped from the released product and that will exist only in the cloud of figure 2. This type of procedure is already standard practice for a variety of census products and raises no new or special concerns. Likewise, the AOS would be made available only to carefully vetted researchers and research projects through federal statistical research data centers, again a long-standing and very successful delivery mechanism that raises no new or special concerns.

When the AOS is made available, the demand will likely be so high that existing FSRDCs will have to grow in size, new FSRDCs will have to be opened, and processes for accessing AOS data within the FSRDCs will have to be streamlined within the CEP guidelines.

We obviously cannot rule out the possibility of legitimate first-order concerns. Rather, our point is simply that we are currently unaware of any troubling confidentiality issues that the preceding practices, all of which are standard and ongoing, might raise in the foreseeable future, assuming that the AOS is indeed embedded in the NSDS. Because we could be overlooking legitimate concerns, a crucial part of the debate about the AOS and the NSDS should be an open and wide-ranging discussion of the types of security breaches that might occur and how they might be prevented. The Census Bureau is, for example, currently developing new standards for the disclosure review process in direct response to concerns raised by the data security literature.

Although a full discussion of first-order concerns should be an important part of any deliberations about the AOS, our strong suspicion is that the most pressing worries will prove to be of the second-order variety, especially in light of recent revelations of data misuse by private social media companies. These revelations create a problematic climate for discussing data security even though they do not bear directly on AOS security. That is, most of us very reasonably worry about the public's perception of the AOS, not about any actual compromises to privacy that the AOS might imply. The standard prescription for such misinformation problems, and one to which we default here, is simply a call for a full and frank discussion of the facts of the matter.

We are hopeful that the public will conclude that the benefits are profound and that the risks are minimal and can be contained. If the AOS is successfully developed, it will prove to be a transformative tool that upgrades the country's capacity to evaluate programs and policies, allows for evidence-based debate about our programs and policies, and improves the science of poverty, unemployment, and other social and economic problems.

REFERENCES

Aaronson, Daniel, and Bhashkar Mazumder. 2008. "Intergenerational Economic Mobility in the United States, 1940 to 2000." *Journal of Human Resources* 43(1): 139–72. DOI: 10.3368/jhr.43.1.139.

Aizer, Anna, and Janet V. Currie. 2014. The Intergenerational Transmission of Inequality: Maternal Disadvantage and Health at Birth." *Science* 344 (May): 856.

Aizer, Anna, Shari Eli, Joseph Ferrie, and Adriana Lleras-Mune. 2014. "The Long Term Impact of Cash Transfers to Poor Families." NBER working paper 20103. Cambridge, Mass.: National Bureau of Economic Research. Accessed October 5, 2018. http://www.nber.org/papers/w20103.

Almond, Douglas, and Janet Currie. 2011. "Killing Me Softly: The Fetal Origins Hypothesis." *Journal of Economic Perspectives* 25(3): 153–172. DOI:10.1257/jep.25.3.153.

Almond, Douglas, Janet Currie, and Valerie Duque. 2018. "Childhood Circumstances and Adult Outcomes: Act II." *Journal of Economic Literature* 56(4): 1360–446.

Almond, Douglas, Hilary W. Hoynes, and Diane W. Schanzenbach. 2011. "Inside the War on Poverty: The Impact of Food Stamps on Birth Outcomes." *Review of Economics and Statistics* 93(2): 387–403.

Ananat, Elizabeth O., Anna Gassman-Pines, and Christina Gibson-Davis. 2013. "The Effect of Local Economic Downturns on Teen Births: Evidence from North Carolina." *Demography* December 50(6): 2151–71.

Ananat, Elizabeth O., Anna Gassman-Pines, Dania V. Francis, and Christina M. Gibson-Davis. 2011. "Children Left Behind: The Effects of Statewide Job Loss on Student Achievement." NBER working paper no. 17104. Cambridge, Mass.: National Bureau of Economic Research. Accessed October 5, 2018. http://www.nber.org/papers/w17104.

Autor, David H., Mark Duggan, Kyle Greenberg, and David S. Lyle. 2015. "The Impact of Disability Benefits on Labor Supply: Evidence from the VA's Disability Compensation Program." NBER working paper no. 21144. Cambridge, Mass.: National Bureau of Economic Research. Accessed October 5, 2018. http://www.nber.org/papers/w21144.

Barker, David. 1995. "Fetal Origins of Coronary Heart Disease." *British Medical Journal* 311(6998): 171–74. DOI: 10.1136/bmj.311.6998.171.

Berlin, Gordon. 2016. "Using Evidence as the Driver of Policy Change: The Next Steps in Supporting Innovation, Continuous Improvement, and Accountability." Testimony before the Senate Finance Committee. New York: MDRC. Accessed October 5, 2018. https://www.mdrc.org/sites/default/files/Berlin_testimony_051016.pdf.

Blau, Peter M., and Otis Dudley Duncan. 1967. *The American Occupational Structure*. New York: John Wiley & Sons.

Bollinger, Christopher, Barry T. Hirsch, Charles Hokayem, and James P. Ziliak. 2015. "Measuring Levels and Trends in Earnings Inequality with

Nonresponse, Imputations, and Topcoding." Paper presented at the Joint Meetings of the American Statistical Association. Chicago (August 1, 2016).

Breen, Richard, Carina Mood, and Jan O. Jonsson. 2016. "How Much Scope for a Mobility Paradox?" *Sociological Science* 3(3): 39–60. DOI: 10.15195/v3.a3.

Brown, David W., Amanda E. Kowalski, and Ithai Z. Lurie. 2015. "Medicaid as an Investment in Children: What Is the Long-Term Impact on Tax Receipts?" NBER working paper no. 20835. Cambridge, Mass.: National Bureau of Economic Research. Accessed October 5, 2018. http://www.nber.org/papers/w20835.

Cancian, Maria, Carolyn J. Heinrich, and Yiyoon Chung. 2013. "Discouraging Disadvantaged Fathers' Employment: An Unintended Consequence of Policies Designed to Support Families." *Journal of Policy Analysis and Management* 32(4): 758–84.

Cascio, Elizabeth U., and Diane Whitmore Schanzenbach. 2013. "The Impacts of Expanding Access to High-Quality Preschool Education." *Brookings Papers on Economic Activity* 47 (Fall): 127–92.

Chetty, Raj. 2012. "Time Trends in the Use of Administrative Data for Empirical Research." Paper presented at the 34th Annual NBER Summer Institute. Cambridge, Mass. (July 9–27, 2012).

Chetty, Raj, John N. Friedman, Nathaniel Hilger, Emmanuel Saez, Diane Whitmore Schanzenbach, and Danny Yagan. 2011. "How Does Your Kindergarten Classroom Affect Your Earnings? Evidence from Project Star." *Quarterly Journal of Economics* 126(4): 1593–660.

Chetty, Raj, David B. Grusky, Maximilian Hell, Nathaniel Hendren, Robert Manduca, and Jimmy Narang. 2017. "The Fading American Dream: Trends in Absolute Income Mobility Since 1940." *Science*, April 24, eaal4617. DOI: 10.1126/science.aal4617.

Chetty, Raj, Nathaniel Hendren, and Lawrence F. Katz. 2015. "The Effects of Exposure to Better Neighborhoods on Children: New Evidence from the Moving to Opportunity Experiment." NBER working paper no. 21156. Cambridge, Mass.: National Bureau of Economic Research. Accessed November 28, 2018. http://www.nber.org/papers/w21156.

Chetty, Raj, Nathaniel Hendren, Patrick Kline, Emmanuel Saez, and Nicholas Turner. 2014. "Is the United States Still a Land of Opportunity? Recent Trends in Intergenerational Mobility." *American Economic Review* 104(5): 141–47. DOI: 10.1257/aer.104.5.141.

Commission on Evidence-Based Policymaking (CEP). 2017. *The Promise of Evidence-Based Policymaking: Report of the Commission on Evidence-Based Policymaking*. Washington: U.S. Department of Health and Human Services. Accessed November 28, 2018. https://www.cep.gov/cep-final-report.html.

Council of Economic Advisers. 2015. "The Economics of Early Childhood Investments." January. Washington: Government Printing Office.

Cunha, Flavio, and James J. Heckman. 2008. "Formulating, Identifying and Estimating the Technology of Cognitive and Noncognitive Skill Formation." *Journal of Human Resources* 43(4): 738–82.

Dahl, Gordon B., and Lance Lochner. 2012. "The Impact of Family Income on Child Achievement: Evidence from the Earned Income Tax Credit." *American Economic Review* 102(5): 1927–56.

Decker, Paul T. 2014. "False Choices, Policy Framing, and the Promise of 'Big Data.'" *Journal of Policy Analysis and Management* 33(2): 252–62.

Duncan, Greg J., and Katherine Magnuson. 2013. "Investing in Preschool Programs." *Journal of Economic Perspectives* 27(2): 109–31.

Duncan, Greg J., Katherine Magnuson, and Elizabeth Votruba-Drzal. 2014. "Boosting Family Income to Promote Child Development." *Future of Children* 24(1): 99–120.

Einav, Liran, and Jonathan Levin. 2014. "Economics in the Age of Big Data." *Science* 346(6210): 715–21. DOI: 10.1126/science.1243089.

Evans, William N., and Craig L. Garthwaite. 2014. "Giving Mom a Break: The Impact of Higher EITC Payments on Maternal Health." *American Economic Journal* 6(2): 258–90.

Featherman, David L., and Robert M. Hauser. 1978. *Opportunity and Change*. New York: Academic Press.

Figlio, David, Jonathan Guryan, Krzysztof Karbownik, and Jeffrey Roth. 2014. "The Effects of Poor Neonatal Health on Children's Cognitive Development." *American Economic Review* 104 (December): 3921–55.

Fischer, Claude S., and Michael Hout. 2006. *Century of Difference: How America Changed in the Last One Hundred Years*. New York: Russell Sage Foundation.

Furman, Jason. 2015. "Smart Social Programs" *New York Times*, May 11. Accessed October 5, 2018. http://www.nytimes.com/2015/05/11/opinion/smart-social-programs.html.

Grusky, David B., Timothy M. Smeeding, and C. Matthew Snipp. 2015. "A New Infrastructure for Monitoring Social Mobility in the United States." *Annals of the American Academy of Political and Social Science* 657(1): 63–82.

Harding, David J., Jonah A. Siegel, and Jeffrey D. Morenoff. 2017. "Custodial Parole Sanctions and Earnings After Release from Prison." *Social Forces* 96(2): 909–34. DOI: 10.1093/sf/sox047.

Hart, Nick, and Sandy Davis. 2017. "Fact Sheet: Foundations for Evidence-Based Policymaking Act." *Evidence* (blog), Bipartisan Policy Center, November 30. Accessed October 5, 2018. https://bipartisanpolicy.org/blog/fact-sheet-foundations-for-evidence-based-policymaking-act/.

Haskins, Ron, and Greg Margolis. 2014. *Show Me the Evidence: Obama's Fight for Rigor and Results in Social Policy*. Washington, D.C.: Brookings Institution Press.

Heckman, James, and Stefano Mosso. 2014. "The Economics of Human Development and Social Mobility." *Annual Review of Economics* 6(1): 689–733.

Hokayem, Charles, Christopher Bollinger, and James P. Ziliak. 2015. "The Role of CPS Nonresponse in the Measurement of Poverty." *Journal of the American Statistical Association* 110(511): 935–45. DOI: 10.1080/01621459.2015.1029576.

Hout, Michael. 2015. "A Summary of What We Know About Social Mobility." *Annals of the American Academy of Political and Social Science* 657(1): 27–36.

———. 2018. "Americans' Occupational Status Reflects the Status of Both of Their Parents." *PNAS* 115(38): 9527–32.

Hoynes, Hilary, Marianne E. Page, and Ann Huff Stevens. 2011. "Can Targeted Transfers Improve Birth Outcomes? Evidence from the Introduction of the WIC Program." *Journal of Public Economics* 95(7–8): 813–27.

Hoynes, Hilary, Diane Whitmore Schanzenbach, and Douglas Almond. 2016. "Long Run Economic and Health Impacts of Participation in the Food Stamp Program." *American Economic Review* 106(4): 903–34.

Jacob, Brian, Susan Dynarski, Kenneth Frank, and Barbara Schneider. 2016. "Are Expectations Alone Enough? Estimating the Effect of a Mandatory College-Prep Curriculum in Michigan." NBER working paper no. 22013. Cambridge, Mass.: National Bureau of Economic Research.

Johnson, David S., Catherine Massey, and Amy O'Hara. 2015. "The Opportunities and Challenges of Using Administrative Data Linkages to Evaluate Mobility." *Annals of the American Academy of Political and Social Science* 657(1): 247–64.

Kille, Leighton Walter. 2015. "Major Administrative Datasets of the U.S. Government — All in One Place." *Journalist's Resource*, January 15. Shorenstein Center, Kennedy School, Harvard University. Accessed October 5, 2018. https://journalistsresource.org/tip-sheets/research/websites-u-s-federal-government-administrative-datasets.

Lee, Chul-In, and Gary Solon. 2009. "Trends in Intergenerational Income Mobility." *Review of Economics and Statistics* 91(4): 766–72.

Lee, Keun Bok, David J. Harding, and Jeffrey D. Morenoff. 2017. "Trajectories of Neighborhood Attainment After Prison." *Social Science Research* 66 (August): 211–33.

Looney, Adam, and Nicholas Turner. 2018. "Work and Opportunity Before and After Incarceration." Washington, D.C.: Brookings Institution. Accessed October 5, 2018. https://www.brookings.edu/wp-content/uploads/2018/03/es_20180314_looneyincarceration_final.pdf.

Manza, Jeff, and Clem Brooks. 2016. "Why Aren't Americans Angrier About Rising Inequality?" *Pathways Magazine*, 2016, 22–26. Accessed November 28, 2018. https://inequality.stanford.edu/sites/default/files/Pathways_Presidential_Anger.pdf.

Massey, Catherine G., and Amy O'Hara. 2014. "Person Matching in Historical Files Using the Census Bureau's Person Validation System." CARRA working paper no. 2014-11. Washington: U.S. Census Bureau. Accessed October 5, 2018. https://www.census.gov/library/working-papers/2014/adrm/carra-wp-2014-11.html.

Mazumder, Bhashkar. 2015. "Estimating the Intergenerational Elasticity and Rank Association in the US: Overcoming the Current Limitations of

Tax Data." FRB of Chicago working paper no. 2015-04. Chicago: Federal Reserve Bank. Accessed October 5, 2018. http://ssrn.com/abstract=2620727.

Mervis, Jeffrey. 2014. "How Two Economists Got Direct Access to IRS Tax Records." *Science*, May 22. Accessed October 5, 2018. http://news.sciencemag.org/2014/05/how-two-economists-got-direct-access-irs-tax-records.

Meyer, Bruce D., Wallace K.C. Mok, and James X. Sullivan. 2015. "Household Surveys in Crisis." *Journal of Economic Perspectives* 29(4): 199–226.

Milligan, Kevin, and Mark Stabile. 2009. "Child Benefits, Maternal Employment, and Children's Health: Evidence from Canadian Child Benefit Expansions," *American Economic Review* 99(2): 128–32.

Mitnik, Pablo A., Erin Cumberworth, and David B. Grusky. 2016. "Social Mobility in a High Inequality Regime." *Annals of the American Academy of Political and Social Science* 663(1): 140–84. DOI: 10.1177/0002716215596971.

Mitnik, Pablo A., Victoria Bryant, David B. Grusky, and Michael Weber. 2015. "New Estimates of Intergenerational Mobility Using Administrative Data." Statistics of Income working paper. Washington: Internal Revenue Service. Accessed October 5, 2018. https://www.irs.gov/pub/irs-soi/15rpintergenmobility.pdf.

National Academies of Sciences, Engineering, and Medicine (NASEM). 2017. *Innovations in Federal Statistics: Combining Data Sources While Protecting Privacy*. Washington, D.C.: National Academies Press.

National Research Council (NRC). 2005. *Experimental Poverty Measures: Summary of a Workshop*. Washington, D.C.: National Academies Press.

———. 2016. "Using Linked Census, Survey, and Administrative Data to Assess Longer-Term Effects of Policy: Proceedings of a Workshop—in Brief." Washington, D.C.: National Academies Press. Accessed October 5, 2018. https://www.nap.edu/catalog/23583/using-linked-census-survey-and-administrative-data-to-assess-longer-term-effects-of-policy.

Noyes, Jennifer. 2015. "Using Linked Administrative Data to Improve Child Welfare Programs: The Wisconsin Experience." Paper presented at the Mathematica Policy Research CIRE Forum Connecting the Dots. Washington, D.C. (November 5, 2015). Accessed October 5, 2018. https://www.mathematica-mpr.com/events/cire-forum-child-welfare-programs-nov-2015.

Office of the Mayor. 2014. *The CEO Poverty Measure, 2005–2012*. New York: The City of New York. Accessed October 5, 2018. https://www1.nyc.gov/assets/opportunity/pdf/14_poverty_measure_report.pdf.

Price, David J., and Jae Song. 2018. "The Long-Term Effects of Cash Assistance." Industrial Relations Section working paper 621. Princeton, N.J.: Princeton University. Accessed January 28, 2019. https://dataspace.princeton.edu/jspui/handle/88435/dsp01ng451m210.

Reamer, Andrew, and Julia Lane. 2018. "A Roadmap to Nationwide Data Infrastructure for Evidence-Based Policymaking." *Annals of the American Academy of Political and Social Science* 675(1): 28–35.

Shaefer, H. Luke, Sophie Collier, Greg Duncan. Kathryn Edin, Irwin Garfinkel, David Harris, Timothy M. Smeeding, Jane Waldfogel, Christopher Wimer, and Hiro Yoshikawa. 2018. "A Universal Child Allowance: A Plan to Reduce Poverty and Income Instability Among Children in the United States." *RSF: The Russell Sage Foundation Journal of the Social Sciences* 4(2): 22–42.

Smeeding, Timothy M., and Katherine A. Thornton. 2017. "Wisconsin Poverty Report: The Recovery from the Great Recession Lowers Poverty Rates in 2015." Ninth Annual Report of the Wisconsin Poverty Project. Madison: Institute for Research on Poverty, University of Wisconsin–Madison. Accessed October 5, 2018. https://www.irp.wisc.edu/resource/wisconsin-poverty-report-the-recovery-from-the-great-recession-lowers-poverty-rates-in-2015/.

Stevens, Ann, Michal Kurlaender, and Michel Grosz. 2015. "Career Technical Education and Labor Market Outcomes: Evidence from California Community Colleges." NBER working paper no. 21137. Cambridge, Mass.: National Bureau of Economic Research. Accessed October 5, 2018. http://www.nber.org/papers/w21137.

Tam, Siu-Ming, and Frederic Clarke. 2015. "Big Data, Official Statistics and Some Initiatives of the Australian Bureau of Statistics." *International Statistical Review* 83(3): 436–48.

Trépanier, Julie, Jean Pignal, and Don Royce. 2014. "Administrative Data Initiatives at Statistics Canada." Paper presented at the 2013 Federal Committee on Statistical Methodology Research

Conference. Washington, D.C. (November 5, 2013).

Warren, John Robert. 2015. "Potential Data Sources for a New Study of Social Mobility in the United States." *Annals of the American Academy of Political and Social Science* 657(1): 208–46.

Weeden, Kim A., and David B. Grusky. 2005. "The Case for a New Class Map." *American Journal of Sociology* 111(1): 141–212.

———. 2012. "The Three Worlds of Inequality." *American Journal of Sociology* 117(6): 1723–85.

Wherry, Laura R., Sarah Miller, Robert Kaestner, and Bruce D. Meyer. 2015. "Childhood Medicaid Coverage and Later Life Health Care Utilization." NBER working paper no. 20929. Cambridge, Mass.: National Bureau of Economic Research. Accessed October 5, 2018. http://www.nber.org/papers/w20929.

Wimer, Christopher, Marybeth Mattingly, Sara Kimberlin, Jonathan Fisher, Caroline Danielson, and Sarah Bohn. 2016. "Using Tax Policy to Address Economic Need: An Assessment of California's New State EITC." Stanford Center on Poverty and Inequality Research Brief (December 2016). Accessed November 28, 2018. https://inequality.stnford.edu/sites/default/files/EITC-california.pdf.

Wimer, Christopher, Marybeth Mattingly, Matt Levin, Caroline Danielson, and Sarah Bohn. 2013. "A Portrait of Poverty Within California Counties and Demographic Groups." Stanford, Calif.: Stanford Center on Poverty and Inequality. Accessed October 5, 2018. http://web.stanford.edu/group/scspi/poverty/cpm/CPMBrief_CPI.pdf.

———. 2014. "Poverty and Deep Poverty in California." Stanford, Calif.: Stanford Center on Poverty and Inequality. Accessed October 5, 2018. http://web.stanford.edu/group/scspi/poverty/cpm/CPM_Brief_Poverty-Deep-Poverty.pdf.

Yiu, Chris. 2012. "The Big Data Opportunity." London: The Policy Exchange. Accessed October 5, 2018. http://www.policyexchange.org.uk/the-big-data-opportunity.

Educational Opportunity in Early and Middle Childhood: Using Full Population Administrative Data to Study Variation by Place and Age

SEAN F. REARDON

I use standardized test scores from roughly forty-five million students to describe the temporal structure of educational opportunity in more than eleven thousand school districts in the United States. Variation among school districts is considerable in both average third-grade scores and test score growth rates. The two measures are uncorrelated, indicating that the characteristics of communities that provide high levels of early childhood educational opportunity are not the same as those that provide high opportunities for growth from third to eighth grade. This suggests that the role of schools in shaping educational opportunity varies across school districts. Variation among districts in the two temporal opportunity dimensions implies that strategies to improve educational opportunity may need to target different age groups in different places.

Keywords: educational opportunity, inequality of opportunity, school effects

Are public schools in the United States engines of mobility or agents of inequality? Can schools in low-income communities provide a pathway out of poverty, or are the constraints of poverty too great for schools to overcome? Such questions are at the heart of debates about the role of education in social mobility in the United States. Despite decades of research, however, we still lack clear answers.

In this article, I provide new evidence to inform these debates. It suggests that the lack of a clear answer to the question is explained in part by the substantial variation in the role of schooling in shaping educational opportunity

---

Sean F. Reardon is Endowed Professor of Poverty and Inequality in Education at the Stanford Graduate School of Education, Stanford University.

© 2019 Russell Sage Foundation. Reardon, Sean F. 2019. "Educational Opportunity in Early and Middle Childhood: Using Full Population Administrative Data to Study Variation by Place and Age." *RSF: The Russell Sage Foundation Journal of the Social Sciences* 5(2): 40–68. DOI: 10.7758/RSF.2019.5.2.03. The research described here was supported by grants from the Institute of Education Sciences (R305D110018), the Spencer Foundation (Award #201500058), the William T. Grant Foundation (Award #186173), the Bill and Melinda Gates Foundation, and the Overdeck Family Foundation. The paper would not have been possible without the assistance of Ross Santy, Michael Hawes, Marilyn Seastrom, and Jennifer Davies, who facilitated access to the EDFacts data. This paper benefited substantially from ongoing collaboration with Andrew Ho, Erin Fahle, and Ben Shear and from the research assistance of Joseph Van Matre and Richard DiSalvo. Some of the data used in this paper were provided by the National Center for Education Statistics (NCES). The opinions expressed here are my own and do not represent views of NCES, the Institute of Education Sciences, the U.S. Department of Education, the Spencer Foundation, the William T. Grant Foundation, the Bill and Melinda Gates Foundation, or the Overdeck Family Foundation. Direct correspondence to: Sean F. Reardon at sean.reardon@stanford.edu, 520 CERAS Building #526, Stanford University, Stanford, CA 94305.

Open Access Policy: *RSF: The Russell Sage Foundation Journal of the Social Sciences* is an open access journal. This article is published under a Creative Commons Attribution-NonCommercial-NoDerivs 3.0 Unported License.

across places. Early childhood conditions are more important in some places, educational opportunities during the elementary and middle school years more important in others.

The article also provides a demonstration of how administrative test score data can be used to construct high-resolution place- and age-based measures of educational outcomes, despite a number of major limitations of available administrative data. In particular, the standardized tests used in schools vary across place, grade, and year; the resulting scores are typically coarsened into a small number of ordinal categories whose definitions also vary across place, grade, and year; and the scores are reported only in repeated cross-sectional aggregate format rather than as student-level longitudinal records. Although these features of educational testing and reporting limit some potential uses of administrative test score data, the data can nonetheless provide useful information about the spatial and temporal structure of educational opportunity in the United States.

In this article, I first use standardized test scores from roughly forty-five million public school students tested during the school years 2008–2009 through 2014–2015 to construct measures of the temporal structure of educational opportunity in more than eleven thousand school districts—almost every district in the United States. By a school district, I mean the geographically defined community—including all of its local institutions—served by a public administrative school district. When I refer to the opportunities available in a district, I therefore mean the opportunities available to children living in that district, including the educational opportunities they have in their homes, neighborhoods, childcare and preschool programs, afterschool programs, and their public schools.

For each school district (read "community"), I construct two measures: the average academic performance of students in grade three and the within-cohort growth in test scores from grade three to eight. I argue that average test scores in a school district can be thought of as reflecting the average cumulative set of educational opportunities children in a community have had up to the time when they take a test.

Seen this way, the average scores in grade three can be thought of as measures of the average extent of "early educational opportunities" (reflecting opportunities from birth to age nine) available to children living in a school district. Research suggests that these early opportunities are strongly related to the average socioeconomic resources available in children's families in the district. They may also depend on other characteristics of the community, including neighborhood conditions, the availability of high-quality childcare and preschool programs, and the quality of schools in grades K–3.

The growth in average test scores from grades three to eight can likewise be thought of as a measure of the average extent of middle childhood educational opportunities available to children living in a school district when they are roughly age nine to fourteen. Given the prominence of schooling in children's lives at these ages, these opportunities may depend in large part on the quality of the local elementary and middle schools. They may also depend on average family resources, of course, as well as other local conditions, including neighborhood characteristics and the availability of afterschool programs.

Given these two measures, average scores in eighth grade are then understood to reflect the cumulative set of early and middle grade educational opportunities available to children in a school district. The decomposition of eighth grade average scores into the two components, reflecting early opportunity and middle grades opportunity, provides insight into the temporal structure of educational opportunity. The availability of these two measures for more than eleven thousand school districts yields unprecedented insight into the geographic and temporal structure of childhood educational opportunity in the United States.

In the second part of this essay, I describe both the relationship between these two measures and their association with socioeconomic characteristics of school districts. I find that the two measures are largely uncorrelated; early and middle grade opportunities appear to be distinct and separable dimensions of local educational opportunity structures. Among districts with a given level of average test scores in third grade, variation in growth in average scores from third to eighth grade is wide. Moreover, although both dimensions of opportunity are positively associated with district socioeconomic conditions, the correlation is much weaker for the middle grades growth dimension. Many low-income school districts have relatively high measures of growth and many affluent districts have relatively low growth. Finally, I also examine the temporal opportunity structure separately by racial-ethnic group and for poor and nonpoor students.

I conclude with two discussion sections. The first reflects on the value and limitations of the administrative data I use here, the process of obtaining the data and constructing the measures I use, and other potential uses of these data. The second reflects on the substantive patterns evident in the data, linking them to several scholarly and policy discussions. These patterns suggest that the role of schooling (and factors that shape children's academic progress during the years they are in school) in shaping educational opportunity (and perhaps social mobility) varies across communities. The answer to the question of whether schools exacerbate or ameliorate socioeconomic inequality may be "it depends on where you live." Moreover, the variation among districts in the two temporal opportunity dimensions implies that strategies to improve educational opportunity may need to target different age groups in different places. Finally, one implication of the low correlation between growth rates and average third-grade scores is that measures of average test scores are likely very poor measures of school quality. The growth measure I construct does not isolate the contribution of schools to children's academic skills but is likely closer to a measure of school effectiveness than measures of average test scores are.

BACKGROUND

Educational outcomes vary widely by socioeconomic status and race-ethnicity in the United States. Children in high-income families, and those whose parent or parents have college degrees, systematically score higher on standardized tests and are more likely to attend and graduate from college than lower-income students and students whose parents did not attend college. Similar disparities are evident between white and Asian students and African American, Hispanic, and Native American students (Chetty et al. 2017; Reardon 2011; Reardon, Robinson-Cimpian, and Weathers 2015; Sirin 2005; Ziol-Guest and Lee 2016). This inequality in average group outcomes is prima facie evidence of systematic between-group differences in opportunity because average academic capacities do not differ among groups (Nisbett 2011; Nisbett et al. 2012; Nisbett 1998). But disparities in outcomes alone do not indicate the ways in which opportunities differ, nor the developmental stage when they are most salient. In particular, they do not tell us to what extent schools—and inequalities in schools—are to blame for these patterns. Here I briefly discuss two strands of scholarship that are relevant to this question: debates about the role of schools in shaping inequality, and evidence regarding place-based opportunity structures.

Schools as "the Great Equalizer" in the United States

The debate regarding schools' role in providing educational opportunity and facilitating social mobility has a long history, particularly among sociologists. Three dominant arguments shape the debate. One position holds that schools reduce inequality of opportunity. The stark inequality in children's family backgrounds creates large differences in children's opportunities to learn, but school environments—in this argument—are less unequal than children's home environments. Evidence for this view comes from research showing, for example, that racial or socioeconomic achievement gaps widen in the summer when children are not in school, but narrow (or at least do not grow) when children are in school (Alexander, Entwisle, and Olson 2001, 2007; Downey and Condron 2016; Downey, von Hippel, and Broh 2004; Entwisle and Alexander 1994). This evidence is sensitive to the scale used to measure academic performance, however: not all studies show these same patterns (von Hippel, Workman, and Downey 2017). Additional support for this argument comes from studies showing that poor children benefit more from expanded time in school—via universal preschool enrollment, universal kindergarten, full-day kindergarten, and extended school days—than nonpoor children (Raudenbush and Eschmann 2015).

A second position is that schools have relatively little effect on the inequality of educational outcomes; family background is a far stronger force than schooling. In this view, most educational inequality is produced early in children's lives and by differences in family resources. This was the conclusion of the 1966 Coleman report, and was, to some extent, the argument of Christopher Jencks and his colleagues (Coleman et al. 1966; Jencks 1972). Additional evidence for this view comes from studies that find that socioeconomic or racial achievement gaps are large when children arrive in formal schooling in kindergarten, and do not change appreciably during the schooling years (Reardon 2011; Reardon, Robinson-Cimpian, and Weathers 2015).

Related to this argument is extensive evidence documenting the developmental importance of early childhood experiences. Family income when children are young is particularly consequential, relative to family income when children are older, for children's educational development (Duncan and Brooks-Gunn 1997; Duncan, Brooks-Gunn, and Klebanov 1994). Early childhood interventions can have significant and lasting impacts on children's outcomes (Duncan and Magnuson 2016; Heckman, Pinto, and Savelyev 2013). And, conditional on income, where one lives as a young child appears to have more effect on college attendance and income in young adulthood than where one lives as an adolescent (Chetty, Hendren, and Katz 2016). The salience of early childhood experiences may mean that experiences during middle childhood and adolescence are relatively unimportant in comparison.

Counter to this argument, however, are case studies and evaluations showing that schooling interventions or policies can have significant effects on achievement gaps, at least in some schools or as a result of specific interventions (Abdulkadiroglu et al. 2011; Bloom and Unterman 2012; Dobbie and Fryer 2011). Lottery-based studies of charter schools, likewise, reveal considerable heterogeneity in both charter and traditional public schools' effectiveness (CREDO 2015; Tuttle, Gleason and Clark 2012). This implies that malleable features of schools can have sizeable effects on students' academic performance.

The third view is that schools are powerful agents of inequality. In this view, not only can schools have sizeable effects on student achievement, but social policies and economic forces also conspire to ensure that schools in high-poverty neighborhoods are systematically inferior to those in affluent communities. In this view, schools exacerbate social inequalities, in large part because society systematically invests little in poor children's schools. Evidence for this comes from studies showing that schools in low-income communities have less-qualified teachers (Boyd et al. 2005; Lankford, Loeb, and Wyckoff 2002) and weaker curricula (Darling-Hammond 1998). An older strain of research argues that high-poverty schools have systematically fewer financial resources (see, for example, Kozol 1967, 1991), though in many—but not all—states this is no longer true, at least in terms of average per-pupil financial resources (Chingos and Blagg 2017). An alternate, neo-Marxist version of this argument holds that capitalism requires an unequal schooling system to prepare students of different class background for their future roles in a capitalist economy (Bowles and Gintis 1976).

Each of these arguments has both supporting and countervailing evidence. This is both because there is some truth to each of them and because the role of schooling varies across place.

Geographic Variation in Educational Opportunity

Much of the discussion of the role of schools or the importance of early childhood is concerned primarily with the average patterns of educational opportunity available to different socioeconomic or demographic populations. But recent research demonstrates that educational opportunity also varies significantly by location, even conditional on family income. Children's educational outcomes—test scores, high school graduation rates, and college enrollment and attendance rates—vary widely across the United States. Raj Chetty and his colleagues, using tax records of twelve million children born in the United States in the early 1980s, demonstrate that this variation is substantial, even conditional on family income (2014). Among children born to families at the 25th percentile of the income distribution, for example, college enrollment rates range from less than 25 percent to more than 65 percent across the 709 commuting zones they study.[1] That is, educational opportunity is a function of both place and family resources.

This is consistent with research on neighborhood effects, which argues that neighborhood contexts play a role in shaping educational outcomes (Chetty, Hendren, and Katz 2016; Harding 2003; Sampson, Sharkey, and Raudenbush 2008; Wodtke, Harding, and Elwert 2011). Much of this literature, however, focuses on the effects of neighborhood economic conditions; research has been less successful at identifying the mechanisms through which neighborhood contexts and community institutions shape educational opportunity. Chetty and his colleagues note that upward economic mobility of children born to low-income families is lower in places with lower test scores and in more segregated places (2014). Both of these are consistent with a story in which the quality of local schools shapes opportunities for mobility: in segregated areas, poor children are more concentrated in a subset of high-poverty schools; these schools may be lower in quality, leading to lower test scores, which reduce future educational opportunities and may be reflected in lower wages. But the evidence is far from definitive. Indeed, in another paper, Chetty and his colleagues show that children's neighborhood contexts when they are young are more influential than their neighborhood conditions after age ten, a finding that suggests schools may not play a central role in shaping mobility (Chetty, Hendren, and Katz 2016).

In short, the evidence is increasingly clear that educational opportunity and social mobility vary spatially. Less clear, however, is the role of schooling in shaping those patterns. Local contexts shape academic skills and human capital, but how? I provide evidence to help answer that question by describing evidence of the timing of these effects. By measuring average academic skills at different ages in each school district, I provide information on how educational opportunity varies by age across communities.

Temporal Patterns of Educational Opportunity

Suppose we characterized each community on two dimensions of opportunity: opportunities available to children in early childhood and opportunities available during their middle childhood. Early opportunities might depend on experiences that children have in their homes, in childcare, and in preschool. These will be strongly influenced by the average family resources in a community (income, social capital, educational attainment), but may also depend on neighborhood conditions and local context. For example, two equally poor communities may differ in the extent to which children are exposed to lead paint or other environmental toxins. Two equally affluent communities may differ in the quality of available preschool programs. Middle childhood opportunities may depend substantially on children's schooling experiences and the quality of the local schools, but also may be shaped by family resources and neighborhood conditions, the availability of afterschool activities, neighborhood safety, and so on.

Given these two dimensions, consider five potential patterns of the distribution of educational opportunities among communities. Each of these five corresponds to a panel in figure 1, and each is characterized by three features: the variance of early childhood opportunities, the variance of middle childhood opportunities, and the correlation between the two. The top portion of figure 1 illustrates patterns of early and middle childhood opportunities; the bottom portion shows the corresponding stylized patterns of outcomes at the end of early and middle childhood that would result.

Early experiences largely shape outcomes. In this case, early childhood educational opportunities vary widely among communities, but middle childhood opportunities are similar across places. This might occur if, for example, early opportunities depend heavily on private resources (parental income and investments of

---

1. Commuting zones are collections of counties similar to metropolitan areas but covering the entire United States. The average commuting zone includes about four counties.

Figure 1. Stylized Associations Between Early and Middle Childhood Opportunity and Between Early and Middle Childhood Educational Outcomes

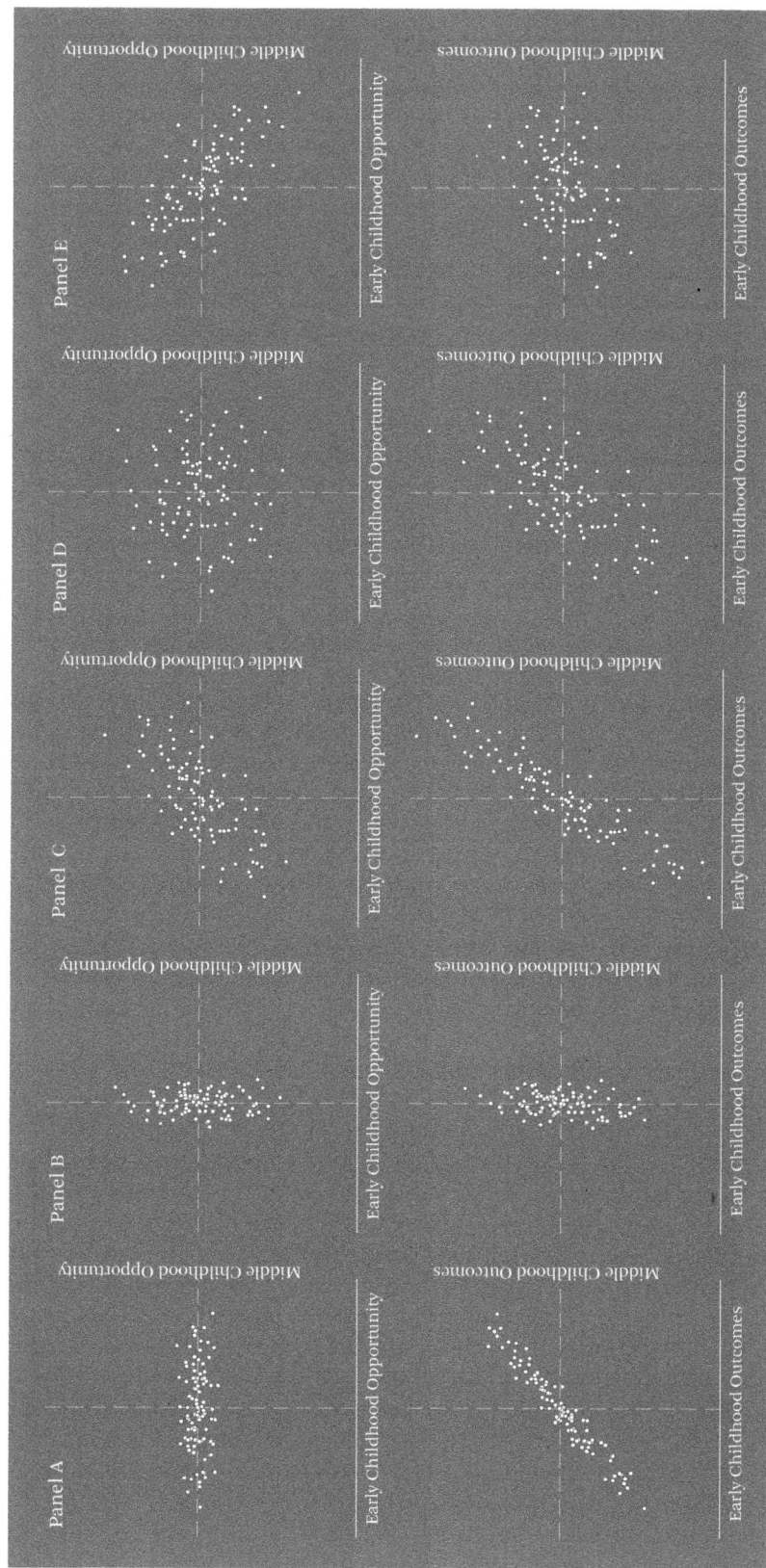

Source: Author.

Note: In each panel, the top figure represents a stylized pattern of the distribution of early and middle childhood educational opportunities. The bottom figure represents the pattern of educational outcomes we would observe at the end of early and middle childhood. In panel A, for example, middle childhood educational opportunities vary little among communities. As a result outcomes at the end of middle childhood are highly correlated with outcomes at the end of early childhood: inequality neither grows nor shrinks. In panel C, however, middle childhood opportunities are both variable and correlated with early childhood opportunities. As a result, inequality grows during middle childhood: middle childhood outcomes are more unequal then early childhood outcomes. The opposite pattern is shown in panel E.

time and money in children's development) and middle childhood opportunities are structured by public institutions (such as schools) that are much more equal in the opportunities they provide than are families. This pattern would be consistent with the view that schools are equalizing forces in society, at least relative to out-of-school experiences.

Middle childhood experiences largely shape outcomes. In this case, educational opportunities in early childhood are much less variable than those in middle childhood. This might occur if school quality were highly variable but preschool quality and parenting practices were not related to family resources. Such a scenario is admittedly not very likely given what we know about the world and the substantial impact of family resources on early childhood opportunities and development (Duncan and Brooks-Gunn 1997; Phillips and Shonkoff 2000).

Both early and middle childhood opportunities vary considerably and are positively correlated. Here, there is really only a single dimension of opportunity: communities where children have above-average early opportunities tend to be those where middle childhood opportunities are also high, and vice versa. This might occur if school quality depended on average family socioeconomic resources, for example, or if family resources continue to play a powerful role in children's educational development while they are in school. In this scenario, inequality of outcomes would grow from early to middle childhood.

Both early and middle childhood opportunities vary considerably, but are uncorrelated. In this case, the factors that shape early childhood opportunities (such as family resources, preschool quality, environmental hazards) are not the same as those that shape later opportunities (such as schools or afterschool programs). As a result, in some communities both early and middle childhood opportunities are high; in some both are low; and in some one is high and the other low. The presence of two distinct temporal dimensions of opportunity would suggest that strategies for improving opportunity might need to be targeted by both age and place.

Both early and middle childhood opportunities vary considerably and are negatively correlated. In this case, middle childhood experiences tend to be compensatory. Those communities that provide low opportunities early in childhood—because of, for example, low family resources or few or low quality preschools—do provide high opportunities later, and vice versa.

In the remainder of this article, I construct a version of figure 1 empirically. Specifically, I use aggregated test score data to construct two measures for each school district in the United States: a measure of average third-grade test scores (which can be thought of as the result of educational opportunities prior to third grade), and a measure of average learning rates from third grade to eighth grade (which can be thought of as the result of educational opportunities during late elementary and middle school). The underlying data represent virtually all U.S. third through eighth graders' scores on state accountability tests from 2009 to 2015. I use these data to construct measures of average initial (third grade) test scores and growth rates of average scores in each district. Essentially, I partition each district's average eighth-grade scores into two components—initial third-grade levels and growth from third through eighth grade. This partition provides information about the temporal structure of educational opportunity in each school district.

DATA

The test score data I use come from the Stanford Education Data Archive (SEDA), which includes estimates of the average test scores—by school district, grade, year, subject, and race-ethnicity—of students in almost every public school district in the United States (Reardon, Ho et al. 2017). These estimates are based on roughly three hundred million state accountability test scores (taken by roughly forty-five million students) on math and English language arts (ELA) tests in grades three through eight from 2009 through 2015 in every public school district in the United States. The SEDA data are publicly available.[2] Cells with fewer than twenty students are suppressed in public SEDA data.

---

2. Stanford Education Data Archive, http://seda.stanford.edu (accessed October 10, 2018).

The SEDA data are constructed from administrative data, but are not simple tabulations of administrative records. The raw test score data used to construct the SEDA data come from the federal ED*Facts* data collection system, which were provided by the National Center for Education Statistics under a restricted data-use license. The data include, for each public school in the United States, counts of students scoring in each of several academic proficiency levels, often labeled along the lines of below basic, basic, proficient, and advanced. These counts are disaggregated by race-ethnicity, grade (grades three through eight), test subject (math and ELA), and year (school years 2008–2009 through 2012–2015).

Using these proficiency category counts, my colleagues and I estimate average scores in each school district. The algorithm is described in the SEDA documentation (Fahle et al. 2018). Charter schools' test scores are included in the public school district in which they are formally chartered or, if not chartered by a district, in the district in which they are physically located. Thus, here I conceptualize a school district as a geographic catchment area that includes students in all local charter schools as well as in traditional public schools. Virtual schools—online schools that do not enroll students from any well-defined geographic area—are dropped from the sample. Such schools enroll fewer than half of 1 percent of all students in the United States.

The test scores in each state, grade, year, and subject are placed on a common scale so that performance can be meaningfully compared across states, grades, and years. First, each state's test scores are linked to the math and reading scales of the National Assessment of Education Progress (NAEP). The NAEP scale is stable over time and is vertically linked from fourth to eighth grade; this allows comparison of test scores among districts in different states and within a district across grades or years. Second, the NAEP scale is transformed linearly to facilitate grade-level interpretations. In this new scale, the national average fourth-grade NAEP score in 2009 is anchored at 4; the national average eighth-grade NAEP score in 2013 is anchored at 8. A one-unit difference in scores is interpretable as the national average difference between students one grade level apart (for much more detail on the linking method and scale, see Reardon, Kalogrides, and Ho 2016). Details on the source and construction of the estimates are available on the SEDA website.

Any description of test score growth or change depends on the test metric used. The NAEP scale (or the linear transformation of it used here) is useful because it was developed to allow comparisons over time, across states, and across grades. Nonetheless, it is not the only defensible scaling of test scores. Another potential metric is one in which test scores are standardized relative to the national student test score distribution within each grade. In this scale, the average test score in each grade is 0 and the standard deviation is fixed at 1 in each grade. This is useful for comparing the relative magnitude of differences in test scores in one grade to another grade but may distort information about relative growth rates. If the variation in true skills grows over time, the standardized metric will necessarily compress that growth and bias it toward zero, inducing a negative correlation between initial status and growth. Here I use both the NAEP metric (rescaled to grade-equivalent units) and a standardized metric, though I focus primarily on the vertically linked NAEP metric because it allows meaningful changes in variance across grades. I use the standardized metric as a sensitivity check.[3]

Estimating Average Test Scores and Growth in Average Test Scores

Each school district includes as many as eighty-four grade-year-subject specific measures of average test scores (six grades, seven years, and two subjects). I use these estimates to construct measures of the average performance of students in a given grade (pooling across years and subjects) and the within-cohort growth rate of

---

3. Other scalings of the test metric are defensible, of course. The indeterminacy of test metrics poses a challenge to any analysis of growth rates (Bond and Lang 2013; Ho 2008; Ho 2009; Reardon 2008). For more discussion of the sensitivity of the estimates to alternative test scalings, see the appendix.

average scores across grades (pooling across cohorts and subjects). This approach is conceptually similar to that used by Paul Hanselman and Jeremy Fiel in their study of test score growth rates among California schools (2017).

First, I define a cohort of observations as the set of observations corresponding to sequential grades in sequential years. Therefore, for example, one cohort is composed of students in third grade in 2009, fourth grade in 2010, fifth grade in 2011, and so on, through eighth grade in 2014. The next cohort consists of those in third grade in 2010 (eighth grade in 2015), and so on. Formally, I define a cohort as the spring of the year in which a group of students would have been in kindergarten (so that $cohort = year - grade$); thus the 2005 cohort describes students who were in kindergarten in spring of 2005 (and who therefore appear in the SEDA data from fourth grade in 2009 through eighth grade in 2013). Twelve cohorts are represented in the SEDA data, from the 2001 cohort (in eighth grade in 2009) through the 2012 cohort (in third grade in 2015).

Note that this definition of cohort does not necessarily correspond to a constant group of students. That is, the students in eighth grade in 2014 in district d are not the same set of students who were in third grade in district d in 2009. Some students may have been retained in grade or skipped a grade; some may have left the district; others may have moved in. Such in- and out-migration may add random or systematic noise to our estimates of average growth rates; we may underestimate growth in places where those who leave are disproportionately higher-achieving than those who move in. Conversely, we may overestimate growth in places with the opposite in- and out-migration patterns or with high retention rates. This is a limitation inherent in the raw ED*Facts* data, which do not include student longitudinal records.

Let $\hat{\mu}_{dygb}$ and $\omega_{dygb} = se(\hat{\mu}_{dygb})$ indicate the estimated average test score and its standard error for students in district d in year y, grade g, and subject b. Let $grd \in (3,4,5,6,7,8)$ and $coh \in (2001, \ldots, 2012)$ be continuous measures of grade and cohort, and let $math \in (0,1)$ be a binary indicator variable denoting the subject of an observation. Using data from all districts, years, grades, and subjects, I fit versions of the following precision-weighted multilevel model:

$$\hat{\mu}_{dygb} = \beta_{0d} + \beta_{1d}(grd_{dygb} - 3) + \beta_{2d}(coh_{dygb} - 2005) + \beta_{3d}(math_{dygb} - .5) + u_{dygb} + e_{dygb}$$

$$\beta_{0d} = \gamma_{00} + \mathbf{X}_d \Gamma_0 + v_{0d}$$
$$\beta_{1d} = \gamma_{10} + \mathbf{X}_d \Gamma_1 + v_{1d}$$
$$\beta_{2d} = \gamma_{20} + \mathbf{X}_d \Gamma_2 + v_{2d}$$
$$\beta_{3d} = \gamma_{30} + \mathbf{X}_d \Gamma_3 + v_{3d}$$

$$e_{dygb} \sim N(0, \omega^2_{dygb}); \; u_{dygb} \sim N(0, \sigma^2); \; \begin{bmatrix} v_{0d} \\ v_{1d} \\ v_{2d} \\ v_{3d} \end{bmatrix} \sim MVN(0, \tau^2). \quad (1)$$

I fit these models via maximum likelihood, treating ω^2_{dygb} as known (it is the square of the standard error of $\hat{\mu}_{dygb}$). The variance term σ^2 and the τ^2 matrix are estimated.

I first fit this model with no district-level covariates ($\mathbf{X}_d$). This model provides estimates of a number of parameters of interest: the average third-grade test score in each district d (β_{0d}), the average within-cohort growth rate of test scores from grades three to eight in district d (β_{1d}), the variances of these two parameters in the population of all districts, and the correlation between grade-three average scores and growth rates. Given the stated framework, we can think of β_{0d} as a measure of the average educational opportunities children in district d have prior to the end of grade three. Likewise, we can think of β_{1d} as a measure of the average educational opportunities children have to learn the tested material between grades three and eight. The predicted average test scores in district d in eighth grade are therefore the sum of average grade-three scores and five years of growth: $\beta_{0d} + 5\beta_{1d}$.

Because $\hat{\mu}_{dygb}$ is scaled to have an average value of 4 among fourth graders in 2009 and an average of 8 among eighth graders in 2013, the coefficients β_{0d} and β_{1d} reflect grade-level units. Note that $\beta_{0d} = 3$ implies that students in district d have the same average scores in third grade as the average 2008 third grader in the United States. Likewise, $\beta_{1d} = 1$ implies that students in district d have the same average learning rate from grade three to grade eight as the average

U.S. student in the 2005 cohort. A value of $\beta_{1d} = 1.1$ or $\beta_{1d} = 0.90$, for example, would imply that the performance of the average student in district d improves or declines, respectively, 10 percent (one-tenth of a grade-level per year) faster or slower, respectively, than the average U.S. public school student from the third to the eighth grade.

Of particular interest here is the joint distribution of β_{0d} and β_{1d}. This is given by $\left[\begin{pmatrix}\gamma_{00}\\\gamma_{10}\end{pmatrix}, \tau^2_{[01]}\right]$, where $\tau^2_{[01]} = \begin{bmatrix}\tau_{00} & \tau_{01}\\\tau_{01} & \tau_{11}\end{bmatrix}$ is the 2-x-2 upper-left submatrix of τ^2. This joint distribution is our primary focus: τ_{00} and τ_{11} describe the variances of β_{0d} and β_{1d}, respectively, and their correlation is computed as $r_{01} = \tau_{01}(\tau_{00} \cdot \tau_{11})^{-1/2}$. Note that I estimate the covariance matrix $\tau^2_{[01]}$ via maximum likelihood using the model above, rather than from the observed variances and covariance of the estimated (and therefore error-prone) β_{0d}'s and β_{1d}'s.

In addition to providing estimates of the parameters of the joint distribution of β_{0d} and β_{1d}, the model also provides estimates of β_{0d} and β_{1d} for each district. I use the Empirical Bayes (EB) shrunken estimates of these parameters, denoted $\hat{\beta}^*_{0d}$ and $\hat{\beta}^*_{1d}$. The model provides estimates of the reliability of each of these estimates as well as a measure of their average reliability.

The other coefficients in the model are of less direct interest for our purposes here: β_{2d} indicates the average within-grade (cohort-to-cohort) change per year in average test scores in district d; β_{3d} indicates the average (within grade and year) difference in math and reading scores in district d.

To estimate the association between district characteristics (denoted by the vector X_d) and average test scores (β_{0d}) and test score growth (β_{1d}), I fit models that add X_d as predictors of the district parameters in model (1).

Measuring Average Socioeconomic Status Among Enrolled Students

To measure the socioeconomic characteristics of the families of children, I use data from the American Community Survey (ACS). The ACS includes detailed sociodemographic data for families living in each U.S. school district; these tabulations are available through the School District Demographic System (SDDS). I use data from the 2006–2010 SDDS tabulations because they include tabulations of family characteristics among families with school-age children enrolled in public schools.

In particular, I use six measures of the socioeconomic composition of families living in a district with children enrolled in public schools: median family income; percentage of adults with a bachelor's degree or higher degree; poverty rate; unemployment rate; Supplemental Nutritional Assistance Program eligibility rate; and percentage of families headed by a single mother. Each of these is available separately by race-ethnicity (for racial-ethnic groups of large enough local population size).

I construct a measure of each district's average socioeconomic status as the first principal component of the six measures. This measure is standardized to have a mean of zero and a standard deviation of 1. To give a sense of how this measure is scaled, table 1 describes the average characteristics of school districts at various values of the socioeconomic status (SES) composite.

ANALYTIC SAMPLE

The data I use here include 11,315 school districts for which I am able to compute a socioeconomic status variable and for which the SEDA data include measures of academic achievement. Districts not included in the sample are predominantly very small districts for which samples are too small for SDDS to report socioeconomic characteristics or that have fewer than twenty students total per grade (in which case the SEDA data do not include estimates of average test scores). The ACS SES variable cannot be constructed for 824 districts; these are small districts (averaging forty-three students per grade) and contain fewer than 1 percent of U.S. public school students. The districts in the analytic sample collectively enroll roughly 3.7 million students per grade (roughly 99 percent of all U.S. public school students).

Table 1. Average Family Socioeconomic Characteristics, at Various District SES Composite Values

	SES Composite					
	−3	−2	−1	0	1	2
Median family income	$24,038	$31,026	$39,634	$53,029	$78,644	$136,804
Percent with BA or higher	13.5	14.9	14.6	18.3	32.3	62.4
Poverty rate	48.0	37.6	25.9	14.7	6.0	1.6
SNAP eligibility rate	50.0	39.9	27.6	15.5	5.6	0.2
Unemployment rate	10.5	8.0	6.0	4.5	3.4	2.6
Single parent family rate	51.9	41.9	31.7	22.2	14.6	10.0

Source: Fahle et al. 2018, table 6.
Note: All numbers except income in percentages.

How Do Grade-Three Average Scores and Growth Rates Vary Among Districts?

Model 1 provides estimates of the average grade-three test scores and the average grade-three through grade-eight growth rate in each district. It also provides maximum likelihood estimates of the variances and correlation of these parameters. Recall that we can think of the grade-three test score average as a measure of early educational opportunities in a district; the growth rate serves as a proxy for growth opportunities—the extent of educational opportunities in grades three to eight (though these opportunities may occur in and out of school).

Table 2 presents the parameters describing the joint distribution of these two measures. The left panel reports the results based on the preferred grade-equivalent NAEP scale; the right panel reports comparable results based on the standardized scale. Each panel includes a column for math and ELA score, as well as results from the model that pools the data and estimates a common grade-three level and growth rate for both subjects.

In the average school district, third-grade average test scores are roughly one-sixth of a grade level above the national average, and increase by 0.97 grade levels per grade.[4] By third grade, test scores vary substantially across school districts. The standard deviation of district average third-grade scores is almost one grade level (0.98 grade levels), meaning that roughly one-third of school districts have average third-grade test scores more than one grade level above or below the national average (one-sixth above and one-sixth below).

Perhaps surprisingly, the correlation between average third-grade scores and growth rates is very weak—and negative ($r = -0.13$). This means that knowing a district's average third-grade scores tells us almost nothing about the rate at which average scores change from third to eighth grade. Or, in terms of opportunity structure, the communities where children experience high opportunities to learn in early childhood and early elementary school are not necessarily those where opportunities to learn are high in the elementary and middle school years, and vice versa.[5]

The weak and negative correlation between grade-three levels and growth rates does not imply no association between eighth-grade scores and growth rates. Because average eighth-grade scores are in part the result of growth rates, we would expect them to be positively correlated with growth rates, and they are, though the cor-

---

4. The average district's scores are not equal to the national average for three reasons. First, more small districts have above-average test scores and slightly lower than average growth rates, so the unweighted averages across districts are not identical to the enrollment-weighted averages. Second, some very small districts are not included in the analytic sample. Third, the national average is constructed relative to students in the 2005 cohort (grade four in 2009, grade eight in 2013), but districts' average scores are computed using all cohorts in the SEDA data (cohorts 2001 through 2012). The average third-grade scores over all cohorts were slightly higher than those in the 2005 cohort, whereas the average growth rate was somewhat lower.

5. As noted, this correlation is sensitive to the scale used to measure test scores.

Table 2. Characteristics of the Joint Distribution of Grade-Three Test Scores and Grade-Three Through Grade-Eight Growth Rates

	NAEP (Grade Equivalent) Scale			Standardized Scale		
	Pooled	Math	ELA	Pooled	Math	ELA
Grade three						
Average	3.173	3.172	3.173	0.015	0.054	0.046
SD	0.976	0.919	1.084	0.341	0.361	0.337
Reliability	0.956	0.925	0.937	0.959	0.938	0.932
Growth, grades three through eight						
Average	0.965	0.970	0.964	-0.008	-0.009	-0.005
SD	0.135	0.175	0.123	0.044	0.055	0.040
Reliability	0.859	0.843	0.754	0.854	0.822	0.749
Correlations						
Grade three, growth	-0.130	0.002	-0.365	-0.245	-0.282	-0.241
Average grades three through eight, growth	0.213	0.430	-0.086	0.079	0.100	0.057
Grade eight, growth	0.494	0.690	0.214	0.381	0.443	0.341
Grade three math, reading		0.902			0.909	
Math growth, reading growth		0.661			0.760	
Predicted average scores by district type						
Grade-three average scores						
High early, average growth opportunity	4.149	4.091	4.257	0.392	0.415	0.383
Average early, high growth opportunity	3.173	3.172	3.173	0.051	0.054	0.046
Difference	-0.976	-0.919	-1.084	-0.341	-0.361	-0.337
Grade-eight average scores						
High early, average growth opportunity	8.974	8.941	9.077	0.354	0.367	0.358
Average early, high growth opportunity	8.673	8.895	8.610	0.233	0.280	0.221
Difference	-0.301	-0.045	-0.467	-0.121	-0.088	-0.137
Relative magnitude of 1 SD of high growth to 1 SD high early opportunity on grade-eight scores	0.692	0.950	0.569	0.645	0.757	0.593
N (districts)	11,315	11,315	11,315	11,315	11,315	11,315

Source: Author's calculations based on Stanford Education Data Archive (Reardon, Ho et al. 2017).

relation is moderate ($r = 0.49$). This suggests that eighth-grade average scores carry more signal regarding growth rates than third-grade scores. However, if we estimate the correlation between growth rates and average scores across all grades three through eight (which is more typical of the level of detail publicly available about schools), the correlation is small ($r = 0.21$).

The right panel of table 2 repeats the analysis using the standardized test score scale. In this scale, the correlation between growth rates and grade three average scores is similar, but slightly more negative than the estimate based on the grade-equivalent NAEP scaled scores. Again, average opportunities prior to third grade are a poor predictor of average growth rates.

One additional feature of table 2 is worth noting. The second and third columns of each panel show the estimate separately for math and reading tests. Between-district variation in growth rates is much higher in math scores than in reading (the standard deviation [SD] of growth rates is 40 percent larger in math than in reading), and—at least in the NAEP scale results—much less in third-grade achievement in math than in reading (the SD is 15 percent smaller in math than reading). This is consistent with the commonly held belief that math skills are more affected by schooling, and that reading skills are affected by both home and school environments. Early childhood and early elementary opportunities to learn to read may be more variable than opportunities to learn math skills, but growth in math scores from grade three to eight appears to vary much more than growth in reading scores. Moreover, the correlation of growth and eighth-grade scores is much higher for math than for reading ($r = 0.69$ for math versus $r = 0.21$ for reading). In other words, eighth-grade math scores are a reasonably good proxy for growth rates in math, potentially because students' math skills (particularly those measured by standardized math tests) are shaped largely by opportunities to learn during the elementary and middle school years.

That said, in the interest of parsimony, I focus for the remainder of this article on models that pool the estimates across math and reading. Given the relatively high within-district correlations between math and reading grade-three scores ($r = 0.90$) and between math and reading growth rates ($r = 0.66$), models that pool the results across subjects capture most of the relevant information. Moreover, although growth rates and grade-three levels are estimated reliably in all of the models here (generally above 0.75), they are lower in the subject-specific models than the pooled models (where the grade-three averages are estimated with reliability 0.96 and the growth rates with reliability 0.86). The higher precision of the pooled models allows for sharper distinctions among districts. Although differences may indeed be important in those factors that shape opportunities for math and reading skill development, those issues are outside the scope of this analysis.

How Much Do Growth Rates Vary?

It is clear from table 2 that average test scores in grade three are uninformative as predictors of growth rates, perhaps because variation in growth rates is relatively small. It is useful therefore to quantify the magnitude of the variation in growth rates. The standard deviation of growth rates is 0.135 grade levels per year, or equivalently, 0.675 grade levels from grade three to grade eight. This means that in roughly one-sixth of districts test scores improve by two-thirds or more of a grade level from grades three to eight; in another one-sixth of districts scores fall behind by two-thirds or more of a grade level. Another way to quantify this is that a growth rate of 1.135 indicates that students' scores increase 13.5 percent faster than the national average (an increase of 13.5 percent of a school year is roughly an additional twenty-five school days per year in the typical district, not a trivial amount). So variation among school districts in average growth rates is considerable.

Another way to quantify the relative magnitude is to compare the magnitude of between-district variation in growth rates to that of between-district variation in grade-three test scores. Consider two school districts, one in which students' third-grade scores are at the national average but growth rates are 1 standard deviation above the national average; and one in which students' third-grade scores are 1 standard deviation above the national average but growth rates are at the national average. In which district are students' scores higher by eighth grade, and by how much? These calculations are shown in the bottom panel of table 2.

A standard deviation difference in growth rates experienced over five years from grade three to grade eight is equivalent to a 70 percent of a district standard deviation in grade-three levels. That is, in five years, students in the average-early-opportunity and high-growth-opportunity district make up 70 percent of the grade-three gap relative to a high-early-opportunity and average-growth-opportunity district. These results hold in both the reported scales.

Where Are Growth Opportunities Highest?

Figures 2 and 3 display the geographic patterns of grade-three average scores and grade-three through grade-eight growth rates. Figure 2 shows that opportunities prior to grade three are highest in many of suburban and exurban school districts around metropolitan areas,

Figure 2. Average Third-Grade Test Scores (Math and Reading Averaged), 2009–2015

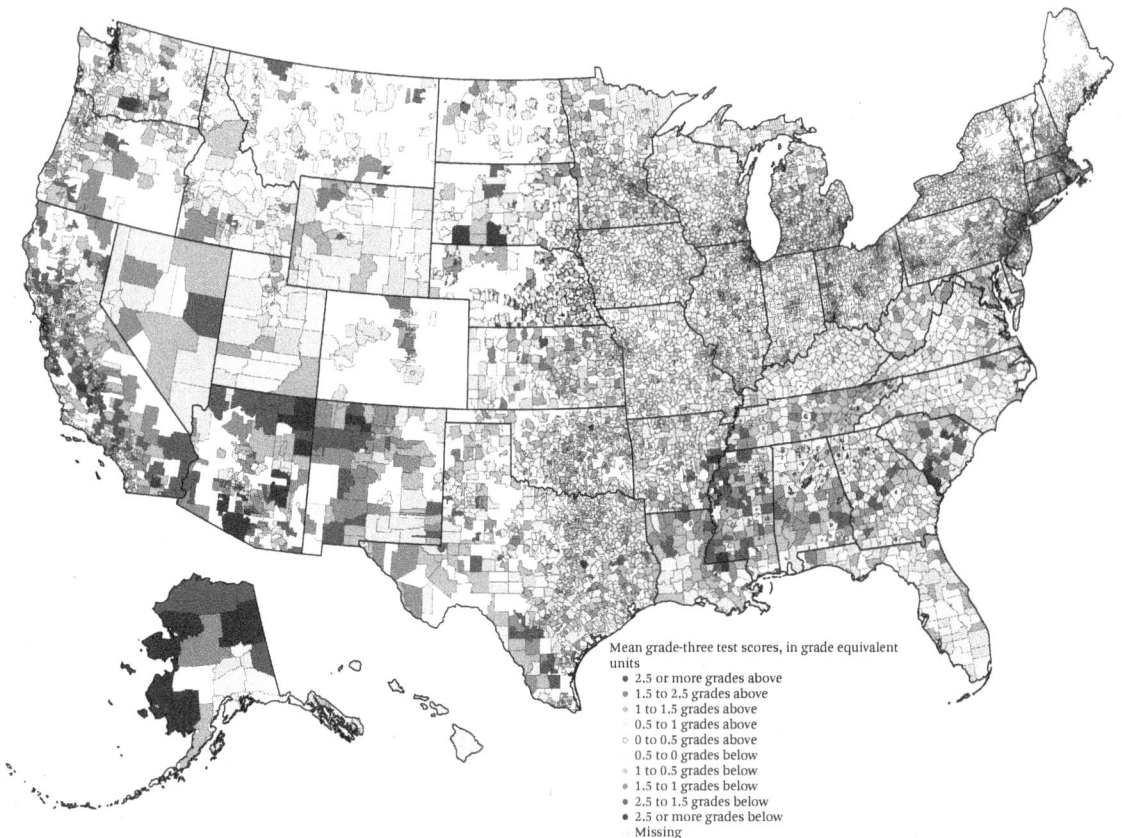

Source: Stanford Education Data Archive (Reardon, Ho et al. 2017).

particularly in the Northeast, Midwest, and the California coast, and are low in much of the Deep South and the rural West. Growth opportunities in contrast are more varied. Tennessee is characterized by moderately low third-grade scores but above-average growth rates; Florida, by contrast, is characterized by slightly above-average scores in grade three but very low average growth.

Table 2 and figures 2 and 3 indicate considerable variation in both grade-three average scores and growth rates, but no high correlation between the two. This is more evident in figure 4, which plots each district's estimated growth rate (on the vertical axis) against its grade-three through grade-eight growth rate. The plot uses the EB estimates $\hat{\beta}^*_{0d}$ and $\hat{\beta}^*_{1d}$; imprecisely estimated values are shrunken toward the overall mean. Note that district estimates with a reliability less than 0.7 are not included in this or other figures (though their data are included in fitting model 1).

Figure 4 makes the very weak relationship between average third-grade test scores and average growth clear. The figure can be divided into four quadrants defined by districts' early educational opportunity and growth opportunities. In the upper right are districts characterized by high early educational opportunity and high growth opportunity, districts where students have high average achievement in grade three and above-average growth rates after grade three. In the lower left are districts characterized by the opposite pattern: low early and low growth opportunity. The off-diagonal quadrants have high early and low growth or low early and high growth opportunity structures, respectively.

The striking feature of figure 4 is the absence of a correlation between growth and initial

Figure 3. Average Test Score Growth Rates (Math and Reading Averaged), 2009–2015

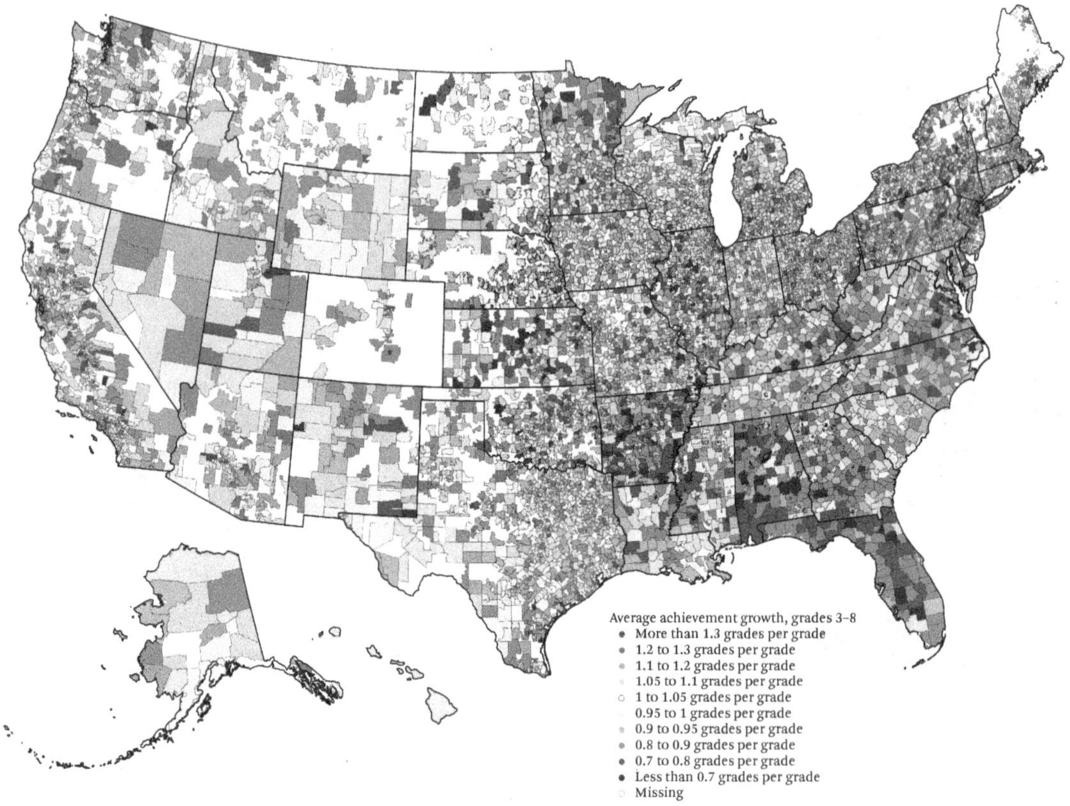

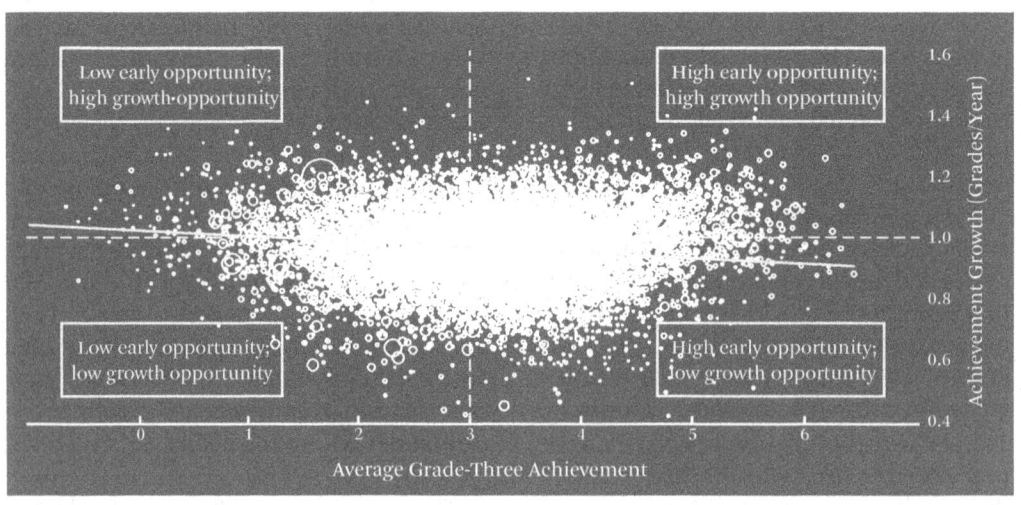

Average achievement growth, grades 3–8
- More than 1.3 grades per grade
- 1.2 to 1.3 grades per grade
- 1.1 to 1.2 grades per grade
- 1.05 to 1.1 grades per grade
- 1 to 1.05 grades per grade
- 0.95 to 1 grades per grade
- 0.9 to 0.95 grades per grade
- 0.8 to 0.9 grades per grade
- 0.7 to 0.8 grades per grade
- Less than 0.7 grades per grade
- Missing

Source: Stanford Education Data Archive (Reardon, Ho et al. 2017).

Figure 4. Achievement Growth Rates by Grade-Three Achievement

Source: Author's tabulations based on Stanford Education Data Archive (Reardon, Ho et al. 2017).

Figure 5. Achievement Growth Rates by Grade-Three Achievement, All Students, With Grade-Eight Achievement Isobars

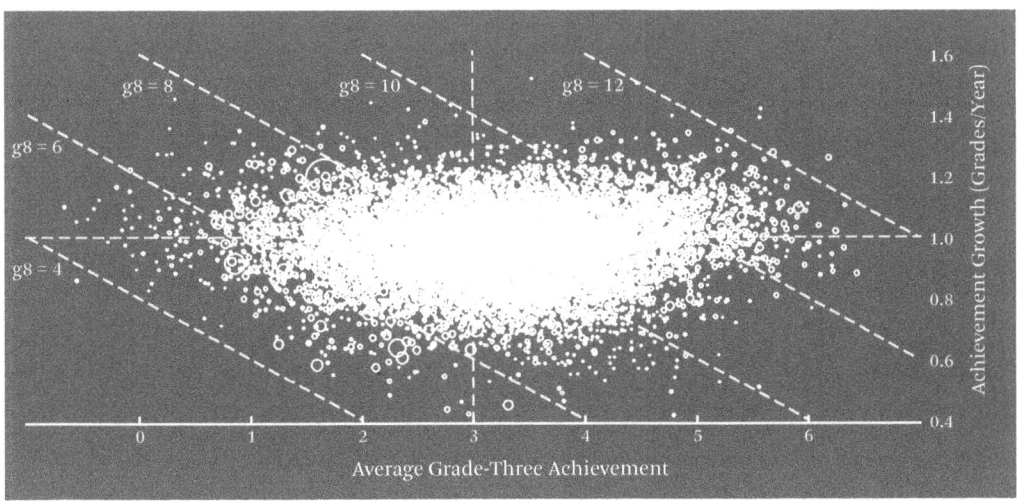

Source: Author's tabulations based on Stanford Education Data Archive (Reardon, Ho et al. 2017).

scores. Among districts with high grade-three scores are many with high growth and many with low growth; the same is true among those with low initial scores. This suggests the lack of a significant floor or ceiling effect in the estimates (which is not surprising, given that the data points reflect district average scores not individual student scores). Even among school districts with very high scores in third grade (three grade levels above average), some districts have very high growth; the same is true among initially low-performing districts.[6]

Another perspective on figure 4 is provided by considering districts with the same eighth-grade average scores. The lack of a substantial correlation between growth and grade-three scores implies that, among districts with the same eighth-grade average scores, some have higher grade-three scores and lower growth and others have lower initial status and higher growth. Figure 5 illustrates this: the plot is the same as figure 4, but includes lines representing levels of grade-eight average achievement drawn as isobars on the plot. Districts that fall anywhere on an isobar have the same average eighth-grade achievement, despite differences in initial status and growth rates. For example, a district where initial scores are one grade level below average and the average growth rates is 1.2 will have the same average eighth-grade scores as one where initial scores are one grade level above average but growth rates are 0.8 (both districts will fall on the g8 = 8 line).

Chicago, for example (see figure 6), has average third-grade test scores well below the national average (about 1.4 grade levels below), but very high growth rates. New York City students have both average third-grade scores and average growth rates. And in Henrico County (suburban Richmond), Virginia, third-grade test

---

6. The measures here are not subject to ceiling effects or regression to the mean for several reasons. First, the district average scores in third grade are very precisely estimated because of the large number of scores in each district; as a result, measurement-error induced regression to the mean is not a concern. Second, the district-level means are generally not near the ceiling or floor of the tests; although individual students' scores may in some cases reach a test's floor or ceiling, the average in district does not (even in the highest-score district, average scores are less than 1 standard deviation from the test score mean, placing the average student in that district somewhere near the 80th percentile of the state's test score distribution—so the average student in the district still has room to improve). Third, the methods used to construct the measures rely on the ordinal nature of test scores, and so are less sensitive to floor and ceiling effects than methods based on interval scale measures.

Figure 6. Achievement Growth Rates by Grade-Three Achievement, Hundred Largest School Districts

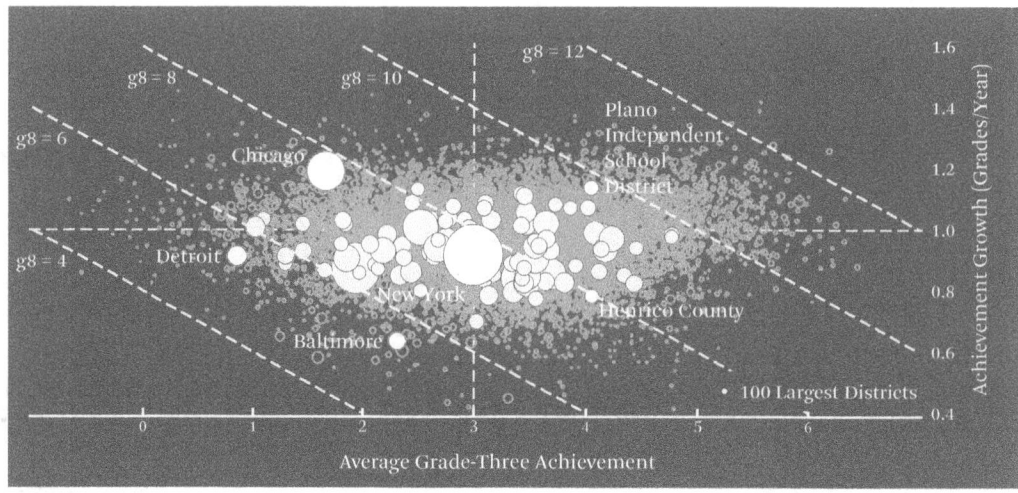

Source: Author's tabulations based on Stanford Education Data Archive (Reardon, Ho et al. 2017).

scores are very high but growth rates are very low. As a result, eighth-grade scores in Chicago, New York, and Henrico County are quite similar (within a half grade level of each other) despite a range of 2.5 grade levels difference in their third-grade scores. Likewise, Detroit and Baltimore eighth-grade test scores are quite similar to one another (and very low, more than 2.5 grade levels below the national average), but in Baltimore the low eighth-grade scores are more the result of low growth opportunities than low early opportunities, the opposite of Detroit.

Figure 6 highlights the hundred largest school districts in the United States. The substantial variation among them on both the early and growth opportunity dimensions suggests that the variation evident in figures 3 through 5 is not simply the result of idiosyncratic variation among small school districts or sampling noise. Each of these districts' estimates are based on hundreds of thousands or millions of test scores (Chicago's is based on more than two million, for example).

How Is Average Test Score Growth Related to District Socioeconomic Status?
Figure 7 displays the association between the socioeconomic status measure and both grade-three average scores (upper figure) and growth rates (lower figure). The fitted lines are estimated from a version of model 1 that includes a cubic function of socioeconomic status (SES) as a predictor of each of the four district-level parameters in the model. SES is positively associated with grade-three scores and growth rates, but the association is much stronger with grade-three average scores ($r = 0.68$) than with growth rates ($r = .32$). These associations are presented in figure 7.

It may seem strange that both grade-three average scores and growth rates are higher, on average, in high-SES districts than in low-SES districts, but the scores and growth are slightly negatively correlated. Figure 8 helps clarify these patterns. Each panel of the figure highlights districts in a given SES quartile. Low-SES districts have generally, but not always, low average scores, and many have lower than average growth rates. High-SES districts, in contrast, generally have above-average scores, but above-average growth rates only slightly more often than below-average growth rates. In sum, socioeconomic status distinguishes where districts fall on the x-axis of figure 8 but is not especially predictive of where districts fall on the y-axis.

How Do Growth Rates Vary by Student Poverty Status, Race-Ethnicity, and Gender?
The preceding analyses demonstrate considerable variation among school districts in both early educational opportunities (as measured

Figure 7. Achievement Patterns and Socioeconomic Status

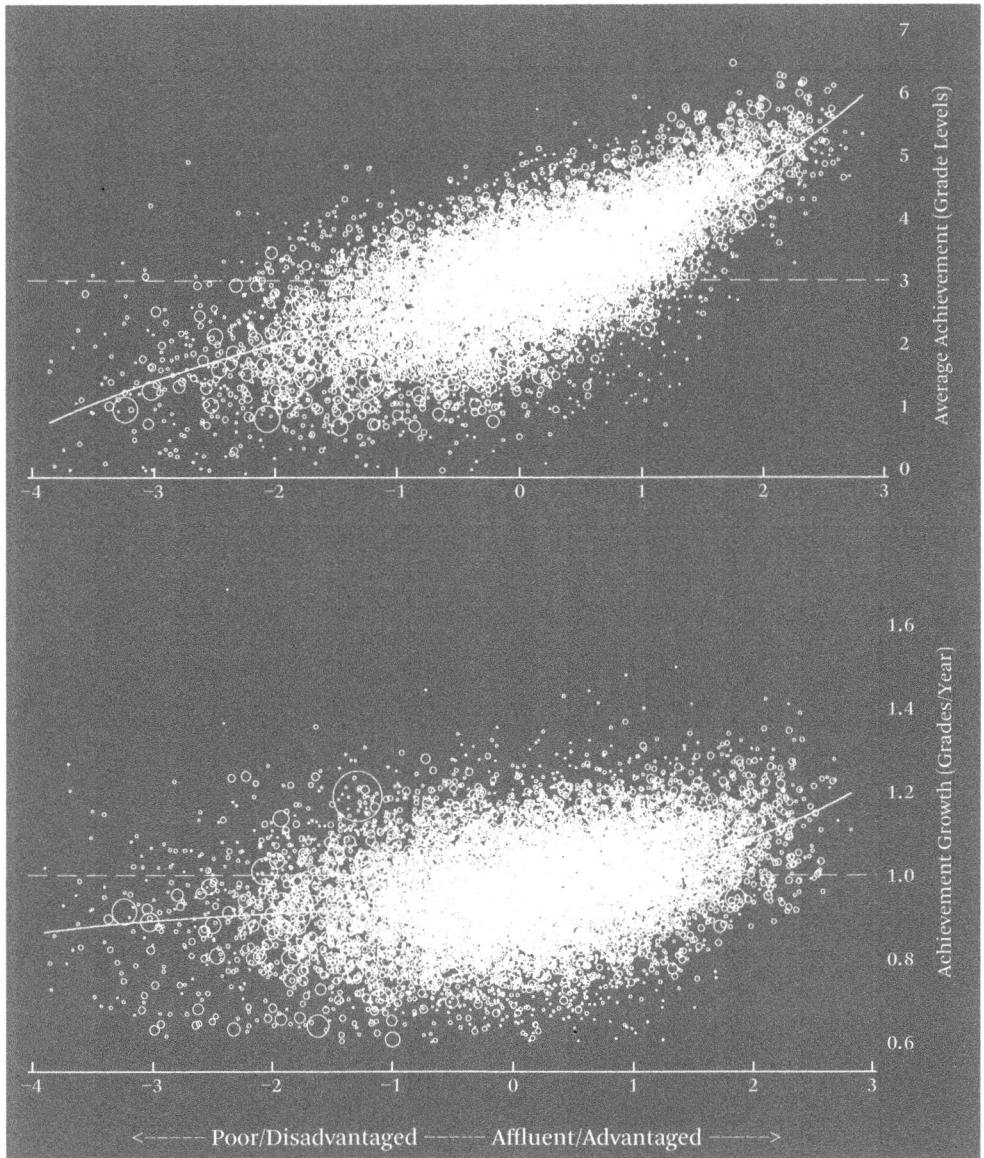

Source: Author's tabulations based on Stanford Education Data Archive (Reardon, Ho et al. 2017).

by average third-grade test scores) and in growth rates from grade three to grade eight. How do these patterns differ by students' poverty status, race-ethnicity, and gender? Figure 9 displays average third-grade test scores (left panel) and growth rates (right panel) for poor and nonpoor students.[7] The left panel compares the average third-grade scores. On average, poor students' average third-grade scores are 1.5 grade levels below those of their nonpoor peers in the same district. Moreover, despite considerable variation in the gap in average

---

7. States report test scores by students' economic disadvantage status; each state can define economic disadvantage differently, though in practice, most use eligibility for free or reduced-price lunch to define economic disadvantage.

Figure 8. Growth Rates and Grade-Three Achievement, by District SES Quartile

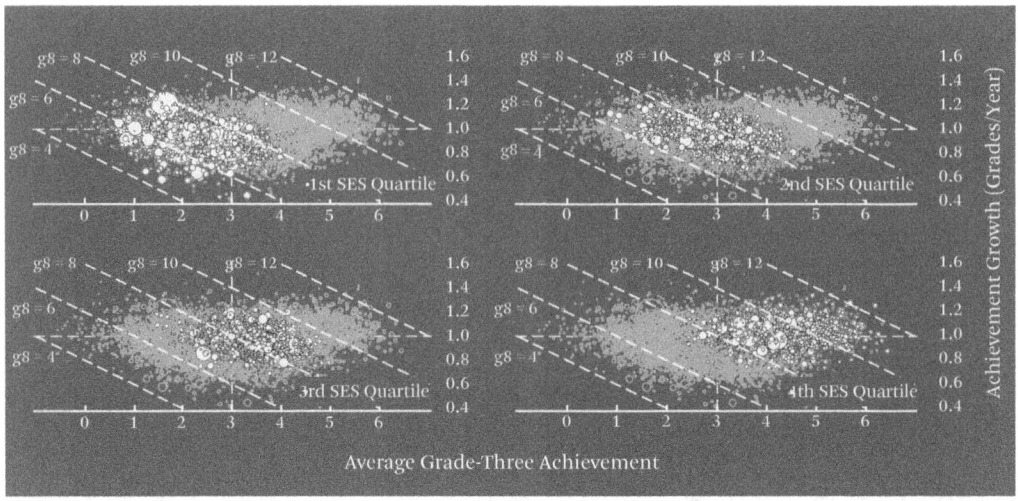

Source: Author's tabulations based on Stanford Education Data Archive (Reardon, Ho et al. 2017).

Figure 9. Levels and Growth for Poor and Nonpoor Students

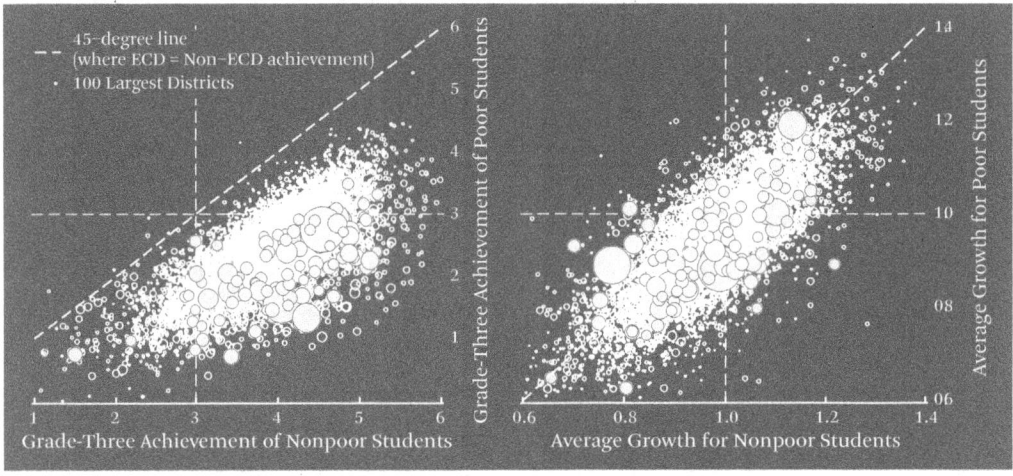

Source: Author's tabulations based on Stanford Education Data Archive (Reardon, Ho et al. 2017).

third-grade scores between poor and nonpoor students, almost every district falls well below the 45-degree line in the figure. Of the roughly ten thousand school districts for which we have enough data to estimate average achievement levels by poverty status, in only a handful do poor and nonpoor students arrive in third grade with equal academic skills (and in most of those few cases, both poor and nonpoor students have low third-grade scores).

The right panel shows that the pattern is quite different when comparing poor and nonpoor students' growth rates. In most school districts, poor students' growth rates are quite similar to those of nonpoor students in the same district (most of the districts fall near the 45 degree line). The average within-district difference in growth rates between nonpoor and poor students is 0.04 grade levels per year. That is, in the average district, poor students have third-grade scores roughly 1.5 grade levels below their nonpoor peers and fall behind by an

Table 3. Characteristics of the Joint Distribution of Grade-Three Test Scores and Grade-Three Through Grade-Eight Growth Rates, by Subgroup

	All	Poor	Nonpoor	White	Black	Hispanic	Asian	Male	Female
Grade-three average									
Average	3.173	2.351	3.803	3.535	1.933	2.177	4.286	3.088	3.274
Standard deviation	0.976	0.779	0.791	0.808	0.762	0.883	1.215	1.000	0.959
Reliability	0.956	0.901	0.913	0.931	0.899	0.881	0.899	0.943	0.941
Growth, grades three through eight									
Average	0.965	0.942	0.985	0.967	0.912	0.992	1.110	0.932	0.998
Standard deviation	0.135	0.134	0.133	0.131	0.131	0.134	0.144	0.137	0.129
Reliability	0.859	0.809	0.811	0.831	0.796	0.770	0.719	0.829	0.819
Correlations									
Corr (grade three, growth)	-0.130	-0.475	-0.167	-0.148	-0.298	-0.431	0.273	-0.089	-0.087
Corr (average grades three through eight, growth)	0.213	-0.050	0.248	0.251	0.138	-0.057	0.508	0.245	0.242
Corr (grade eight, growth)	0.494	0.403	0.563	0.556	0.509	0.341	0.668	0.512	0.505
N (districts)	11,315	9,735	10,180	10,662	3,077	4,102	1,789	10,327	10,233

Source: Author's calculations based on Stanford Education Data Archive (Reardon, Ho et al. 2017).

additional 0.2 grade levels by eighth grade. The difference in the early (before grade three) opportunities of poor and nonpoor students is much larger than the average difference in opportunities to learn in grades three to eight.

Table 3 reports the joint distributions of districts' grade-three average test scores and growth rates by subgroup. Each column describes the distributions for a different group—by poverty status, race-ethnicity, and gender. The top row reveals the large differences in early educational opportunity by poverty status and race-ethnicity: poor students' average scores are 1.5 grade levels below those of nonpoor students in third grade. The racial-ethnic disparities are similarly large: the white-black and white-Hispanic gap are also roughly 1.5 grade levels in third grade.

The second panel of table 3 reports average growth rates. The average growth rate of poor students in the average district is 0.04 grade levels per year lower than that of nonpoor students. The white-black difference in growth rates is -0.055. These are meaningfully large, but not enormous, differences; they imply that the poor-nonpoor and white-black gaps grow by roughly 0.20 to 0.25 grade levels between third and eighth grade, a modest increase relative to the size of the gaps in third grade.[8] The Hispanic average growth rate is actually slightly higher than the white growth rate, meaning that white-Hispanic gaps narrow very slightly (by about one-eighth of a grade) between third and eighth grade. The Asian average growth rates are substantially higher, on average, than any other group, almost 0.15 grade levels per year higher than white growth rates. In the average district, Asian students have average scores roughly 0.7 grade levels higher than white students in grade three. This gap doubles, on average, by eighth grade.[9]

The last two columns report growth rates by

---

8. Hanselman and Fiel conduct a related but different analysis (2017). Using 1998 to 2002 test score data from California, they find that black, Hispanic, and Asian students attend schools where, on average, the overall average growth rates are only slightly lower than in the schools attended by white students. Their analysis does not, however, identify race-ethnicity specific growth rates, so is not directly comparable to the analyses here.

9. Average test score growth rates by subgroup are each estimated on a different sample of districts—those enrolling at least twenty students of that subgroup per grade. Therefore, the differences between subgroups'

Figure 10. Growth Rates and Grade-Three Achievement by Subgroup

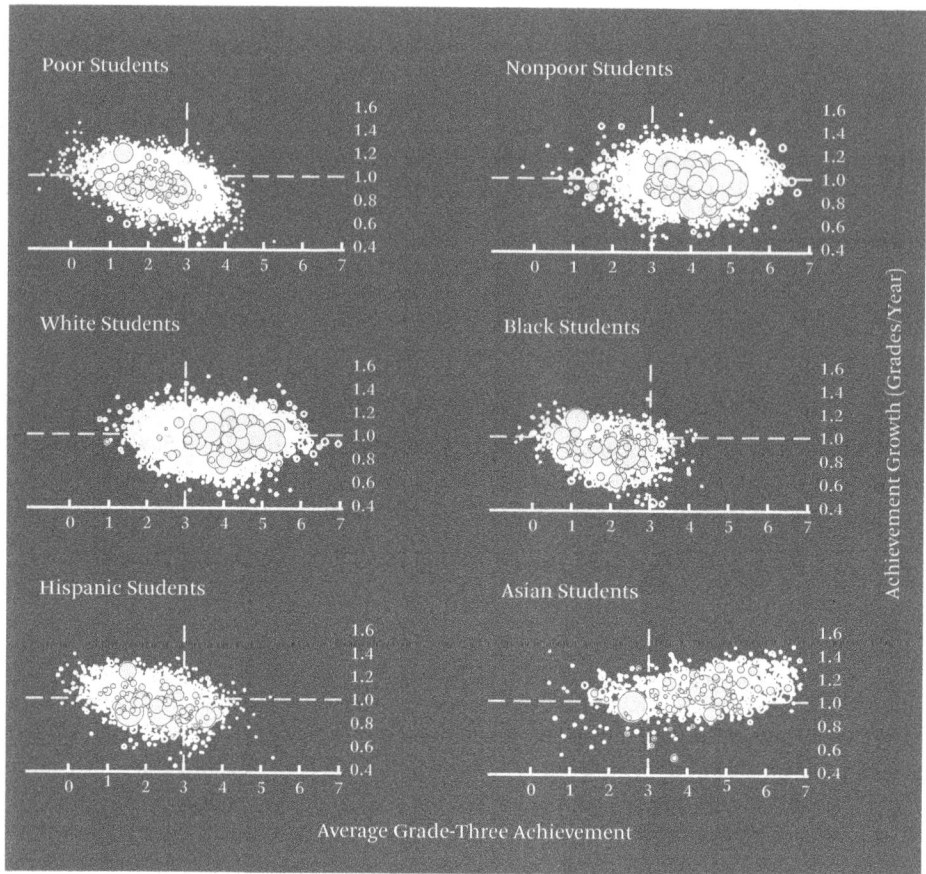

Source: Author's tabulations based on Stanford Education Data Archive (Reardon, Ho et al. 2017).

gender. Girls have, on average, both higher third-grade scores and higher growth rates than boys. By eighth grade, girls' average scores are roughly half a grade level higher than boys. Other research indicates that this difference is primarily due to the fact that girls substantially outperform boys on ELA tests, by nearly a grade level in eighth grade (Reardon et al. 2018).

Figure 10 summarizes the joint distribution of average third-grade scores and growth rates for each subgroup (the gender figures are not shown because the male and female patterns differ relatively little from one another relative to the racial-ethnic and socioeconomic differences). In most school districts, poor students, black students, and Hispanic students all have below-average test scores in third grade; nonpoor, white, and Asian students more commonly have above-average scores. The growth rate patterns differ somewhat. Black students, for example, are generally in districts where both their early opportunities and growth op-

estimated average growth rates in table 3 are not exactly the same as the average within-district average growth difference. One should read the differences in average growth rates here as suggestive of how achievement gaps change from the third to eighth grade, but not definitive. A better description of how gaps change (and how those rates of change are related to the magnitude of the gaps in third grade) could be obtained by limiting the analyses to a subset of districts with large enough populations of the two subgroups of interest, and then estimating the average rate of change of within-district achievement gaps in this sample of districts. That analysis is beyond the scope of this article.

portunities are low (lower left quadrant). The pattern is not so pronounced for Hispanic students and poor students: in many districts they have above-average growth rates despite below-average third-grade scores. More generally, figure 10 makes clear that patterns of both early opportunity and growth opportunity vary substantially by poverty status and race, but that growth opportunities are sometimes quite high for poor and Hispanic students.

DISCUSSION, PART ONE: THE POTENTIAL AND LIMITS OF ADMINISTRATIVE EDUCATION DATA

The data I use here, like most administrative data, are the residuum of a set of federal and state educational bureaucratic processes; they were not designed and collected with social science research needs in mind. Each state tests all students in grades three through eight, and reports their scores—in aggregated and coarsened form—to the U.S. Department of Education through the ED*Facts* system because federal law requires it. As a result, the data have both advantages and limitations.

Perhaps the most significant feature of the ED*Facts* data is their population coverage; the data are based on the test scores of the full population of public school students in grades three to eight in each year from 2008–2009 through 2014–2015 (with some missing data, as noted). Roughly twenty-two million third through eighth graders are enrolled in public school each year in the United States; each takes both a math and ELA test. Over the seven years of data I use, therefore, states administered roughly three hundred million tests to these students. This is more than a hundred times as many tests as administered by NAEP over the same period: roughly six hundred thousand math and reading tests in grades four and eight in each of the years 2009, 2011, 2013, and 2015. Even a school or district with only twenty-five students per grade would be represented by more than two thousand test scores (7 years x 6 grades x 2 subjects x 25 students = 2,100 tests) in the ED*Facts* data, versus only roughly sixteen in the NAEP data. The ED*Facts* data therefore can provide a high-resolution description of test score patterns even in very small schools or school districts.

The full population coverage of the ED*Facts* data make it possible to identify both general patterns of academic performance (such as the magnitude of achievement gaps) and heterogeneity in these patterns among subgroups, schools, districts, grades, and years. Sample-based analyses (even large samples like NAEP) might be able to provide reliable estimates of average test scores and growth rates for the nation as a whole, and by subgroup, or even by state (as is possible with NAEP data), but are generally inadequate to describe the heterogeneity of these patterns across smaller geographic or organizational units, like school districts. As the analyses show, heterogeneity in these patterns among school districts is considerable.

One additional benefit of these data is that they are not just publicly available but also identifiable and linkable to other data. Each school district in the public SEDA data is identified by name and by a unique NCES ID that can be used to merge the data to other data, public and private. As a result, these data allow us not only to quantify the variation among school districts in the key parameters of interest here, but also to identify interesting cases or sets of cases to study further. For example, we might be interested in what community and school characteristics foster high test score growth rates for poor students. We could identify a set of school districts in which poor students' growth rates are high, and then collect additional data, through case studies, about these districts; such case studies might be used to generate causal hypotheses that could be systematically tested in a larger set of districts. In addition, the data can be linked to available data on local policy and context to study the effects of educational and social policies on academic achievement (for examples of papers using the SEDA data to study the effects of social policy and conditions, see Shores and Steinberg 2017; Sorensen et al. 2018; Torats-Espinosa 2018).

That said, the ED*Facts* data are far from ideal in a number of ways. First, the test scores are based on tests that differ across states and grades, and sometimes across years, making them not readily comparable except within a given state-grade-year. Second, the scores are coarsened—reported in broad categories with labels such as basic, proficient, and advanced. Not only does the coarsening destroy some information, but the categories are also not defined in comparable ways across states, grades, and year. Third, the ED*Facts* data are reported in aggregated form, as counts of students in a given subgroup, school, grade, and year who score in each of two to five ordered performance categories; the ED*Facts* data do not include individual student records. This has two drawbacks: it is not possible to link students' scores longitudinally or across subjects in the same grade and year; and no data on individual student characteristics are included in the data. The latter means that we can tabulate the test scores only according to the subgroups reported in the data (which are those that states are required to report by law: race-ethnicity, gender, economic disadvantage, and so on); we cannot construct student-level cross-tabulations (race-by-gender, for example).

These limitations are not trivial. The comparability issues due to differences in states and the definition of coarsened performance categories would seem to damn any attempt to compare performance except within individual state-grade-year-subjects. Further, the coarsening of the data would seem to muddy any statistical comparisons between the test score distributions in different districts, even in the same state-grade-year-subject, because the means and variances of each district's score distribution are not reported. My colleagues and I, however, demonstrate that it is possible to recover reliably estimated test score means and variances in each district-grade-year-subject, and then to link these to a common national scale that enables meaningful comparisons across all districts and across grades and years (Reardon, Kalogrides, and Ho 2016; Reardon, Shear et al. 2017). Using these methods, we constructed the estimated district-specific test score means I use in this article. These estimates are publicly available through the Stanford Education Data Archive.

One additional hurdle constrains the usefulness of the ED*Facts* data for research purposes. The raw ED*Facts* data are not publicly available; they require researchers to obtain a restricted data-use license from the National Center for Education Statistics. Moreover, to avoid disclosure of individually identifiable information, researchers are required to send all analyses to NCES for review before dissemination or publication. The raw ED*Facts* data are unsuppressed, meaning that even if a single student of a given subgroup is in a particular school-grade-year, that student's test score is reported in the raw ED*Facts* data files. NCES reviews research findings prior to dissemination to ensure that no individually identifiable information is released publicly. To enable us to make the estimated test score distributions publicly available through SEDA, NCES and ED*Facts* provided us with a blanket disclosure agreement. Under this agreement, we suppress any estimate based on a cell size of fewer than twenty test scores. In addition, we add a small amount of random noise to all reported estimates to ensure that the estimation algorithm cannot be reverse-engineered to recover the underlying cell counts. With these provisos in place, NCES allows us to release our estimates publicly without further disclosure review. Because of this agreement, we are able to publicly disseminate estimates of the distributions of test scores in grades three through eight from 2009 through 2015, all measured on a common scale, in virtually every U.S. school district. These data are available at the Stanford Education Data Archive.

Despite the value of SEDA, the available data cannot, however, overcome the limitations caused by the lack of student-level longitudinal data. Such data do, of course, exist. Most states now have education data systems that track individual students over time as long as they remain in the state's public education system. One could, in theory, use states' student-level longitudinal data files (and the continuous, uncoarsened test scores they contain) for research, as many scholars have done. The challenge, however, is in negotiating data-use agreements with each of the fifty states; without fifty separate data agreements, the use of student-level longitudinal data comes at the cost of full population coverage. Ideally, states might work together to create common systems for sharing de-identified individual educational records that would make it possible to conduct longitudinal student-level analyses with full population coverage; until that time, researchers will face a trade-off between using inferior data with full population coverage or more complete data in samples or subsets of the population.

DISCUSSION, PART TWO: THE HETEROGENEITY OF OPPORTUNITY

As noted, one of the advantages of having data on the full population of students, as opposed to a relatively small sample of students or districts, is that both general patterns and variation become clear. The analyses demonstrate several key facts, some of which would not be evident without data of this kind.

First, variation is enormous among districts in the extent of early learning opportunities available to children before third grade. These differences are evident in the wide range of average third-grade test scores. Not surprisingly, early opportunities are strongly associated with districts' socioeconomic characteristics; affluent families and districts are able to provide much greater opportunities than poor ones early in children's lives.

What may be surprising, however, is the extent of variation among communities in the kinds of opportunities they provide for students to learn from grades three to eight, and that these growth opportunities are at best weakly correlated with early opportunities and socioeconomic status. This is consistent, however, with other work showing that patterns of achievement do not correspond closely to patterns of test score growth (Hanselman and Fiel 2017). The empirical patterns presented earlier are most similar to the scenario described in panel D of figure 1: both early and middle childhood opportunities vary widely among school districts, but do not covary significantly.

It is tempting to think of growth rates in test scores as a rough measure of the effectiveness of a district's public schools. This is neither entirely inappropriate nor entirely accurate, however. The growth rates better isolate the contribution to learning due to experiences during the schooling years than the grade-three scores. Grade-three average scores are likely much more strongly influenced by early childhood experiences than the growth rates. Growth rates are therefore certainly better as measures of educational opportunities from age nine to fourteen than average test scores in a school district are. But that does not mean they reflect only the contribution of schooling. Other characteristics of communities, including family resources, afterschool programs, and neighborhood conditions may all affect growth in test scores independent of schools' effects. Thus, some caution is warranted in interpreting the average growth rates as pure measures of school effectiveness. Nonetheless, relative to average test scores (at grade three or any other), the growth rates are certainly closer to a measure of school effectiveness. Given that schooling plays a significant role in children's lives from age nine to fourteen (at least in terms of time spent), it is not unreasonable to think that the growth measures carry some signal regarding school quality—and more signal than contained in simple average test score measures.

If we take the growth rates, then, as rough measures of school effectiveness, then neither socioeconomic conditions nor average test scores are especially informative about school effectiveness in a district. Many districts with high average test scores have low growth rates, and vice versa. Similarly, many low-income districts have above-average growth rates. This finding calls into question the use of average test scores as an accountability tool or a way of evaluating schools. Because average test scores, even in eighth grade, are only weakly correlated with growth rates, any system that rewards or sanctions schools or districts on the basis of their average scores will necessarily do so inappropriately in many cases (assuming that we wish to incentivize growth rates). Any information system that makes average test scores publicly available to parents in the hopes that a market for high test score districts will emerge and drive school improvement may instead simply create a market for high-SES districts, increasing economic segregation without improving school systems. To the extent that public information about school quality affects middle- and high-income families' decisions about where to live, information on growth rates might provide very different signals, perhaps leading to lower levels of economic residential and school segregation.

That is not to say the growth rates of the type

I have calculated here—using repeated cross-sectional aggregated data—are ideal, but they almost certainly are better signals than average test scores of the learning opportunities available in a school district. If we used measures like these as one part of an accountability system or a public information system, school districts in the upper-left quadrant of figure 4 would be preferred (at least in grades three through eight) over districts in the lower-right quadrant. Future research might compare the growth measures I construct here with those based on longitudinal student-level data. Such measures would be immune from the potential noise in my measures that arises because of district in- and out-migration or grade retention, or both.

The findings here also provide some insight into the issues raised in the opening of this paper. Are schools engines of opportunity or agents of inequality? The answer is perhaps more nuanced than the question implies. Some school districts seem to provide high opportunities for children from low-income families during elementary and middle school; others do not. This suggests that our school systems (or other community institutions) have the potential to catalyze opportunity, but that potential is incompletely realized in many places. And although poverty is systematically associated with low opportunities to learn in early childhood, as evidenced by the consistently low average third-grade test scores in low-income districts, poverty very clearly does not strictly determine the opportunities for children to learn in the middle grade years. That said, it is not clear from the patterns here that an effective school system alone can make up for low opportunities in early childhood. The large gaps in students' academic skills between low- and higher-SES districts are so large that even the highest growth rate in the country would be inadequate to closing even half of the gap by eighth grade.

These patterns have implications both for education policy and for our understanding of the potentially equalizing role of schools. In terms of policy, they suggest that levels of student outcomes are a poor measure of school effectiveness. I am certainly not the first to say this, but the data from eleven thousand school districts demonstrate the point very clearly. The findings also suggest that we could learn a great deal about reducing educational inequality from the low-SES communities with high growth rates. They provide, at a minimum, an existence proof of the possibility that even schools in high-poverty communities can be effective. Now the challenge is to learn what conditions make that possible and how we can foster the same conditions for children everywhere.

APPENDIX: SCALE SENSITIVITY OF CORRELATIONS BETWEEN GROWTH AND STATUS

The correlation between initial status (grade-three test average test scores in our case) and growth (change in average scores from grade three to grade eight here) is sensitive to the relative scales in which initial and final scores are measured. To see this, let $Y3$ and $Y8$ represent scores in grades three and eight, respectively. Let $\Delta = Y8 - Y3$ the change in scores. Let $\tau_3 = Var(Y3)$; $\tau_\Delta = Var(\Delta)$; and $C = Cov(Y3, \Delta)$ Note that the correlation of growth and initial status is then $r_{\Delta 3} = Corr(Y3, \Delta) = \dfrac{C}{\sqrt{\tau_3 \tau_\Delta}}$.

Now suppose we transform by a linear transformation, where $b > 0$:

$$Y8' = a + bY8.$$

The change as measured in this new metric is

$$\Delta' = a + bY8 - Y3 = a + b\Delta + (b-1)Y3.$$

The variance of changes in the new metric is

$$\tau_{\Delta'} = b^2 \tau_\Delta + (b-1)^2 \tau_3 + 2b(b-1)C.$$

And now the correlation of $Y3$ and Δ' will be

$$r' = \frac{Cov(Y3, \Delta')}{\sqrt{\tau_3 \tau_{\Delta'}}}$$

$$= \frac{bC + (b-1)\tau_3}{\sqrt{\tau_3(b^2 \tau_\Delta + (b-1)^2 \tau_3 + 2b(b-1)C)}}$$

$$= \frac{rb\sqrt{\tau_\Delta} + (b-1)\sqrt{\tau_3}}{\left[(b\sqrt{\tau_\Delta} + (b-1)\sqrt{\tau_3})^2 + 2b(b-1)(r-1)\sqrt{\tau_3 \tau_\Delta}\right]^{\frac{1}{2}}}. \quad (A1)$$

Figure A1. Grade-Three Growth Correlation as a Function of Grade-Eight/Grade-Three SD Ratio, Theoretical and Observed

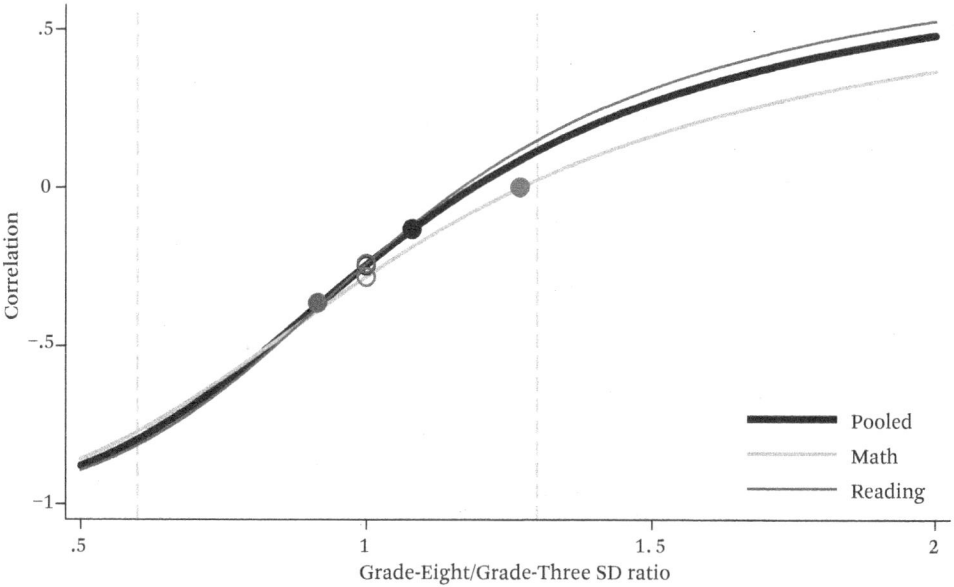

Source: Author's calculations.

Now, given τ_3, τ_Δ, and C (or r), r' is a continuous, monotonically increasing function of b. Note that

$$\lim_{b \to \infty} r' = Corr(Y3, Y8)$$

$$\lim_{b \to 0} r' = -1.$$

If we take the estimated values of τ_3, τ_Δ, and C estimated from model 1 using the standardized test scale (the scale in which $\tau_3 = \tau_8$), we can plot the equation (A1) as a function of b (see figure A1).

The red line, for example, displays the correlation between math average third-grade scores and growth rates as a function of b. In the standardized scale (corresponding to $b = 1$ on the figure), the estimated correlation is −0.282 (as shown by the hollow red circle). In the NAEP scale, the estimated correlation is 0.002, indicated by the solid red dot. This occurs at a value of about $b = 1.25$, which is very close to the ratio of the eighth-grade NAEP math standard deviation to the fourth-grade standard deviation. In other words, NAEP scale has a value of roughly $b = 1.25$ in math (and a value of $b = 0.94$ in reading).

To produce a correlation of $r' > 0.25$, we would need $b > 1.5$ in reading and $b > 1.7$ in math. In other words, if the eighth-grade metric were stretched by a factor of 1.7 or 1.5 in reading or math, respectively, the estimated correlation would be positive 0.25 rather than −0.25—still a low correlation but with the opposite sign as we observe in the standardized scale. Is a factor of $b > 1.5$ plausible?

One way to assess this is to examine other vertically scaled tests. Nathan Dadey and Derek Briggs examine sixteen vertically scaled tests used in state assessment programs (2012). For these tests, the value of b—the ratio of the eighth-grade standard deviation of scores to the third-grade standard deviation—ranges from 0.6 to almost 1.3 (though most of the reading ratios are between 0.8 and 1.0; most of the math ratios are between 0.9 and 1.1). Howard Bloom and his colleagues report standard deviations for seven vertically equated reading tests; the grade-eight to grade-three standard deviation ratios in those tests range from 0.87 to 1.04 (2008). Of the twenty-three vertically scaled assessments for which data are available, none have $b > 1.3$. The vertical gray dashed lines in the figure show the range of values of b reported by Dadey and Briggs (2012) and Bloom his colleagues (2008). The possible correlations these values of b would produce in the SEDA data range from −0.80 to +0.15. This suggests that no plausible vertical scale would yield a moderate or high positive correlation between grade-three test scores and growth rates.

REFERENCES

Abdulkadiroglu, Atila, Joshua Angrist, Susan Dynarski, Thomas J. Kane, and Parag Pathak. 2011. "Accountability and Flexibility in Public Schools: Evidence from Boston's Charters and Pilots." *Quarterly Journal of Economics* 126(2): 699–748.

Alexander, Karl L., Doris R. Entwisle, and Linda S. Olson. 2001. "Schools, Achievement, and Inequality: A Seasonal Perspective." *Educational Evaluation and Policy Analysis* 23(2): 171–91.

Alexander, Karl L., Doris R. Entwisle, and Linda Steffel Olson. 2007. "Lasting Consequences of the Summer Learning Gap." *American Sociological Review* 72 (April): 167–80.

Bloom, Howard S., Carolyn J. Hill, Alison Rebeck Black, and Mark W. Lipsey. 2008. "Performance Trajectories and Performance Gaps as Achievement Effect-Size Benchmarks for Educational Interventions." *Journal of Research on Educational Effectiveness* 1(4): 289–328.

Bloom, Howard S., and Rebecca Unterman. 2012. "Sustained Positive Effects on Graduation Rates Produced by New York City's Small Public High Schools of Choice." New York: MDRC.

Bond, Timothy N., and Kevin Lang. 2013. "The Black-White Education-Scaled Test-Score Gap in Grades K-7." NBER working paper no. 19243. Cambridge, Mass.: National Bureau of Economic Research.

Bowles, Samuel, and Herbert Gintis. 1976. *Schooling in Capitalist America: Educational Reform and the Contradictions of Economic Life*. New York: Basic Books.

Boyd, Donald, Hamilton Lankford, Susanna Loeb, and James Wyckoff. 2005. "Explaining the Short Careers of High-Achieving Teachers in Schools with Low-Performing Students." *American Economic Review* 95(2):166–71.

Center for Research on Education Outcomes (CREDO). 2015. "National Charter School Study." Stanford, Calif.: Stanford University.

Chetty, Raj, John N. Friedman, Emmanuel Saez, Nicholas Turner, and Danny Yagan. 2017. "Mobility Report Cards: The Role of Colleges in Intergenerational Mobility." NBER working paper no. 23618. Cambridge, Mass.: National Bureau of Economic Research.

Chetty, Raj, Nathaniel Hendren, and Lawrence F. Katz. 2016. "The Effects of Exposure to Better Neighborhoods on Children: New Evidence from the Moving to Opportunity Experiment." *American Economic Review* 106(4): 855–902.

Chetty, Raj, Nathaniel Hendren, Patrick Kline, and Emmanuel Saez. 2014. "Where Is the Land of Opportunity? The Geography of Intergenerational Mobility in the United States." NBER working paper no. 19843. Cambridge, Mass.: National Bureau of Economic Research.

Chingos, Matthew M., and Kristin Blagg. 2017. "Do Poor Kids Get Their Fair Share of School Funding?" Washington, D.C.: Urban Institute.

Coleman, James S., Ernest Q. Campbell, Carol J. Hobson, James McPartland, Alexander M. Mood, Frederick D. Weinfeld, and Robert L. York. 1966. *Equality of Educational Opportunity*. Washington: U.S. Department of Health, Education, and Welfare, Office of Education.

Dadey, Nathan, and Derek C. Briggs. 2012. "A Meta-Analysis of Growth Trends from Vertically Scaled Assessments." *Practical Assessment, Research & Evaluation* 17(14): 1–13.

Darling-Hammond, Linda. 1998. "Unequal Opportunity: Race and Education." *Brookings Review* 16(2): 28–32.

Dobbie, Will, and Roland G. Fryer Jr. 2011. "Are High-Quality Schools Enough to Increase Achievement Among the Poor? Evidence from the Harlem Children's Zone." *American Economic Journal: Applied Economics* 3(3): 158–87.

Downey, Douglas B., and Dennis J. Condron. 2016. "Fifty Years Since the Coleman Report: Rethinking the Relationship Between Schools and Inequality." *Sociology of Education* 89(3): 207–20.

Downey, Douglas B., Paul T. von Hippel, and Beckett A. Broh. 2004. "Are Schools the Great Equalizer? School and Non-School Influences on Socioeconomic and Black/White Gaps in Reading Skills." *American Sociological Review* 69(5): 613–35.

Duncan, Greg J., and Jeanne Brooks-Gunn. 1997. *Consequences of Growing Up Poor*. New York: Russell Sage Foundation.

Duncan, Greg J., Jeanne Brooks-Gunn, and Pamela Kato Klebanov. 1994. "Economic Deprivation and

Early Childhood Development." *Child Development* 65(2): 296–318.

Duncan, Greg J., and Katharine A. Magnuson. 2016. "Can Early Childhood Interventions Decrease Inequality of Economic Opportunity?" *RSF: The Russell Sage Foundation Journal of the Social Sciences* 2(2): 123–41.

Entwisle, Doris R., and Karl L. Alexander. 1994. "Winter Setback: The Racial Composition of Schools and Learning to Read." *American Sociological Review* 59(3): 446–60.

Fahle, Erin M., Benjamin R. Shear, Demetra Kalogrides, Sean F. Reardon, Richard DiSalvo, and Andrew D. Ho. 2018. "Stanford Education Data Archive: Technical Documentation, Version 2.1." Center for Education Policy Analysis, Stanford University. Accessed October 10, 2018. https://stacks.stanford.edu/file/druid:db586ns4974/SEDA_documentation_v21.pdf.

Hanselman, Paul, and Jeremy E. Fiel. 2017. "School Opportunity Hoarding? Racial Segregation and Access to High Growth Schools." *Social Forces* 95(3): 1077–104.

Harding, David J. 2003. "Counterfactual Models of Neighborhood Effects: The Effect of Neighborhood Poverty on Dropping Out and Teenage Pregnancy." *American Journal of Sociology* 109(3): 676–719.

Heckman, James, Rodrigo Pinto, and Peter Savelyev. 2013. "Understanding the Mechanisms Through Which an Influential Early Childhood Program Boosted Adult Outcomes." *American Economic Review* 103(6): 2052–86.

Ho, Andrew D. 2008. "The Problem with "Proficiency": Limitations of Statistics and Policy Under No Child Left Behind." *Educational Researcher* 37(6): 351–60.

———. 2009. "A Nonparametric Framework for Comparing Trends and Gaps Across Tests." *Journal of Educational and Behavioral Statistics* 34(2): 201–28.

Jencks, Christopher. 1972. *Inequality: A Reassessment of the Effect of Family and Schooling in America*. New York: Basic Books.

Kozol, Jonathan. 1967. *Death at an Early Age: The Destruction of the Hearts and Minds of Negro Children in the Boston Public Schools*. New York: Penguin.

———. 1991. *Savage Inequalities: Children in America's Schools*. New York: Crown.

Lankford, Hamilton, Susanna Loeb, and James Wyckoff. 2002. "Teacher Sorting and the Plight of Urban Schools: A Descriptive Analysis." *Educational Evaluation and Policy Analysis* 24(1): 37–62.

Nisbett, Richard E. 1998. "Race, Genetics, and IQ." In *The Black-White Test Score Gap*, edited by Christopher Jencks and Meredith Phillips. Washington, D.C.: Brookings Institution Press.

———. 2011. "The Achievement Gap: Past, Present & Future." *Daedalus* 140(2): 90–100.

Nisbett, Richard E., Joshua Aronson, Clancy Blair, William Dickens, James Flynn, Diane F. Halpern, and Eric Turkheimer. 2012. "Group Differences in IQ Are Best Understood as Environmental in Origin." *American Psychologist* 67(6): 503–04.

Phillips, Deborah A., and Jack P. Shonkoff. 2000. *From Neurons to Neighborhoods: The Science of Early Childhood Development*. Washington, D.C.: National Academies Press.

Raudenbush, Stephen W., and Robert D. Eschmann. 2015. "Does Schooling Increase or Reduce Social Inequality?" *Annual Review of Sociology* 41(1): 443–70.

Reardon, Sean F. 2008. "Thirteen Ways of Looking at the Black-White Test Score Gap." IREPP working paper. Stanford, Calif.: Stanford University.

———. 2011. "The Widening Academic Achievement Gap Between the Rich and the Poor: New Evidence and Possible Explanations." In *Whither Opportunity? Rising Inequality, Schools, and Children's Life Chances*, edited by Greg J. Duncan and Richard J. Murnane. New York: Russell Sage Foundation.

Reardon, Sean F., Erin M. Fahle, Demetra Kalogrides, Anne Podolsky, and Rosalia Zarate. 2018. "Gender Achievement Gaps in US School Districts." CEPA working paper no. 18-13. Stanford, Calif.: Center for Education Policy Analysis, Stanford University. Accessed October 10, 2018. https://cepa.stanford.edu/sites/default/files/wp18-13-v201806_0.pdf.

Reardon, Sean F., Andrew D. Ho, Benjamin R. Shear, Erin M. Fahle, Demetra Kalogrides, and Richard DiSalvo. 2017. "Stanford Education Data Archive, Version 2.1." Accessed October 10, 2018. http://purl.stanford.edu/db586ns4974.

Reardon, Sean F., Demetra Kalogrides, and Andrew D. Ho. 2016. "Linking U.S. School District Test Score Distributions to a Common Scale, 2009-2013." CEPA working paper no. 16-09. Stanford, Calif.: Center for Education Policy Analysis,

Stanford University. Accessed October 10, 2018. https://cepa.stanford.edu/sites/default/files/wp16-09-v201604.pdf.

Reardon, Sean F., Joseph P. Robinson-Cimpian, and Ericka S. Weathers. 2015. "Patterns and Trends in Racial/Ethnic and Socioeconomic Academic Achievement Gaps." In *Handbook of Research in Education Finance and Policy*, edited by Helen Ladd and Margaret Goertz. Mahwah, N.J.: Lawrence Erlbaum.

Reardon, Sean F., Benjamin R. Shear, Katherine E. Castellano, and Andrew D. Ho. 2017. "Using Heteroskedastic Ordered Probit Models to Recover Moments of Continuous Test Score Distributions from Coarsened Data." *Journal of Educational and Behavioral Statistics* 42(1): 3–45.

Sampson, Robert J., Patrick Sharkey, and Stephen W. Raudenbush. 2008. "Durable Effects of Concentrated Disadvantage on Verbal Ability Among African-American Children." *Proceedings of the National Academy of Sciences* 105(3): 845–52.

Shores, Kenneth, and Matthew Steinberg. 2017. "The Impact of the Great Recession on Student Achievement: Evidence from Population Data." CEPA working paper no. 17-09. Stanford, Calif.: Stanford Center for Education Policy Analysis, Sanford University. Accessed October 10, 2018. https://cepa.stanford.edu/sites/default/files/wp17-09-v201708.pdf.

Sirin, Selcuk R. 2005. "Socioeconomic Status and Academic Achievement: A Meta-Analytic Review of Research." *Review of Educational Research* 75(3): 417–53.

Sorensen, Lucy C., Ashley M. Fox, Heyjie Jung, and Erika G. Martin. 2018. "Lead Exposure and Academic Achievement: Evidence from Childhood Lead Poisoning Prevention Efforts." *Journal of Population Economics*. Published online May 24, 2018. DOI: 10.1007/s00148-018-0707-y.

Torats-Espinosa, Gerard. 2018. "Crime and Inequality in Academic Achievement across School Districts in the United States." Stanford, Calif.: Stanford Center for Education Policy Analysis, Sanford University. Accessed October 10, 2018. http://cepa.stanford.edu/sites/default/files/torrats-espinosa-seda-crime.pdf.

Tuttle, Christina Clark, Philip Gleason, and Melissa Clark. 2012. "Using Lotteries to Evaluate Schools of Choice: Evidence from a National Study of Charter Schools." *Economics of Education Review* 31(2): 237–53.

von Hippel, Paul T., Joseph Workman, and Douglas B. Downey. 2017. "Are Schools (Still) a Great Equalizer? Replicating a Summer Learning Study Using Better Test Scores and a New Cohort of Children." Social Science Research Network. Accessed October 10, 2018. https://papers.ssrn.com/sol3/papers.cfm?abstract_id=3036094.

Wodtke, Geoffrey T., David J. Harding, and Felix Elwert. 2011. "Neighborhood Effects in Temporal Perspective: The Impact of Long-Term Exposure to Concentrated Disadvantage on High School Graduation." *American Sociological Review* 76(5): 713–36.

Ziol-Guest, Kathleen M., and Kenneth T.H. Lee. 2016. "Parent Income–Based Gaps in Schooling." *AERA Open* 2(2): 1–10.

PART II
Child Welfare

Building Connections: Using Integrated Administrative Data to Identify Issues and Solutions Spanning the Child Welfare and Child Support Systems

LANIKQUE HOWARD, LISA KLEIN VOGEL, MARIA CANCIAN, AND JENNIFER L. NOYES

We analyze the role of newly integrated data from the child support and child welfare systems in seeding a major policy change in Wisconsin. Parents are often ordered to pay child support to offset the costs of their children's stay in foster care. Policy allows for consideration of the "best interests of the child." Concerns that charging parents could delay or disrupt reunification motivated our analyses of integrated data to identify the impacts of current policy. We summarize the results of the analyses and then focus on the role of administrative data in supporting policy development. We discuss the potential and limitations of integrated data in supporting cross-system innovation and detail a series of complementary research efforts designed to support implementation.

Keywords: integrated administrative data, administrative data analysis, cost-benefit analysis, cross-program evaluation, innovative policy solutions

Lanikque Howard is the founder of Children First Strategy Group and the early childhood special projects coordinator at First 5 Alameda County. **Lisa Klein Vogel** is a researcher at the Institute for Research on Poverty at the University of Wisconsin–Madison and a graduate student in the School of Social Work at the University of Wisconsin–Madison. **Maria Cancian** is professor of public affairs and social work at the University of Wisconsin–Madison. **Jennifer L. Noyes** is associate dean for operations and staff, College of Letters and Science, and Distinguished Researcher, Institute for Research on Poverty at the University of Wisconsin–Madison.

© 2019 Russell Sage Foundation. Howard, Lanikque, Lisa Klein Vogel, Maria Cancian, and Jennifer L. Noyes. 2019. "Building Connections: Using Integrated Administrative Data to Identify Issues and Solutions Spanning the Child Welfare and Child Support Systems." *RSF: The Russell Sage Foundation Journal of the Social Sciences* 5(2): 70–85. DOI: 10.7758/RSF.2019.5.2.04. The authors thank the editors and reviewers for helpful comments on earlier drafts, Carol Chellew, Steven Cook, Mai Seki, Rebekah Selekman, and Lynn Wimer for contributions to earlier research on which this article draws, as well as colleagues at the Institute for Research on Poverty and the Wisconsin Department of Children and Families for their ongoing support of the Wisconsin Data Core and the collaborative research initiative discussed in this article. Any opinions expressed are those of the authors. Direct correspondence to: Lanikque Howard at llhoward@wisc.edu, 10700 MacArthur Blvd., Suite 2A, Oakland, CA 94605; Lisa Klein Vogel at lmklein@wisc.edu, 1180 Observatory Dr., #3438, Madison, WI 53706; Maria Cancian at mcancian@wisc.edu, 2302 17th St. NW, Washington, D.C. 20009; and Jennifer L. Noyes at jennifer.noyes@wisc.edu, University of Wisconsin–Madison, 105A South Hall, 1055 Bascom Mall, Madison, WI 53706.

Open Access Policy: *RSF: The Russell Sage Foundation Journal of the Social Sciences* is an open access journal. This article is published under a Creative Commons Attribution-NonCommercial-NoDerivs 3.0 Unported License.

Our counties have asked, "Where did this data come from?" And when we say, "It's Wisconsin data, it's eWiSACWIS data, it's like our families' data," they're like, "Oh," and it suddenly means something. And, when we say we're going to keep studying it, people are very interested in that. People clearly feel like the research is going to show them something.

    Wisconsin Child Support Policy
    Workgroup Leader

The current demand for data-driven decision making in public programs is widespread. For example, the Commission on Evidence-Based Policymaking, which was established by the bipartisan Evidence-Based Policymaking Commission Act of 2016, issued its recommendations in September 2017 calling for the use of rigorous evidence created as part of routine government operations in constructing public policy (CEP 2017). The commission's call was quickly followed by the introduction of the related Foundations for Evidence-Based Policymaking Act of 2017, introduced by Democratic Senator Patty Murray (S. 2046) and Republican Speaker of the House Paul Ryan (H.R. 4174). In addition, academic conferences on the use of "big data" and related analytic techniques are proliferating, and universities and foundations are making major investments in related programs. Despite the enthusiasm reflected in these initiatives, a number of technical, institutional, and cultural challenges are inherent in using administrative data for social policy development that must be addressed. In this article, we analyze the role of integrated data from the child support and child welfare systems in seeding a major policy proposal in Wisconsin, briefly reviewing the empirical research supported by the data and how it motivated the initial consideration of a policy change, before focusing on implementation challenges and how integrated administrative data, and related qualitative research and analysis, can support cross-system policy innovation.

POLICY ISSUE

Why child support and child welfare programs? These programs were selected because studies of related administrative data reveal that, for low-income, single-parent families, child support is often a crucial source of economic support and stability, and in many cases a significant share of income (Office of Child Support Enforcement 2011). Given that numerous studies have shown that children from low-income families are more likely than their affluent peers to experience child abuse or neglect, we expect that child support can serve as a critical tool for preventing child maltreatment by bringing financial resources into the households of struggling families (Berger 2004; Drake and Pandey 1996; Pelton 1994; Sedlak et al. 2010). Evidence suggests that even modest increases in family income can reduce maltreatment risk (Cancian, Yang, and Slack 2013; Pelton 1994).

However, whereas child support has the potential to serve as a key resource for single-parent households living in poverty, it is possible that the child support system also has the potential to harm rather than help children in these families. In particular, when children are removed from the custodial parent's home and placed in out-of-home care, federal policies allow child support agencies to divert resources from the home to recover a portion of the costs associated with out-of-home care (Chellew, Noyes, and Selekman 2012; Children's Bureau 2012). In Wisconsin, the focus of our analysis, counties operationalize this directive using one of three mechanisms. First, existing orders of support from a noncustodial parent (the parent who lived apart from the child) to the parent with whom the child lived prior to removal can be redirected from the noncustodial parent to the county. Second, the child support system can initiate a new order for support from the custodial parent to the county. Third, an existing order to the custodial parent from the noncustodial parent can be redirected to the county and a new order can be established for the custodial parent. In other words, for example, if a child living with her mother, and receiving child support from her father, is placed in foster care, the father's child support may be redirected, and a new child support order could be put in place for the mother, so that both parents make payments to the county to offset the costs of foster care.

Given that we know that poverty often contributes to foster care placements, the loss of income due to changes to existing child support orders and the creation of new orders to offset foster care costs may be a cause for concern (Office of Child Support Enforcement 2017; Wulczyn, Hislop, and Harden 2002). However, the effects of this practice are apparent only when data and outcomes are examined across rather than within systems. This article highlights the findings of analyses of longitudinal, integrated data from both the child welfare and child support systems that in tandem identified the implications of child support referrals for child welfare outcomes. Our analysis informed the development of policy solutions to preclude the charging of families for foster care costs, which our analysis revealed was counterproductive for both families and the state. But, as we discuss, this was only an initial step in the policy change process and just one context in which integrated data can support innovation.

THE ROLE OF ADMINISTRATIVE DATA MANAGEMENT AND ANALYSIS IN SUPPORTING A RESEARCHER-PRACTITIONER PARTNERSHIP

Researchers at the Institute for Research on Poverty (IRP) have a long-standing relationship with State of Wisconsin agencies to support policy-related research. Of particular interest to this article is the close collaboration between IRP researchers and the Wisconsin Department of Children and Families (DCF).[1] As part of the long-standing Child Support Research Agreement, researchers at IRP and practitioners and policymakers in the DCF Bureau of Child Support work together to identify a set of research projects aimed at improving policy and practice as they relate to the child support system, the families the system serves, and the agencies and programs with which the system interacts. These projects include research reviews, applied research to address specific policy and practice concerns, exploratory research to fuel innovations within the system, and program evaluation. A key advantage of this collaboration is the ability of researchers and practitioners to work together to share questions and ideas for answering them, and to develop and evaluate potential policy and practice innovations.

Research conducted under the Child Support Research Agreement is facilitated by the integrated data system maintained at IRP known as the Wisconsin Data Core. The Wisconsin Data Core was initially created through a joint effort between IRP and DCF that has now expanded to include other state agencies. The Wisconsin Data Core, generated annually by IRP analysts, draws data from the state's public assistance, child welfare (eWiSACWIS), child support, unemployment insurance, and incarceration (Wisconsin Department of Corrections and Milwaukee County Jail) administrative data systems. At the heart of the Wisconsin Data Core is the Multi-Sample Person File (MSPF), which identifies each individual that appears in the administrative data and then matches those individuals across all of the program data systems in order to create a unique record for each individual. The MSPF also includes demographic information and county-level location information on each individual. The MSPF can be linked to program case and participation files, resulting in the creation of analysis files that include administrative data from multiple sources and across time. Separate files indicate family relationships (mothers and fathers) for those individuals for whom these relationships can be determined from the available data.

By linking individual-level administrative data from multiple human service agencies, across time, the Wisconsin Data Core provides researchers with the opportunity to create a more complete picture of service needs and outcomes, identify clients who are served by multiple systems, examine participation trends over time, and support cross-program evaluation and analysis. Additionally, by leveraging records from multiple systems that serve par-

---

1. The Wisconsin Department of Children and Families is responsible for providing (and overseeing county provision of) services to assist children and families, including child abuse and neglect investigations, adoption and foster care services, the Wisconsin Works program, the childcare subsidy program, and child support enforcement and paternity establishment, among other programs and services.

ents and children (such as Medicaid birth records and paternity establishment from the child support system) and using this information to link parents to their children, it is possible to construct longitudinal household and family participation records. This is a particularly important advantage because many families are served by multiple systems; however, administrative records from many systems have historically not been shared or linked, thereby severely limiting examination of cross-system effects.

The availability of data through the Wisconsin Data Core has played a crucial role in facilitating the researcher-practitioner partnership between IRP and DCF. The data were, and continue to be, an essential component of the researcher-practitioner collaboration in Wisconsin. The availability of the data was critical to the collaborative effort discussed in this article.

USE OF INTEGRATED ADMINISTRATIVE DATA TO ASSESS POLICY ISSUES

The collaboration reflected here was born out of concern about the potential effects of a current U.S. federal law that requires states to take steps to secure child support from biological parents who have a child in foster care. Although federal policy allows for consideration of the best interests of the child when determining whether to pursue child support to offset the costs of foster care, decisions about child support often focus on the responsibility of both parents to provide financial support and on the ostensible cost savings of charging parents for their children's care (Chellew, Noyes, and Selekman 2012). Given that poverty often contributes to foster care placements (Office of Child Support Enforcement 2017; Wulczyn, Hislop, and Harden 2002), and consistent with experimental evidence suggesting that child support payments to custodial parents reduces child welfare involvement (Cancian, Yang, and Slack 2013), DCF staff raised concerns that diverting child support or requiring formerly resident parents to pay child support could delay or disrupt reunification efforts (that is, children's return to their parents). The most salient policy question is whether it is cost effective to order resident parents (typically mothers) to pay child support, and to divert child support payments from noncustodial parents (typically fathers), when children are placed in foster care. In particular, are the foster care costs that are thereby "recovered" by the child support system on behalf of the county greater than the related administrative and program costs? Of particular concern, given that poverty is a significant factor in many child welfare cases, was whether the obligation to pay child support would create a financial barrier to children returning to their parents. Given the high costs of providing foster care, if child support obligations delayed reunification, the net impact was expected to be an increase in public costs.

Using statewide, longitudinal, integrated data from both the child welfare and the child support systems available through the Wisconsin Data Core, we were able to analyze the interactions between the child support and child welfare systems to address these questions.[2] Three types of analyses were completed: descriptive, causal, and cost-benefit.

Initial descriptive analysis demonstrated that children in foster care whose mothers were required to pay child support had, on average, longer spells out of home (Cancian and Seki 2010). However, identifying whether child support orders have a causal effect on the length of time children spend in foster care is challenging because the positive relationship between child support orders and the length of out-of-home placements could potentially stem from a number of factors. Based on conversations with state and local child welfare agency staff, we expected that the relationship could simply reflect an appropriate assessment of the likely length of an out-of-home placement. For example, if a child welfare worker knows that a child is likely to be in an out-of-home placement for a significant period, the welfare worker may be more likely to pursue an order for the

---

2. Although not all of the researchers who contributed to this and other analyses summarized are listed as authors, the article uses *we* throughout to refer to the body of work generated during the IRP-DCF partnership.

preplacement resident parent (the parent with whom the child lived before being placed in foster care), or to redirect an established child support order from the preplacement resident parent to the child welfare system. In that case, the positive relationship between child support orders and length of placement could simply reflect the higher rate of referrals to child support for families with children expected to be out of home for a longer period. On the other hand, for disadvantaged families who are required to address an income-related deficiency as part of the requirements to be reunified with their child, such as finding adequate housing, charging the preplacement resident parent child support may create barriers to meeting the permanency plan requirements, which can impede reunification. The implications for policy depend on identifying the causal relationship.

Using the statewide longitudinal data available in the Wisconsin Data Core, we were able to identify and exploit the natural variation in county child support referral practices to estimate the causal effect of referring parents to child support on the duration of out-of-home placements. Although Wisconsin operates a state-supervised child welfare system, child welfare agencies are county run, and variation in policy interpretation and implementation across counties is substantial. Analysis of administrative records allowed us to identify significant differences in the proportion of mothers referred to child support throughout the state, some counties referring virtually all foster care cases to child support, and other counties rarely, if ever, making a referral. Using variation in referral rates as an instrument, we estimated the effect of child support orders on foster care spells—essentially comparing differences in time to reunification for children of mothers who live in low-probability counties, where they are less likely to be referred to child support, versus those in high-probability counties, where they are more likely to be referred to child support (Cancian et al. 2017). We found that charging preplacement custodial mothers (the parent the child lived with before being placed in foster care) or redirecting the child support income the preplacement custodial mothers receive to the county results in a substantial loss in resources for families. Further, our estimates suggested that a $100 child support order to offset foster care costs is associated with a 6.6-month delay in reunification or other permanency options. This finding is important, not only because the extra time in care is financially costly for counties operating child welfare systems, but also because it delays reunification for the families, which is a priority for the child welfare system (Child Welfare Information Gateway 2012).

For these findings to better inform policy, it was important to estimate the extent to which the additional financial costs associated with a delay in reunification would be offset by the child support collections made to the county following an out-of-home placement. Again, integrated administrative data available through the IRP Data Core were important, and were used for a cost-benefit analysis (Chellew, Noyes, and Selekman 2012). The cost-benefit analysis found that 55 percent of children in the child welfare system were associated with a child support order. These orders totaled $11.8 million, which, if fully collected, would have recovered 8 percent of child welfare expenditures in 2011. However, of all of the out-of-home placements made in 2011, only 18.2 percent of cases were associated with at least one child support payment, totaling $3.0 million. Additionally, $1.1 million was collected in arrears. Therefore, on average, counties recovered less than 3 percent of child welfare expenditures in 2011.[3] Given the small percentage of child welfare expenditures recovered by associated child support pay-

---

3. Because child welfare agencies provide a multitude of services that are interrelated, it is challenging to disaggregate case management and program services into discrete activities. This, along with the fact that child welfare services are financed through various funding mechanisms, led us to use a very conservative estimate of out-of-home costs. We did not account for administrative or facility costs or the long-term societal costs of having children in the child welfare system for an extended period. Instead, we calculated only the costs of payments to care providers using state administrative data and county fiscal data. In addition to these estimates,

ments and the estimated delay in reunification associated with child support orders, we concluded that ordering parents whose children have been removed from their custody to pay child support was not cost effective.

In this example, administrative data, integrated across programs and data systems, were essential in identifying the consequences of the interaction between two relatively siloed programs. These data also allowed researchers to observe systematic differences in practice across counties, and to leverage those differences to estimate the impact of alternative approaches. The results of that analysis, with the related cost-benefit analysis, provided a basis for leadership in the Wisconsin Department of Children and Families to consider a new approach to serving families dually engaged in the child welfare and child support systems.

UNDERSTANDING THE PROCESSES REVEALED BY THE ANALYSIS OF ADMINISTRATIVE DATA

In Wisconsin, discretion in the referral of child welfare–involved families to child support enforcement rests entirely with the child welfare agency. Child welfare staff are expected to have the information needed to support an assessment of the steps most consistent with the best interests of the child. Once they make their assessment, the child support referral is automatically generated. Although the analysis of administrative data highlighted key differences in outcomes of the referral process—some agencies referring almost all cases, and others rarely referring any—it provided far less insight into the differences in policy and practice that accounted for the variation across counties. We turned to a qualitative study of agency practice to better understand county processes for referring cases to child support following an out-of-home placement. We wanted to understand workers' perspectives regarding the relevant policies and also to determine whether agency practice is influenced by the information technology. This understanding was essential to the development of potential policy modifications regarding the referral process.

State Policy

In Wisconsin, at the time of removal, and before a foster home can be determined, county child welfare workers respond to three questions in the Wisconsin Statewide Automated Child Welfare Information System, which then automatically determines whether a referral to child support will be made. The questions are as follows:

Is this referral in the best interests of the child?

Is the placement expected to be long term?

Is the worker aware of a court order for child support or is this otherwise an appropriate case to refer for child support services?

As noted in figure 1, a positive response to questions 1 and 2 in combination will result in a referral to child support. Alternatively, a positive response to question 3 will also initiate a referral to child support regardless of how the other questions were answered. If question 1 or question 3 is marked *yes*, then the *referral applies to* field is displayed and becomes required. Child protective service workers can then choose among three choices. The choices are both parents, father only, and mother only. Once a referral is made to child support, the child support agency must take the requisite action and work the case.

In most cases, the mother is the preplacement resident parent and the father is the noncustodial parent (the parent who lived apart from the child). Therefore, when a child welfare worker selects *mother only*, it typically means they are referring the preplacement resident parent to child support. Referring the preplacement resident parent to child support generates a new child support order that requires the preplacement resident parent to pay a monthly fee to the county to offset the costs of care for

---

we calculated the amount of child support collected for all foster care cases during 2011, including arrears, using administrative data from the child support enforcement system.

Figure 1. Current System Flow

When entering placements in the eWiSACWIS, child welfare staff use three questions to determine if a child support referral is appropriate.

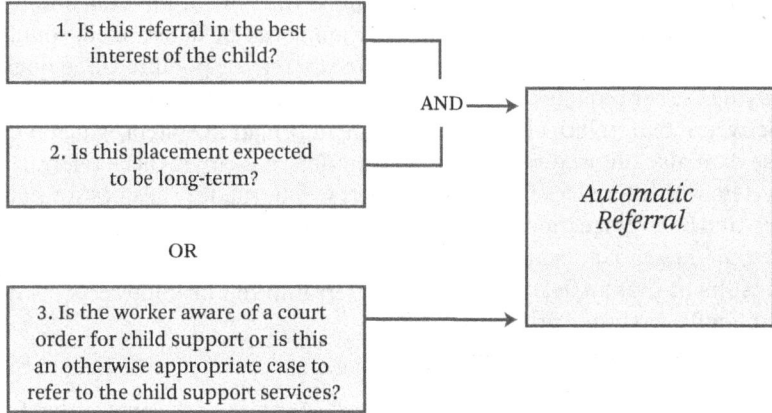

At least one parent of the child in OHP must be identified in order for a referral to occur.

Source: Authors, in collaboration with Wisconsin Department of Children and Families staff and leadership.

their child. On the other hand, when a child welfare worker selects *father only*, it usually refers to the noncustodial parent and the system prompts the child support worker who receives the case to determine if there is already a child support order in place.[4] If the custodial parent already has a child support order established, the child support worker will redirect the order from the custodial parent to the county. If an order is not in place, the child support worker will attempt to locate the noncustodial parent and establish an order. Finally, if the child welfare worker indicates that both parents should be referred to child support, the child support worker will open cases for both parents, or open a case for the preplacement resident parent and redirect the preplacement resident parent's child support payments to the county, if an order is already in place for the noncustodial parent.

County Practices

Even though Wisconsin has a policy regarding the referral of out-of-home placement cases to child support that emphasizes the best interests of the child and the expected duration of the placement, most child welfare workers reported, through in-depth, semi-structured interviews, that they refer all cases to child support and do not exercise their discretion when making the decision (Chellew, Noyes, and Selekman 2012). This practice is based on the belief that child support payments are an important source of revenue for the county and that referrals to child support help hold parents responsible for their children while their children are in foster care. Among those workers who reported exercising some discretion, variation in practice was substantial. For example, some county workers did not refer cases that they thought would last for less than six months; others, who reported having good working relationships with their child support agency, worked with child support workers to determine the appropriateness of a referral based on factors related to both the child welfare and child support records (Howard, Noyes, and Cancian 2013). Staff noted that their county referral practices reflected a compromise between doing what is in the best interests of the child and the county's need to recover costs.

4. In some cases, though less prevalent, the father is the resident parent and the mother is the noncustodial parent.

Figure 2. Chart of Preplacement Resident Parent Referral Questions

For cases where the out-of-home placement is expected to be longer than six months and/or reunification with the preplacement resident parent is the primary goal.

Start Here:

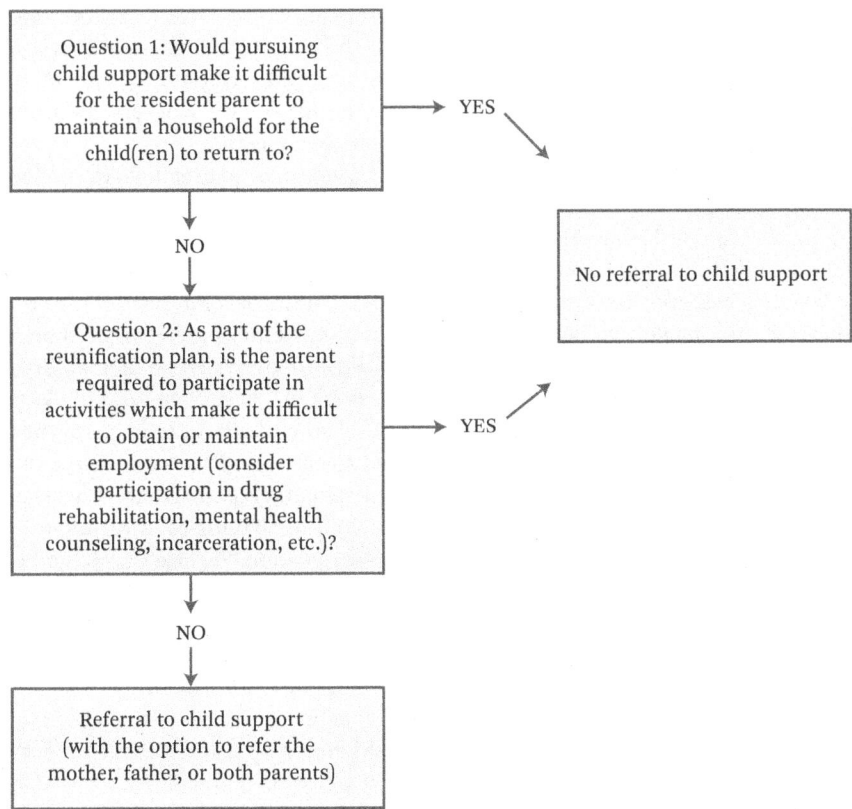

Source: Authors, in collaboration with Wisconsin Department of Children and Families staff and leadership.

IDENTIFYING PRACTICE OPTIONS

The quantitative analysis of integrated administrative data confirmed concerns about redirecting child support payments from noncustodial parents to the county, or requiring custodial parents to pay child support to the county, when a child is placed in foster care. The initial qualitative interviews helped explain county variation in the application of the policy. Although these analyses supported identification of the policy problem, developing an appropriate solution and an implementation strategy again required information well beyond that available from administrative data analysis. To support that effort, sixty child welfare staff from eleven counties were interviewed. Counties were invited to participate based on their geographical location, population size, poverty levels, relationship with child support staff, and—here, leveraging the analysis of administrative data—the frequency of out-of-home placement cases referred to child support. A flowchart developed by IRP researchers in consultation with DCF staff was used as a tool to assist county staff in thinking about what the best interests of the child may mean as well as the potential timing of a referral.

The flowchart, reflected in figure 2, asked child welfare workers to think about two questions as they worked through a figurative case in which the out-of-home placement is expected to be longer than six months or reunification with the preplacement resident parent is the primary goal:

Would pursuing child support make it difficult for the resident parent to maintain a household for the child(ren) to return to?

As part of the reunification plan, is the parent required to participate in activities that make it difficult to obtain or maintain employment (consider participation in drug rehabilitation, mental health counseling, incarceration)?

In many instances, child welfare workers were able to identify cases for which such a decision-making structure would have been useful, given that paying child support did severely affect the families and may have interfered with reunification. In considering the first question, for example, child welfare workers noted that charging parents child support after their child is removed from their home only adds to the distress of the family, because doing so decreases the resources available to being able to maintain housing and access services necessary prior to allowing the child to return to the home. Further, charging child support may undermine the ability for a parent to continue a relationship with a child who is placed out of home. One worker noted, for instance, that although the agency encourages parents to visit their children and still purchase items for them, such as their winter coat or favorite food, it becomes increasingly difficult for parents to continue to do so if they are paying child support. Another worker noted a particular case in which, after receiving a child support order, a mother stopped visiting her child, who was placed in a residential treatment facility far from her home, because she could not afford the costs of such visits while also paying child support.

However, despite recognizing the challenges that charging child support may create for families, many workers expressed concern about being able to distinguish between parents who have a hard time paying child support because of poor money management, or some other personal action, versus those parents who truly cannot afford child support, despite their best efforts. Underlying these concerns was the issue of the timing of the referral to child support, given the need to determine the best interests of the child. Over the course of the interviews, child welfare workers identified three key sets of concerns.

Developing adequate information. In counties where intake is separated from ongoing case management within child welfare, intake workers were uncomfortable with thinking about what might be in the best interests of the child in determining whether parents should be referred to child support based on their ability to pay.[5] These workers felt that they did not know the families well enough and did not want to get into questions related to income at the time of removal. Ongoing child welfare workers seemed much more willing to think about the best interests question because they felt better able to assess the financial situation of the family. They felt that after working with the family for a time, they would know whether a family could afford to pay child support.

Assessing potential length of removal. Most workers did not feel able to determine the length of a placement during the initial removal of a child. Workers reported not knowing whether a case was going to last more than six months when a child was initially removed. Others remarked that they felt answering *yes* went against their programmatic goal to reunify children as quickly as possible.

Establishing reunification activities. Some workers stated that they try to think about the parent's ability to maintain employment when assigning reunification activities. Those who said that they did not consider reunification requirements when making referrals were still able to give examples of cases where it was im-

---

5. In some counties, child welfare services are provided by two different staff members: intake and ongoing child welfare workers. In these cases, intake staff assess allegations of child abuse and neglect and determine whether the allegations are substantiated. An intake worker who determines that maltreatment has occurred is responsible for removing the child from the home and locating an out-of-home placement. Once this occurs, the case is transferred to an ongoing child welfare worker who has oversight of out-of-home placement cases. The ongoing worker is responsible for conducting a family assessment, creating a permanency plan, assisting with reunification efforts, and evaluating the parent's progress toward the goals outlined in the permanency plan.

possible for parents to maintain employment and follow the permanency plan activities. Many child welfare workers ultimately agreed that it is important to know what the reunification activities will require before referring parents to child support.

The interviews highlighted the importance of the timing of referrals for determining what is in the best interests of the child. The process of discussing the flowchart in figure 2 yielded important information to be considered in potentially modifying state policy and providing guidance regarding its implementation to county child welfare workers. However, although workers indicated that delaying referrals has a number of potential advantages, many child welfare workers contested changes in the timing of referrals due to concerns related to cost recovery and parental responsibility.

INFORMING POLICY DEVELOPMENT AND IMPLEMENTATION

Proponents of the researcher-practitioner model argue that research-practice partnerships facilitate greater use of research in agency decision making (Tseng 2012). Developing research with implications for policy and program improvement is a central goal of the IRP-DCF collaboration. In many cases, the Wisconsin Data Core and access to its integrated administrative data make it possible for the partnership to thrive and be successful. This is the case for the policy problem discussed here. Without the integrated administrative data, we would not have been able to identify and examine patterns of cross-system program participation. Even though DCF staff noted an area of concern, without statewide data for a large sample, our ability to find a potential instrument and identify the causal relationship between child support orders and time in care would have been quite limited. In the absence of the analysis of state administrative data and county fiscal data, the child support recovered from parents was easily quantified, but the delay in reunification, and associated costs, were invisible. The administrative data analysis provided DCF with an opportunity to better understand their child support referral policy and its implications. Moreover, these findings, in combination with the qualitative studies of county child support referral practices, allowed researchers at IRP to not only analyze current practice, but also help inform the discussion of options for change.

Seeding Collaboration

IRP researchers discussed the findings with DCF officials in a variety of settings. After consideration, the DCF Division of Economic Security, which has responsibility for the child support enforcement system, and the DCF Division of Safety and Permanence, which has responsibility for the child welfare system, made the joint decision to work with IRP researchers to begin to develop alternatives to current policy and practice. This collaboration not only represents a promising and novel approach to addressing an unintended policy consequence, but also constitutes a major milestone in efforts for the two systems to work jointly to coordinate policy and practice.

This collaborative endeavor was made possible by a number of factors (Howard 2018). The following are the four most prominent:

A new administrative structure established in 2008 brought the administrations of child welfare and child support, along with other human service programs, into a single department, the Wisconsin Department of Children and Families. In theory, having the two systems under the same administrative structure increased opportunities for coordination.

Guidance at the federal level encouraged collaboration between child welfare and child support systems. For instance, even though federal policy states it is the state child welfare agency's responsibility to determine which cases to refer based on a determination of the best interests of the child, the federal government issued guidance in 2012 encouraging child welfare and child support agencies "to work together to develop criteria for appropriate referrals in the best interests of the child involved" (Office of Child Support Enforcement 2012).

The cross-program analysis conducted by IRP, through its partnership with DCF, showed how policies and practices in the child welfare system affect clients served by the child support system and vice versa.

Strong leadership, with endorsement of the value of research to inform policy and practice by DCF's leadership, specifically the department's secretary, greatly facilitated the collaborative project.

Developing Policy Alternatives

Building on the administrative data analysis, cost-benefit analysis, and qualitative studies, the two DCF divisions and IRP staff developed a framework for modifying the Wisconsin child support policy and delaying referrals to child support from the initial foster care placement to six months after the initial placement. This time frame was selected because, at the six-month mark, child welfare workers are required to establish a permanency plan for children in out-of-home care. The plan outlines the activities parents are required to complete to be reunified with their children. During interviews conducted as part of the qualitative research components, child welfare workers noted that at this point they have a better sense of the family's lifestyle, their likely cooperation with the permanency plan and reunification activities, and their connection with their children. That allows them to assess whether a family is moving toward reunification, what the parents' priorities are, and whether charging child support would be in the best interests of the child. This understanding of child welfare practice was central to the development of the policy recommendations. Other factors in support of the delay emerged more clearly from the analysis of caseload dynamics. In particular, many entries into foster care are short term; cases that remain open at six months are less likely to close in the time it will take to establish an order. By contrast, if cases are immediately referred to child support, the order may go into effect after a child and the parents already reunited. Once a child support order is initiated, it can be costly and time consuming to stop the order, and if the order remains in place after reunification, it may increase the risk of the child reentering the child welfare system.

The plan received immediate support from DCF's senior leadership. The modified policy framework was approved, and DCF assembled a workgroup to flesh out the details of the policy modifications and determine how best to implement it. The workgroup, which comprised county and state child welfare and child support representatives, drew on research from IRP and on additional agency analysis of administrative data. The final recommendations from the workgroup, which are currently under review, call for referrals to child support to be delayed for at least six months, and indefinitely if the parents are actively working toward reunification.

Importance of Research

During the summer and fall of 2017, we conducted semi-structured interviews with members of the policy implementation workgroup. The interview sample included all twenty-eight workgroup members. Four members of the workgroup had left their position either before the start of the research study or during the data collection phase. Eighty-five percent of the potential sample of all workgroup members participated in an interview. One of the primary themes explored during the interviews was the role of research during the policy development, modification, and implementation phases. The workgroup facilitators underscored the significance of the research for both identifying possible innovations and engaging workgroup members. One staff member explained that it is "rare [for DCF] to look at the data before jump[ing] in and work[ing] on [a] policy change." Instead, the department usually makes policy decisions based on practice experience. However, the staff member noted that having Wisconsin-based research that shows that pursuing child support delays reunification efforts allowed the agency to use "actual research as the basis for making a policy decision." Moreover, when describing how they used the research to obtain buy-in and motivate workgroup members, one of the facilitators noted, "I always start the conversation with the research. Every conversation I have had about this policy, I [have] start[ed] with the research." For this facilitator, the research represented an objective middle ground. Understanding the strong convictions some child welfare workers and counties have about the role of child support in both holding parents responsible for their children and offsetting the costs of out-of-home placements, the facilitator used the research to focus policy discussions on the empirical evidence of the impact of current practice. Further, another workgroup leader explained that DCF used the research as a tool to facilitate engagement with stakeholders and obtain buy-in from child welfare and child support staff. She explained, "Our counties have asked, 'Where did this data come from?' And when we say, 'It's Wisconsin data, it's eWiSACWIS data, it's like our families' data,' they're like, 'Oh,' and it suddenly means something. And, when we say we're going to keep studying it, people are very interested in that. People clearly feel like the research is going to show them something." The responses from the workgroup leaders suggest that having research on the very population served by practitioners helped to establish credibility among caseworker staff and other stakeholders.

In addition to workgroup leaders, workgroup members have indicated that grounding the policy change in research has been helpful for building momentum around the new policy. For instance, one explained, "I think it's a really smart policy and then if you can get buy-in from different stakeholders by showing them the research and appealing to people's sense of not wanting kids to stay in out-of-home care longer than they need to, then you can build consensus and build good will about the policy. And, then you can move forward. Any time we have an opportunity to create policy that's grounded in research, we should because it's smart. It's a really, really smart thing to do." Further, despite the range of beliefs around the use and need for child support orders, another workgroup member noted, "I think that everyone who was in the workgroup was genuinely interested in hearing the research and working together to create a policy that would work and to share the expertise that they had." The research therefore provided leaders with a vehicle not only for launching discussions on the research findings, but also for engaging practitioners in a dialogue about the implications of implementing a policy based on their experiences working with clients.

Preparing for Implementation

Regardless of the evidence base for a policy change, understanding stakeholders' perspectives is critical to assessing potential barriers and facilitators to implementation. In the case of the modified child support referral policy, county child welfare agencies will be responsible for implementing the policy redesign. Therefore, their view of the policy is important because their buy-in is likely to shape how well, and to what extent, they implement the modified policy (Bartlett and Vavrus 2017; Lipsky 1980; Zacka 2017). Moreover, our early interviews suggested that some child welfare workers strongly believe that they need to refer parents to child support in order to recover costs associated with out-of-home care (Howard, Noyes, and Cancian 2013). This tension may lead some counties to find a work-around, which would interfere with the fidelity of policy implementation and be expected to compromise effectiveness (Durlak and DuPre 2008).

To assess stakeholders' perceptions of the appropriateness and usefulness of the modified policy, and their beliefs on the causes of poverty and child maltreatment, we administered a survey to child welfare workers statewide.[6] The survey was sent to all child welfare intake and ongoing staff, as well as to supervisors, throughout Wisconsin. Individuals in these roles were selected as the sample population because they are usually responsible for determining if a child should be removed from their home, if a child support order should be made, and reunification goals. Ultimately 1,159 individuals participated in the survey, for a response rate of 58 percent. Most of the questions in the survey were based on the Consolidated Framework for

---

6. This survey, known as the Wisconsin Child Support Policy Redesign Implementation Survey was a web based, Qualtrics survey, administered by the University of Wisconsin Survey Center during the summer of 2017 approximately six months before the scheduled statewide implementation of the modified child support policy. The instrument underwent two rounds of pilot testing to ensure face-validity and ease of use before it entered the field. The survey was in the field for four weeks.

Implementation Research, and were devoted to either understanding the respondents' perceptions on the validity of the evidence for the policy redesign or their perceptions on the appropriateness and usefulness of the modified policy (Damschroder et al. 2009).[7]

Only one in four survey respondents (24.7 percent) indicated that they were aware of the child support policy redesign prior to taking part in the survey. Of those who were aware, 36.4 percent specified that they understood the purpose of the redesign somewhat well, and about 20.0 percent indicated that they understood very or extremely well.

Perceptions on the Evidence That Led to the Redesign

Relatively few of all survey respondents (15.3 percent) indicated that they were aware of the research from IRP on the relationship between child support referrals and the amount of time children spend in foster care prior to taking the survey.[8] The respondents who were aware of the research conducted by IRP were asked how well they remember the research; if they were surprised by the research findings, based on their previous experiences making child support referrals for families involved in the child welfare system; and the extent to which the research findings changed their perspective. As shown in table 1, about one in four (27.1 percent) of these respondents indicated that they remembered the research somewhat well and about 10 percent noted that they remembered it very or extremely well. Additionally, 11 percent of respondents reported that they were either very or extremely surprised by the research findings. Many respondents (38.4 percent) were at least somewhat surprised by the research results, and about half (47.2 percent) reported that their perspective was at least somewhat changed by the research.

All respondents, regardless of their familiarity with the IRP research, were asked two general questions about the role of economic resources on the risk of child maltreatment. As shown in table 1, more than 85 percent of respondents believe that economic resources affect a child's risk of maltreatment at least somewhat, and more than half indicate that economic resources affect it quite a bit or a very great deal. The same percentage believe economic resources affect a family's involvement in the child welfare system.

In sum, relatively few respondents were aware of the original research that contributed to the policy redesign, and six months prior to the proposed implementation only about one in four were aware of the modified policy. Yet, more than 85 percent believe that economic resources affect a child's risk of maltreatment and a family's involvement in the child welfare system at least somewhat, and more than half believe that economic resources affect both situations quite a bit or a very great deal. These results indicate that the majority of child welfare workers agree that there is a connection between economic resources and child maltreatment and child welfare involvement, even though relatively few were aware of the child support policy redesign, its purpose, and the evidence base.

CONCLUSION

High-quality data are in great demand as policymakers seek to make decisions about programs and funding using evidence-based strategies. As a result, universities and other research organizations have invested substantial effort, time, and financial resources in creating systems and analyzing data in such a way that meets these needs. In Wisconsin, comprehensive administrative data is the cornerstone of the researcher-practitioner model. IRP and Wisconsin state agencies, particularly DCF, have supported this model through investment in and sustained maintenance of the Wisconsin Data Core in the context of a long-standing collaborative partnership.

The child support referral policy analysis described in this article illustrates the advantages of a joint effort that brings together linked ad-

---

7. The Consolidated Framework for Implementation Research (CFIR) provides a framework of constructs that are associated with effective implementation. Each of the child support policy redesign-specific questions were mapped to a CFIR construct.

8. The respondents who were aware of the redesign were more likely to be aware of the research from IRP.

Table 1. Staff Perceptions of Child Welfare Practice, Economic Resources, and Child Outcomes

Relationship Between Child Support Referrals and the Length of Time in Foster Care[a]

Question	Response Categories and Responses				
How well do you remember the research shared by the Institute for Research on Poverty or DCF about the relationship between child support referrals and the amount of time children spend in foster care? (N = 177)	Not at all well	A little bit well	Somewhat well	Very well	Extremely well
	16.9%	45.8%	27.1%	9.6%	
Based on your previous experience, how surprised were you by the research findings? (N = 171)	Not at all surprised	A little bit surprised	Somewhat surprised	Very surprised	Extremely surprised
	30.4%	30.9%	27.4%	7.0%	4.0%
To what extent did the research findings change your perspective? (N = 169)	None	A little	Somewhat	Quite a bit	A very great deal
	28.9%	23.6%	29.5%	17.7%	0%

Relationship Between Economic Resources and Child Maltreatment[b]

Question	Response Categories and Responses				
How much does a family's income and other economic resources affect a child's risk for maltreatment? (N = 995)	None	A little	Somewhat	Quite a bit	A very great deal
	1.6%	9.5%	29.3%	42.1%	17.3%
How much does a family's income and other economic resources affect a family's involvement in the child welfare system? (N = 994)	None	A little	Somewhat	Quite a bit	A very great deal
	3.1%	8.7%	27.8%	44.8%	15.3%

Source: Authors' calculations.
[a]All survey respondents were asked if they were aware of any research shared by the Institute for Research on Poverty or DCF about the relationship between child support referrals and the amount of time children spend in foster care. Survey respondents who selected "yes" (n = 177) were then asked questions about the relationship between child support referrals and the length of time in foster care.
[b]All respondents, regardless of if they were aware of the policy redesign or the research from IRP, were asked these questions.

ministrative data and related qualitative research to support the efforts of those establishing as well as implementing the policy. An important lesson to be drawn is that, although the Wisconsin Data Core played a crucial role in facilitating policy-relevant research, its creation was just a first step toward evidence-based policymaking. Using the research to inform policy and practice changes required an additional investment in understanding the policy context—an effort that required a substantial investment in qualitative research drawing on field work. Efforts to assist with policy development also involved assessing and taking into account the perspectives of local agency staff who are most directly responsible for implementing policy revisions. These types of investments may be essential to the success of initiatives designed to promote data-driven decision making.

REFERENCES

Bartlett, Lesley, and Frances Vavrus. 2017. *Rethinking Case Study Research: A Comparative Approach.* New York: Routledge.

Berger, Lawrence M. 2004. "Income, Family Structure, and Child Maltreatment Risk." *Children and Youth Services Review* 26(8): 725–48.

Cancian, Maria, and Mai Seki. 2010. "Child Support and the Risk of Child Welfare Involvement: An Initial Assessment of Relationships." Report submitted to the Wisconsin Department of Children and Families. Madison: Institute for Research on Poverty, University of Wisconsin–Madison.

Cancian, Maria, Mi-Youn Yang, and Kristen Shook Slack. 2013. "The Effect of Additional Child Support Income on the Risk of Child Maltreatment." *Social Service Review* 87(3): 417–37.

Cancian, Maria, Steven T. Cook, Mai Seki, and Lynn Wimer. 2017. "Making Parents Pay: The Unintended Consequences of Charging Parents for Foster Care." *Children and Youth Services Review* 72:100–10.

Chellew, Carol, Jennifer L. Noyes, and Rebekah Selekman. 2012. "Child Support Referrals for Out-of-Home Placements: A Review of Policy and Practice." Report to the Wisconsin Department of Children and Families. Madison: Institute for Research on Poverty, University of Wisconsin–Madison.

Children's Bureau. 2012. *Child Welfare Policy Manual.* Washington: U.S. Department of Health and Human Services, Administration for Children and Families. Accessed November 1, 2018. https://www.acf.hhs.gov/cwpm/public_html/programs/cb/laws_policies/laws/cwpm/policy.jsp.

Child Welfare Information Gateway. 2012. "Reunifying Families." Accessed November 1, 2018. https://www.childwelfare.gov/topics/permanency/reunification.

Commission on Evidence-Based Policymaking (CEP). 2017. *The Promise of Evidence-Based Policymaking: Report of the Commission on Evidence-Based Policymaking.* Washington, D.C.: CEP. Accessed November 1, 2018. https://www.cep.gov/content/dam/cep/report/cep-final-report.pdf.

Damschroder, Laura J., David C. Aron, Rosalind E. Keith, Susan R. Kirsh, Jeffery A. Alexander, and Julie C. Lowery. 2009. "Fostering Implementation of Health Services Research Findings into Practice: A Consolidated Framework for Advancing Implementation Science." *Implementation Science* 4:50. DOI: 10.1186/1748-5908-4-50.

Drake, Brett, and Shanta Pandey. 1996. "Understanding the Relationship Between Neighborhood Poverty and Specific Types of Child Maltreatment." *Child Abuse & Neglect* 20(11): 1003–18.

Durlak, Joseph A., and Emily P. DuPre. 2008 "Implementation Matters: A Review of Research on the Influence of Implementation on Program Outcomes and the Factors Affecting Implementation." *American Journal of Community Psychology* 41(3–4): 327–50.

Howard, Lanikque. 2018. "Righting Our Wrongs: A Mixed Methods Case Study of a Collaboration Between Human Service Agencies to Address an Unintended Policy Consequence and Increase the Well-Being of Children." Ph.D. diss., University of Wisconsin–Madison.

Howard, Lanikque, Jennifer L. Noyes, and Maria Cancian. 2013. "The Child Support Referral Process for Out-of-Home Placements: Potential Modifications to Current Policy." Report submitted to the Wisconsin Department of Children and Families. Madison: University of Wisconsin–Madison, Institute for Research on Poverty.

Lipsky, Michael. 1980. *Street-Level Bureaucracy: Dilemmas of the Individual in Public Services.* New York: Russell Sage Foundation.

Office of Child Support Enforcement. 2011. "Custodial Parents and Child Support Receipt: Story Behind the Numbers." Fact Sheet No. 2. Washington: U.S. Department of Health and Human Services, Administration for Children and Families.

———. 2012. "Requests for Locate Services, Referrals, and Electronic Interface." Informational Memorandum IM-12-2. Washington: U.S. Department of Health and Human Services, Administration for Children and Families. Accessed November 1, 2018. https://www.acf.hhs.gov/css/resource/requests-for-locate-services-referrals-and-electronic-interface.

———. 2017. *FY 2015 Annual Report to Congress: Office of Child Support Enforcement*. Washington: U.S. Department of Health and Human Services, Administration for Children and Families. Accessed November 1, 2018. https://www.acf.hhs.gov/css/resource/fy-2015-annual-report-to-congress.

Pelton, Leroy H. 1994. "The Role of Material Factors in Child Abuse and Neglect." In *Protecting Children from Abuse and Neglect: Foundations for a New National Strategy*, edited by Gary B. Melton and Frank D. Barry. New York: Guilford Press.

Sedlak, Andrea J., Jane Mettenburg, Monica Basena, Ian Petta, Karla McPherson, Angela Greene, and Spencer Li. 2010. *Fourth National Incidence Study of Child Abuse and Neglect (NIS-4): Report to Congress*. Washington: U.S. Department of Health and Human Services, Administration for Children and Families.

Tseng, Vivian. 2012. "The Uses of Research in Policy and Practice." *Social Policy Reports* 26(2): 3–16.

Wulczyn, Fred, Kristen B. Hislop, and Brenda J. Harden. 2002. "The Placement of Infants in Foster Care." *Infant Mental Health Journal* 23(5): 454–75.

Zacka, Bernardo. 2017. *When the State Meets the Street: Public Service and Moral Agency*. Cambridge, Mass.: Harvard University Press.

Understanding Vulnerable Families in Multiple Service Systems

ROBERT M. GOERGE AND EMILY R. WIEGAND

We analyze Illinois families facing multiple barriers and their interactions with public-sector services. Using administrative data from five state agencies to identify families' receipt of child welfare, mental health, and substance abuse services as well as adult and juvenile incarcerations, we identify individuals across systems using probabilistic record-linkage techniques, defining family clusters based on networks of individuals who share child welfare and food stamp cases. We show that 23 percent receive services in two or more of these areas. This concentration accounts for 86 percent of the funding for these services used by the entire sample. They experience more and more severe problems. This population is otherwise heterogeneous, engaging with different types of services and clustered in certain parts of the state.

Keywords: multiproblem families, multisystem families, human services, government programs, public policy

The public system that has developed over the past half century to address social issues such as criminal behavior, juvenile delinquency, child maltreatment, mental illness, and substance abuse is a set of fragmented funding mechanisms, services, and programs (Wilkins 2012). These problems affect both the individual and their family members. Multiple family members with these problems are likely to increasingly challenge a family's most basic normative roles. Having a deeper understanding of families' circumstances is critical to any community's approach to using the scarce resources available to address the needs of vulnerable families. We aspire to characterize the involvement of multiple systems in families' lives as a way to understand overall need of families as well as to quantify the share of the total government effort and funding spent on multisystem families.

Robert M. Goerge is a senior research fellow at Chapin Hall at the University of Chicago. **Emily R. Wiegand** is a researcher at Chapin Hall at the University of Chicago.

© 2019 Russell Sage Foundation. Goerge, Robert M., and Emily R. Wiegand. 2019. "Understanding Vulnerable Families in Multiple Service Systems." *RSF: The Russell Sage Foundation Journal of the Social Sciences* 5(2): 86–104. DOI: 10.7758/RSF.2019.5.2.05. We gratefully acknowledge Cheryl Smithgall, Roopa Seshadri, and Peter Ballard for assistance with the data preparation and analyses described in this article. We also thank our agency partners at the Illinois Department of Human Services, Illinois Department of Child and Family Services, Illinois Department of Healthcare and Family Services, Illinois Department of Juvenile Justice, and Illinois Department of Corrections for their collaboration and support, which made this study possible. Direct correspondence to: Robert M. Goerge at rgoerge@chapinhall.org, 1313 E. 60th St., Chicago, IL 60637; and Emily R. Wiegand at ewiegand@chapinhall.org, 1313 E. 60th St., Chicago, IL 60637.

Open Access Policy: *RSF: The Russell Sage Foundation Journal of the Social Sciences* is an open access journal. This article is published under a Creative Commons Attribution-NonCommercial-NoDerivs 3.0 Unported License.

Understanding the number and characteristics of multisystem families requires multiple sources of data because primary data collection from a general population or even a targeted one would not be feasible from either a cost or data quality perspective. Simply the question of who in a household would be able to report reliably on the participation of each family member in the government programs listed already takes addressing this question to a higher degree of difficulty. Multiple household members would have to recall their participation in these programs. It has been shown that household members cannot accurately recall participation in the food stamp program, and the participation of vulnerable individuals, often with disabilities, in these five programs makes collecting the data needed for this study an even more difficult task (Meyer and Goerge 2011).

Therefore, we rely on state agency administrative data. Just as Andrew Penner and Kenneth Dodge write that "it is difficult to imagine survey data tracking all of the classmates that a student had" (2019), it is difficult to imagine survey data tracking all of the service experiences of multiple household members. Beginning with more than three million Supplemental Nutrition Assistance Program (SNAP) and child protective services participants, we are able to connect their experiences in the juvenile and adult criminal justice systems, publicly funded treatment for mental health and substance abuse problems, and the child welfare system. Moreover, that connections among individuals are captured in these datasets allows us to identify individuals who constitute families in various combinations over a period of time. This, too, would be a challenge for survey research.

The administrative data allow us to provide detailed analyses of experiences as well as cost estimates. We show that, for low-income families participating in government programs, these five publicly provided services are concentrated in a fraction—23 percent—of families, and those families use 86 percent of the fiscal resources that are spent on these services for these families. This indicates a disproportionate concentration of resources and interventions. Given that too few resources are available to address the problems, additional clarity about these families' experiences is necessary to develop appropriate public responses to avoid the ongoing cumulative effects of the conditions as well as policy and programmatic fragmentation. In this study, we only begin to tap the richness of the administrative data and provide a set of analyses that would guide additional policy and programmatic interventions for this large, vulnerable group.

BACKGROUND

Although health and human services systems are designed to address specific problems, individuals often experience co-occurring challenges and conditions that complicate attempts to address any single problem. For example, the parent of a child in foster care may also be receiving substance abuse services and another family member may be incarcerated or newly unemployed. These individuals live in the context of a family and a community, which determine, to a large extent, their current and future well-being. A premise of this article is that U.S. family policy, as operationalized in what government does for individual and families, does not incorporate the fact that families have multiple challenges as well as multiple assets.

Interventions designed to serve families with more holistic approaches can address these kinds of complex and interrelated concerns. "The family as a unit should be one of the basic foci of all interventions . . . individual services will be more effective when viewed in this context," Andrew Selig argues (1976, 527). It is crucial to recognize families' complex needs because these families require services that run both horizontally, across a variety of service domains, and vertically, across generations (Spratt 2011).

Just as familial and environmental factors can make it difficult to address an individual's problem in a vacuum, so too improving family circumstances and dynamics can improve individual challenges. Family members can be positive influences on one another (Selig 1976). Qualitative work shows how a history of trauma or mental illness for a parent can adversely affect other family members and how therapeutic interventions that address adults' histories can mitigate these adverse impacts (Krumer-Nevo 1998; Sacco, Twemlow, and Fonagy 2008).

Families facing pressures from multiple directions are particularly important places to intervene because, left unassisted, they set the stage for children to grow up with "fewer chances to permanently fend off in a constructive way the negative consequences of life events that put pressure on them" (Tausendfreund et al. 2016, 9).

This article measures and characterizes the population of families that face multiple barriers and the ways those families interact with public-sector services. We present the results of a rigorous descriptive analysis using administrative data from several public agencies in Illinois—the Department of Human Services, the Department of Healthcare and Family Services, the Department of Children and Family Services, the Department of Corrections, and the Department of Juvenile Justice—to identify families that interact with two or more of those systems and to characterize those families and their needs.

Ultimately, we show that nearly 25 percent of families served by the state programs that address households and families have members involved in at least two of the costliest programs of the state, a group of families that accounts for 86 percent of the funding for these programs used by all the families in our study population. These families experience more and more severe problems than the other families served by these systems. But apart from the scale of their service use, these families are a diverse group; they are clustered in a few areas around the state and they engage with different combinations of the five programs we analyze.

In the nearly ten years since this work began, we have found that these findings are of significant interest to Illinois state leadership. Actionable applications of these results have been limited, however. The nature of federal financing, privacy concerns, information sharing, and the siloed structure of the public sector makes integrated operations at the scale necessary to address the multiple problems of family members out of reach (Potter et al. 2005).

This research was an important first step in quantifying at a systemic level the extent of cross-system overlap at the family level. Recognizing the heterogeneity of this population, however, we believe that additional analysis is needed to unpack patterns and subpopulations in these results for it to have a direct impact on policymakers' decisions. In particular, the recent introduction of network analysis applications in the social sciences suggests promising new methods to uncover additional insights into this population. It is our hope that applying translational data science to explore the underlying patterns will suggest targeted opportunities for the public sector to integrate resources, data, and expertise across systems in specific applications, reaching families where these methods can make the biggest difference.

UNDERSTANDING MULTIPLE SYSTEM INVOLVEMENT

The concept of families that face multiple areas of challenge and engage with public services through a variety of means has a rich basis in literature from psychology, social work, sociology, and public policy. Various terms have been used to describe these families, but the most frequently used is *multiproblem families*.

The early literature on what would later be called multiproblem families developed in the 1950s and focused on the social deviance and isolation of these families, and particularly on chaos, disorganization, and dysfunction as their primary characteristics (Matos and Sousa 2004; Sousa, Ribeiro, and Rodrigues 2007). In child maltreatment literature, scholars developed the concept of multiproblem families when they began to focus on parental characteristics that increased the risks of harm to children, leading to an increasing awareness that child abuse could be a seen as a product of parental circumstances, experiences, and particularly traumas (Spratt 2011). Frack Sacco, Stuart Twemlow, and Peter Fonagy describe this as "transgenerational transmission of trauma" (2008, 34).

The multiproblem family label comes most directly from literature that classifies families with a certain number of defined barriers or challenges, such as mental and physical health conditions, problems in school, problems in the family, and legal problems (Mazer 1972; Sharlin and Shamai 1995). Different articles have considered the necessary quantity, variety, complexity, severity, and persistence of problems necessary to merit inclusion in the multiproblem family definition (Tausendfreund et al. 2016). The phrase *multiproblem family* does not have an agreed upon definition, making it difficult to compare descriptive research on these families across studies or to quantify incidence in the general population.

In particular, scholars disagree on whether poverty is part of defining multiproblem families. Ana Matos and Liliana Sousa argue that the interplay of problems within a family transcends class (2004). Shlomo Sharlin and Michal Shamai assert that the concept of multiproblem families is rooted in "poverty culture"—the dysfunction that is inherited across generations in these families represents "poverty personality." Sharlin and Shamai agree that middle-class families can be multiple problem families, but only when they "have not managed to overcome the values and habits that characterize lower-class multiproblem families" (1995, 94). Some researchers take a middle approach, using household poverty and related characteristics (such as housing instability) as contributing *problems* in their definition of *multiproblem*.

In more recent years, the traditional multiproblem family concept as defined through a set of barriers and challenges has been criticized as a *deficit* view, focusing on what families lack and where they struggle rather than their strengths and opportunities. Instead, researchers are beginning to move toward language that focuses on the external circumstances and environments that affect these families—using terms such as stress, trauma, and recurring crises (Sousa, Ribeiro, and Rodrigues 2007). Similarly, Tim Tausendfreund and his coauthors point out that in the German context, scholars avoid the concept of multiproblem families because they think this label situates the problem at the family level and ignores the role the broader environment and systemic factors have to play, both in creating the problems the families face and in helping address them. Tausendfreund and his colleagues opt to use the phrase "families in multiproblem situations" as a compromise between respecting that environmental factors create multiproblem families and recognizing "the complexity of interactions between socioeconomic and psychosocial problems"—the interplay of systemic and familial factors that characterizes these families (2016, 5).

Another way of viewing multiproblem families, and an approach that is closely related to our work, is to define the families in the context of the systems they engage. Milton Mazer characterizes this as the conventional approach to defining multiproblem family: "[a family] that becomes known to social and welfare agencies because of the multiple and long-term services it requires" (1972, 792). Defining multiproblem families as those that engage with multiple systems emphasizes the need for, and corresponding lack of, coordinated care for these families (Sousa, Ribeiro, and Rodrigues 2007). However, it also runs the risk of defining problems based not on families' true circumstances but instead on bureaucratic distinctions in service delivery (Spratt 2011). To the extent that systems engagement is used to define multiproblem families, they can be defined not only in the breadth of systems they engage, but also by the extent and complexity of support that they need, and the corresponding difficulty siloed agencies have in providing that support (Tausendfreund et al. 2016).

Some scholars have articulated that in addition to engaging a breadth of systems, multiproblem families have particular ways of interacting with those systems. They may be particularly likely to be referred to service systems by alerts from other systems, rather than by directly reaching out and seeking support (Matos and Sousa 2004). They also often fall into one of two groups, either resisting interventions and exiting systems quickly, or receiving steadily increasing and diverse services, public agencies becoming enmeshed in the life and network of the family (Matos and Sousa 2004; Tausendfreund et al. 2016).

A precise operationalization of the construct of participation in multiple programs is problematic because of how many ways it might be conceptualized. Ultimately, any particular characterization of multiprogram participation depends on the research question or policy issues at hand. However, across disciplines and definitions, the core idea that some portion of the population with a given challenge is struggling on multiple fronts at the same time remains clear.

For this analysis, we concentrate on the type, breadth, and relative cost of public-sector services received by the family. Our analysis is targeted specifically toward policymakers at the state and federal levels and is intended to help policymakers and public-sector managers understand overlaps in service provision and opportunities to design interventions around a high need portion of the population. We capture only a set of the problems and challenges families face and for which they have engaged assistance. To clearly distinguish between this approach and a traditional multiproblem family classification, we use the term *multisystem family*.

We characterize multisystem participation at the family rather than at the individual level because the family or household is the case, or the entire family is affected by any member participating in any of the programs.

However, literature is minimal on the definition of family in these multiple problem or multiple system engagement circumstances. The family or household unit is discussed as discrete and static although we know that is not the case, particularly for this population. As noted, there is no single way to operationalize this concept so there are no studies that characterize the incidence of multiproblem families in the general population (Spratt 2011).

DATA SOURCES

We use administrative data, data collected for administrative purposes (that is, service provision) by public agencies, for this analysis. These data include the universe of individuals and families at a point in time that engage with these public-sector services, the key population for our research goal. Survey data on public benefit receipt and engagement with social service systems is prone to underreporting (Meyer and Goerge 2011) and likely subject to social desirability bias. And, to identify the multiplicity of combinations, a population-based sample survey would be infeasible because of cost and complexity.

Cross-system analyses like this one require access to data from multiple agencies. Accessing the data from the relevant state agencies involves challenges (Goerge 2018). Also, linking data from disparate sources, which range from data manipulation to implementing record-linkage algorithms, entails technical challenges. The work described here was made feasible by Chapin Hall's Integrated Database on Child and Family Programs in Illinois (IDB), which compiles microdata from Illinois, Cook County, and Chicago government agency sources over three decades (Goerge, van Voorhis, and Lee 1994; Kitzmiller 2013). Chapin Hall stewards and manages data for the agencies, and Chapin Hall researchers use the data to address questions approved by the data providers (government agencies) under strict conditions specified in data-sharing agreements. The multisystem families project was funded in part by the state of Illinois.

The database is a linked set of files (tables) rather than an online transactional system that would lend itself to rigorous in-depth exploration of an individual or family. Our focus for this analysis is to generally understand the program participation of individuals in families rather than the specific trajectories that individual or families might have within particular programs, which is also possible with the data in the integrated database.

One frequently mentioned limitation of administrative data for use for research purposes is that data quality may be inconsistent or poor, with duplicate records and fields left blank or entered incorrectly (Hotz et al. 1998). However, researchers generally agree that administrative data are most reliable for fields that are directly applied to the work for which the data were originally collected. This study analyzes program participation and benefit receipt. These topics are fundamental to program operations. As a result, we have confidence in the quality and validity of the relevant data points—a confidence shared by our agency partners, who use the same fields in their regular reporting. We do believe that the data include duplicate records, particularly when a person is engaged with the program, leaves, and subsequently returns. We address this limitation with our record-linkage methods, which include logic to de-duplicate individuals within the same program, as well as identifying the same individual in multiple programs.

We selected five areas of treatment or program participation (mental health treatment, substance abuse treatment, juvenile incarceration, adult incarceration, and child welfare) because together these services represent Illinois' costliest areas of targeted social service expenditure. In fiscal year 2008, 29.5 percent of Illinois state expenditures were for Medicaid. A report from the U.S. Department of Health and Human Services' Substance Abuse and Mental Health Services Administration noted that, in 2009, 10.4 percent of national Medicaid spending was for mental health treatment and 1.4 percent for treating substance use disorders (Substance Abuse and Mental Health Services Administration 2014). In fiscal year 2008, 3 percent of Illinois' budget went to corrections (National Association of State Budget Officers 2009).

A general principle of our study is that once an individual is associated with another who has been in one of our five systems, the effects of that experience last a lifetime (Metzler et al. 2017; Shonkoff et al. 2012). The trauma experienced with one of the problems that led to the system involvement can clearly last a lifetime and lead to the need for additional services provided by the public sector, be they one of the five we examined or others, such as the need for workforce training, disability services, special education, or other such programs. Clearly, incarceration has lifetime effects on family members (Wakefield, Lee, and Wildeman 2016). Foster care has effects on both children and parents for a lifetime (Pecora et al. 2006). Substance abuse and mental illness similarly are challenges for an extensive duration, even if treated (Jordan et al. 2002; Teplin 1994).

The following data sources were combined for use in this research. For each source, we describe the population and time frame included.

SNAP participation. One of the primary drivers of our study population was the universe of households participating in the Supplemental Nutrition Assistance Program in Illinois from 1989 to 2008. We received this data as monthly extracts from the Illinois Department of Human Services, which administers food and cash assistance programs in the state.

Because SNAP assistance is provided at the household level (the assistance unit for SNAP is defined as the group of individuals in the home who shop and prepare food together), it is a good source, albeit not without error, of information about which individuals share a household. Case-level records are linked to the individuals who are current or former participants in the assistance case.

The SNAP data also contain monthly records of household addresses and their changes through time. We geocoded these records and used them to locate families spatially. Historically, mailing addresses were where program recipients received their benefits, so the quality of these addresses was considered very high. Since the introduction of an electronic benefit transfer system in 1997, that quality is less certain, although initial addresses are verified. However, because we use addresses largely to characterize patterns at regional and county levels, we do not think quality concerns about these data are so significant as to undermine the validity of conclusions.

Child welfare involvement. Child welfare service records from the Illinois Department on Child and Family Services (DCFS) were another source of data for our sample population, and these data also provided information about problems in the family represented by involvement with DCFS. DCFS tracks children and families receiving services. Child welfare service data were included from 1977 to 2008. These data included both cases where children were removed from the home and records about services provided to intact families, where the children remain in the home of their parent or parents and DCFS provides supports to the household. We also looked at substantiated allegations of abuse and neglect as recorded by DCFS. Abuse and neglect records were included from the early 1980s.

Incarceration. Incarceration records were included from both the Illinois Department of Corrections (adult incarcerations) and the Illinois Department of Juvenile Justice (juvenile incarcerations). Records were pulled from data on admissions and exits from 1990 to 2008—anyone who began or ended a spell of incarceration during those years would be included in the sample. These data sources reflect only confinement in state prisons, not time spent in county jails or detention centers or on probation. Including less severe measures of involvement with the criminal justice system would likely only increase the number of connections found between family involvement with criminal justice and involvement in other service systems.

Medicaid claims. We identified individuals receiving publicly funded mental health and substance abuse treatments through Medicaid claims records from 1994 to 2008. We also used claims data to look at intentional injuries.

Record linkage. One of the significant technical challenges involved in creating an integrated longitudinal database to conduct this research is accurately linking the records of individual clients across agencies and over time. This process is complicated by the fact that no single identifier, even social security number (SSN), can be completely relied upon to establish the identity of a client across the records of all agencies, although Social Security Act Title programs like SNAP do typically verify and validate SSNs. Probabilistic record-matching, first developed by researchers in the fields of demography and epidemiology, allows such linkages to be made reliably (Fellegi and Sunter 1969; Newcombe et al. 1959).

Probabilistic record-matching is based on the assumption that no single match between variables common to the source databases will identify a client with complete reliability. Instead, this approach calculates the probability that two records belong to the same client using multiple pieces of identifying information. Such identifying data may include name, social security number, birth date, gender, race-ethnicity, and residential address. When multiple pieces of identifying information from two databases are comparable, the probability of a correct match is increased.

Once a match has been determined, a unique number is assigned to the matched record so that each record can be uniquely identified. The end result of a record-matching exercise is a series of crosswalk files between each agency's client identification number and a multisystem identifier (the new unique number assigned to the entity).

Chapin Hall routinely uses record linkage to create the IDB, which was used for this project (Goerge, van Voorhis, and Lee 1994). In the design of the IDB, each component dataset is unduplicated against itself, and then datasets are matched against each other. In the cross-system matches, one and only one match is allowed for each unique individual to reduce the chances of multiplying error.

METHODOLOGY FOR DEFINING FAMILIES

We began with two groups of individuals from which to build our population of households.

One population was drawn from the universe of SNAP families. However, to limit this to families that had received SNAP in a recent year, we chose an index population of all women in the SNAP population during fiscal year 2007–2008 who were eighteen to forty-five years of age. We included everyone in the index population and everyone who ever shared a case with an index person.[1] The women who served as index individuals did not have to be on SNAP for the entire time, but needed to appear active at some point during that window. We chose these women because we believed they were most likely to have belonged to families with children. This selection also included nearly all families who received Temporary Assistance for Needy Families and nearly all families who received Medicaid with an income of below 130 percent of the federal poverty level, given that these families were highly likely to have received SNAP.[2] This process yielded a pool of 318,927 families.

The second population was all families receiving child welfare services at any point from 1977 to 2008, a population that has been shown in the literature to have many additional problems other that the placement of children in

---

1. This index approach allowed us to limit the study to families that had received SNAP in a recent year while still taking advantage of the rich historical SNAP data allowing us to identify the extended family networks of the index participants.

2. An alternative was to choose all families in Medicaid, but because Medicaid eligibility is at the individual, rather than household, level, this would have reduced the number of poor nonparent-nonchild individuals included in our populations. Using SNAP allowed us to represent the universe of extended family members who live together.

Figure 1. Identifying Families

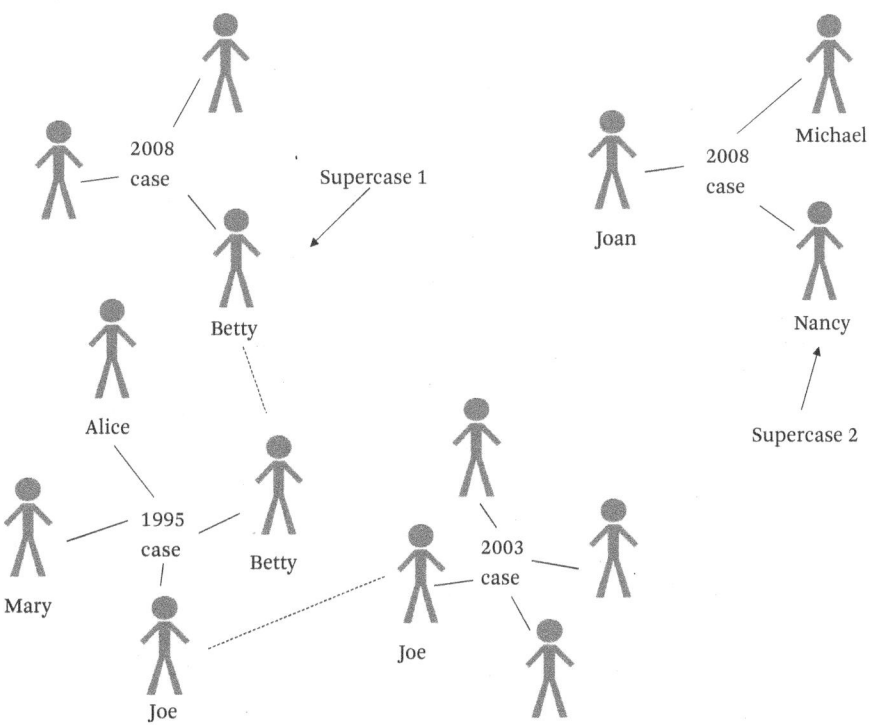

Source: Authors' rendition.

the foster care system, and the effects of the maltreatment and foster care, in most cases, have an impact on their future well-being and service use (Metzler et al. 2017). This process yielded 286,408 families.

The key analytic unit is the family network. This *family* is defined through the analytic concept of a *supercase*, a connected component of the graph of all individuals in these two populations where edges represent shared membership in a case. All individuals who share a case are grouped in the same supercase and individuals in a supercase do not share cases with individuals in any other supercase.

Figure 1 demonstrates this process at the individual level with two example cases:

Betty is an index individual from the SNAP data (a woman between the ages of eighteen and forty-five who received SNAP during fiscal year 2007–2008). We find all public assistance cases associated with Betty going back to 1989. She was a child in 1995 on a case with her mother (Alice) and siblings (Joe and Mary); they all become part of her SNAP supercase. Similarly, all individuals on her SNAP case during 2007–2008 are part of her SNAP supercase. Finally, her brother Joe has a SNAP case in the early 2000s with his family—because Betty and Joe were on the same SNAP case in 1995, this case is also considered a part of the same family network.

Nancy is a second index individual from the SNAP data. She is on a SNAP case in 2008 with her children, Michael and Joan. That case is the only public assistance case any of them have been on in Illinois since 1989, so the three people on this case form a discrete family network.

We completed a similar process with child welfare cases and then combined the two groups of supercases into a single, unified set of supercases, representing our ultimate sample of families. Altogether, we identified 502,165 discrete family networks in our sample—the union of the SNAP and child welfare case populations. The result of this process was a dataset containing the unique cross-system identifiers of all the people associated with these families in either public assistance or child welfare data, along with their corresponding assigned supercase or family identifier. We linked information about the five problem domains (child welfare, adult incarceration, juvenile incarceration, mental health services, and substance abuse services) at the individual level. This information was easily aggregated to the family level for our primary results.

Limitations. We believe that our results both are representative of the families engaging with public services in Illinois and are useful for informing human services policy and practice, but we highlight a few limitations stemming from our data and approach.

Ideally, we would use either the full population of Illinois families or the full population that encountered any of the five systems as the base population. The nature of the administrative data available to our analysis significantly limited our opportunities on this point, however. In particular, because our research question is about families rather than individuals, we needed to form our base population from datasets that captured populations of families. Without access to vital records, tax returns, or decennial census records, there is no comprehensive population-level database of families. David Grusky, Michael Hout, Timothy Smeeding, and Matthew Snipp's proposed American Opportunity Survey would provide exactly the kind of base dataset needed for this work in the future (2019). The next best option would be a base population of all families who touched any of the five systems, but only the child welfare system captures relationships among family members in its participation data. We thus used the universe of child welfare families combined with the universe of food stamp families (to provide a broad sample of Illinois families) to comprise our base population.

The limited nature of our base population limits the interpretation of population-level statistics. However, a primary goal of our work is to provide policymakers and program administrators with evidence about the populations they encounter across systems. For this purpose, being able to characterize the rate of multiple system involvement within a group of families that routinely interact with the state through two of its largest human service systems is of great value. Although using our results to define the prevalence of multisystem families in the general population is difficult, the results demonstrate the high rates of multiple system involvement among the very families with whom the state already works.

To contextualize the extent to which our population is representative of the state of Illinois, we can compare our total count of families (502,165) with the estimates from the 2008 American Community Survey (ACS). The 2008 ACS counted 3,138,757 family households in Illinois (households containing at least two people related by marriage, birth, or adoption), of which fewer than half are families with children younger than eighteen. Our sample included households from the child welfare system and the households of women of childbearing age from the SNAP population, so the number of families with children is probably a better proxy than the overall population of families. When we compare with the population of low-income families, the numbers are much closer: 400,751 families were under 130 percent of the federal poverty line in 2008 in Illinois, including 311,900 families with children younger than eighteen. Although it is difficult to compare too precisely our universe of families derived from decades of administrative data to point-in-time populations, it is evident that our sample captures less than one-third of Illinois families overall but likely represents an extremely high proportion of low-income families.[3]

Although the proportion of the overall Illinois population represented in our universe is small, that our population is centered on households living in poverty means that the count of families in our sample in certain communities is very close to the population-level count. This allows us to infer some community-level con-

---

3. All numbers are from the Census Bureau's American FactFinder based on the results of the 2008 ACS one-year estimates (https://factfinder.census.gov).

clusions about the percentage of all families that are multiple system involved, even though we cannot make those conclusions for the full state.

We think using networks to capture families appropriately represents the concept of a family unit. The median supercase (family) size was four family members; the mean was 5.9. However, opportunities exist to further refine this approach in subsequent analyses—in particular, by incorporating temporal information more granularly, to better distinguish close family relationships (that is, people who lived together at more time points). As family size increases, families are more likely to include individuals with various points of system contact. It would strengthen the findings to confirm that these additional contacts are not from individuals who were only tangentially connected with the family.

Another limitation that derives from the use of administrative data is that the sources of data that identify biological relationships among family members frequently omit fathers. Birth certificate data is the single most important source of information needed to obtain a more accurate construction of family units. Although our method for identifying families attempted to include as many adult males as possible, we do not believe that we identified them particularly well. One indicator for that is that only 33 percent of the adults in the corrections population were connected to the families we identified. We believe that this is our largest source of error and that it artificially decreases both the number and percent of multisystem families in our sample and the costs attributed to them.

METHODOLOGY FOR MEASURING SYSTEMS ENGAGEMENT

For the group of families described, we tracked receipt of five areas of service, each of which represented a problem facing the family: child welfare, adult incarceration, juvenile incarceration, mental health services, and substance abuse services. Family members are exposed to individual mental illness, alcohol or substance abuse problems, incarcerated adults or juveniles, and child maltreatment serious enough to require out-of-home placement or are themselves beset with these problems. We defined multisystem families as those that engaged with two or more of these areas of service.

We estimated costs for each service differently depending on data availability. Our goal was not to arrive at a precise accounting of all costs, but to have an estimate consistent across family service and program participation combinations that would allow for relative comparisons. For the Departments of Corrections and Juvenile Justice, we began with the yearly cost of incarceration per individual across all facilities, reported by those departments, and calculated a per diem amount. We multiplied that amount by the numbers of days incarcerated for each individual and summed that over all of the individuals in the family. For youth served by the Department of Juvenile Justice, we also calculated the cost of after-care similarly. For substance abuse, mental health services, and other Medicaid-reimbursed services, we used the paid claim amount for each service received, summing all paid claims for an individual and then for the family. For child welfare costs, we calculated the cost of substitute care per day and applied that to the number of days experienced by each child in the family. For Medicaid and child welfare costs, we do not include administrative costs, which are included in the Corrections and Juvenile Justice estimates. Estimates of Medicaid administrative costs range from 2 to 5 percent (Yong, Saunders, and Olsen 2010). Estimate of administrative costs for foster care is 35 percent (Stoltzfus, Stohl, and Seibold 2011). Given other sources of error described in the limitations section, these would not change the nature of our results greatly.

RESULTS

Of the 502,165 families in our sample, 23 percent were multisystem families, and these families accounted for 86 percent of the funding for health, mental health, criminal and juvenile, and child welfare needs for the full sample of families. Another 34 percent of families received services in one of the five areas and accounted for the remaining funds. Table 1 presents these populations in more detail.

Table 2 presents the five most prevalent combinations of the programs studied. These

Table 1. Total Engagement by Families in Sample

	Number	Percentage
Total families in sample	502,165	100
No systems	216,443	43
One system	171,367	34
Multisystem families	114,355	23
Two systems	67,443	59
Three systems	30,987	27
Four systems	13,803	12
Five systems	2,122	2

Source: Authors' tabulation.

Table 2. Top Five Combinations of Program Use by Multisystem Families

	Percentage All Families	Percentage Multisystem Families
Mental health services and substance abuse treatment	5.7	25.0
Mental health services and child welfare	4.1	18.2
Mental health services, substance abuse treatment, and child welfare	2.6	11.6
Mental health services, substance abuse treatment, adult incarceration, and child welfare	2.2	9.8
Mental health services and adult incarceration	2.2	9.7

Source: Authors' tabulation.

combinations account for 75 percent of all multisystem families. The most common is mental health services and substance abuse treatment (25.0 percent of multisystem families). The second most common is child welfare involvement and mental health services (18.2 percent). The third most common is child welfare involvement, mental health services, and substance abuse treatment (11.6 percent). This is not surprising given that most families in the child welfare system have challenges related to mental illness and substance abuse; these conditions often motivate entry into the system. The fourth most common is child welfare involvement, adult incarceration, mental health services, and substance abuse treatment (9.8 percent). The size and relative intensity of services received by this group presents opportunities for a particularly targeted focus on them, as their cross-system penetration is quite significant and suggests multiple health, psychological, and social challenges.

Of the funding that supported the participation of the multisystem families in these programs, 34 percent was for child welfare service costs, 23 percent for mental health services, 21 percent for adult corrections, 9 percent for substance abuse treatment, and 7 percent for juvenile incarcerations. We also tracked expenses for long-term care paid for by Medicaid since mental health services and substance abuse treatment account for a significant portion of diagnoses of individuals using long-term care. It accounted for 5 percent of the costs for multisystem families (Simon, Lipson, and Stone 2010).

These findings cannot be interpreted as the prevalence of families with multiple challenges in the general population. Our base population was SNAP- and DCFS-involved families, so we assume the rate to which multisystem families are reflected in our sample is significantly higher than it would be in the general population. Furthermore, we measured rates of system involvement for treatment and services, not the prevalence of mental illness, drug abuse, child abuse and neglect, and so on in the population. An uncertain number of other families in the state with the same problems have not received state services.

However, these findings clearly demonstrate that a significant minority of the families that engage with the state through large human service programs are engaging in multiple areas—and they are major cost drivers within those areas. Their cumulative use of these programs greatly exceeds that of the one-system families because the duration of participation is built into the cost calculation. It certainly could be the case that this could not be so disproportionate if the one-system family members were participating in the one system in a more intensive way than members of the multisystem families.

We believe our method of defining supercases effectively captures familial networks, but recognize that it is unlikely that some of the larger "families" constructed from the administrative records are groups that live in the same household at one time. To test the sensitivity of our results to this definition, we restricted family size to a maximum of ten. Looking only at this universe of more traditionally sized families, the percentages do not change substantially. Where 23 percent of all families are multisystem families, 17 percent of the traditionally sized families are multisystem families. We expect this rate to be a little lower because larger families are more likely to be engaged in multiple ways.

Multisystem families experience more and more severe problems than the other families these systems serve. When we compare the multisystem families with other families on problems that go beyond the components of our definition, including inpatient mental health and substance abuse services, substantiated allegations of abuse or neglect, and cases of intentional injury, we find these problems are more frequent and severe for the multisystem families.

More than 56 percent of the multisystem families have experienced an inpatient hospitalization for either mental illness or substance abuse treatment. In fact, 25 percent of all multisystem families have experienced inpatient hospitalization for both reasons.

Although not one of our five primary programs, we analyzed data on family violence and found 73 percent of the multisystem families had had a substantiated investigation of abuse or neglect. This is not just a product of the families with child welfare cases; 63 percent of the families that did not receive child welfare services have had a substantiated investigation of abuse or neglect. Finally, nearly 49 percent of multisystem families have a member who has experienced an injury diagnosed as intentional (according to International Classification of Diseases) for which they received health care reimbursed by Medicaid. Altogether, nearly 82 percent of multisystem families have either a substantiated report of abuse or neglect or an injury due to violence.

The multisystem families are geographically concentrated. Figure 2 shows the percentage of children living in multisystem families by census tract in Cook County.[4] We see that a relative few areas of Chicago exhibit extremely high percentage of children living in families who participate in multiple systems. In a dozen census tracts in Chicago, more than 60 percent of the children, those seventeen years old and younger, live in multisystem families. In a smaller number of tracts, which we do not identify, more than 90 percent of the children live in multisystem families.

To understand the variation across the state, we calculate the percent of households that are multisystem families by county (figure 3). This is a crude measure (see earlier discussion of comparison with census data), but it does show that proportionately more multisystem families are in counties with smaller urban areas and some of the poorer urban counties. This information provides insight for where policymakers might concentrate efforts. Given the effects of living in these households on children, the impact on schools, the health-care system, public safety, and law enforcement in the areas where these families cluster is significant.

The geographic clustering of multisystem

---

4. Figures 2 and 3 reflect where families lived in 2008.

Figure 2. Distribution of Children in Multisystem Families by Census Tract, 2008

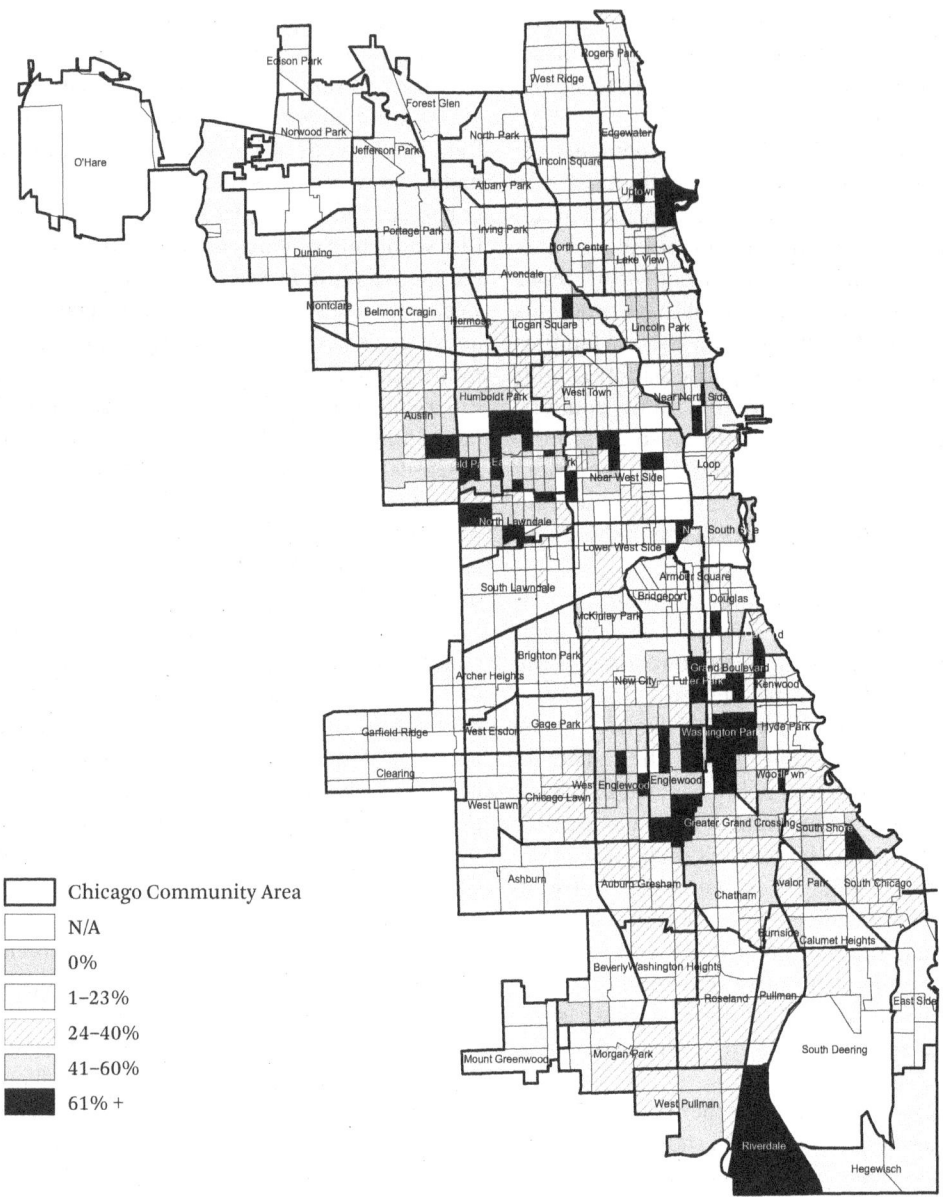

Source: Authors' tabulation.

families suggests the possibility of using geography to target interventions toward these families. It also highlights the variation within multisystem families; these families are concentrated in Chicago and in southern Illinois, but given the very different geographic context it is likely that the specific barriers those families face and the interventions needed will vary. This relates closely to our next finding.

Multisystem families are heterogeneous. As we explore underlying trends around service provision, we must recognize the significant diversity in the quantity, type, and severity of challenges multisystem families face. Table 3 shows the size and percentage of the multisystem population engaged with each service area.

Nearly 94 percent of all multisystem fami-

Figure 3. Distribution of Multisystem Families by County, 2008

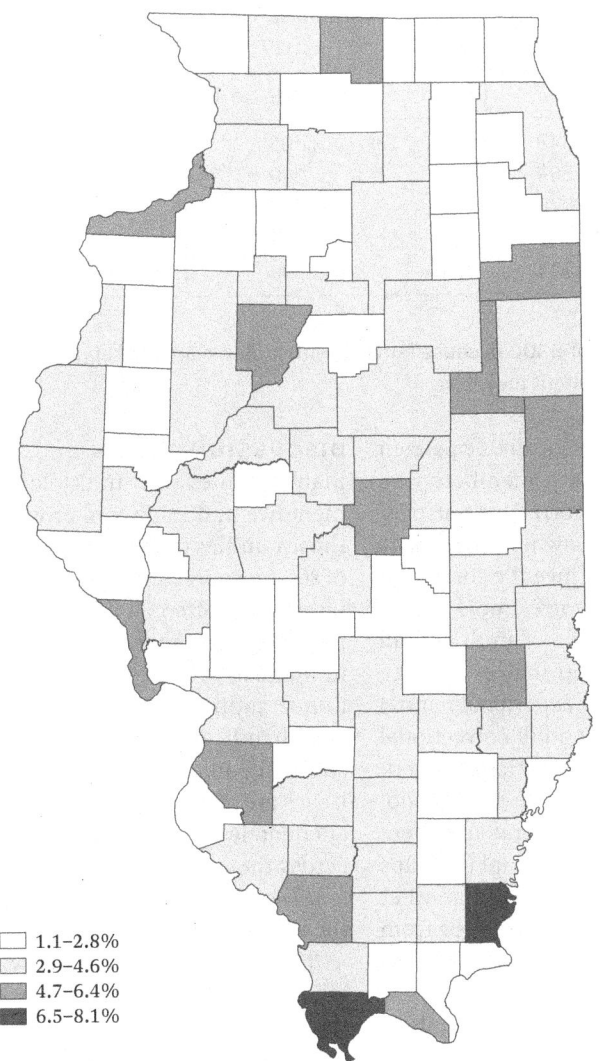

☐ 1.1–2.8%
☐ 2.9–4.6%
☐ 4.7–6.4%
■ 6.5–8.1%

Source: Authors' tabulation.

lies have received mental health services, and about 60 percent have engaged with services in just two of the five areas, so more than half of multisystem families are multisystem because they receive treatment for mental illness and one of the other five. The most common combination is mental health and substance abuse services, which characterizes 25 percent of multisystem families. Another 18 percent are engaged with both mental health and child welfare systems.

The other 40 percent engaged with three or more of the five service areas. In particular, juvenile justice, adult corrections, and substance abuse are unlikely to exist in isolation. Of families with juvenile justice engagement, 96 percent are multisystem. Of those with adult corrections engagement, 85 percent are. For substance abuse, the corresponding rate is 95 percent. By contrast, smaller proportions of the child welfare–involved population of families (57 percent) and the population of families receiving any mental health services (49 percent) were multisystem families.

Although the juvenile justice-involved population is much smaller than the groups engaged with the other service areas, these families overlap, particularly the group engaged

Table 3. Areas of Systems Engagement

	All Families (502,165)		Families, One System (171,368)		Families, Multiple Systems (114,355)	
	Number	Percent	Number	Percent	Number	Percent
Adult incarceration	56,649	11	8,406	5	48,243	42
Juvenile incarceration	8,564	2	366	<1	8,198	7
Mental health	220,878	44	113,321	66	107,557	94
Substance abuse	72,161	14	3,675	2	68,468	60
Child welfare	106,784	21	45,599	27	61,185	54

Source: Authors' tabulation.
Note: Percentages may not total 100 because families with multiple areas of engagement are counted once for each area of engagement they have.

with adult corrections. Specifically, 68 percent of multisystem families with members who have experienced juvenile corrections also experienced adult corrections, whereas about 40 percent of families without juvenile correction experience have had adult correctional experience. Conversely, 11 percent of multisystem families with adult correctional experience have juvenile correctional experience, and 4 percent of families without adult correctional experience have juvenile correctional experience. The correlation is therefore clear of adolescents and adults being incarcerated in these families, either from one individual (perhaps a parent) who was incarcerated and another (perhaps a child) being incarcerated, or from the same individuals being incarcerated as both a child and an adult.

Multisystem families that have members who have been in adult corrections are less likely to have family members who have received mental health services or substance abuse treatment of any kind. For example, 40 percent of families with adult corrections experience also experienced outpatient mental health care, relative to 74 percent of those without adult corrections experience. This may show that families excluded from particular services, such as substance abuse or mental health services, may be the most likely to be involved in the criminal justice system.

Just as the concept of a multiproblem or multisystem family is difficult to isolate across studies, our results demonstrate that the lived situations of these families can be highly variable, even within a single definition.

DISCUSSION

Many families with multiple system involvement live in Illinois, and providing services to those families consumes a significant amount of state resources. Although policymakers and researchers often analyze a single problem, it is obvious that many families at risk must simultaneously address the challenges of economic support, parenting, childcare, health care, handicapping conditions, violence, and substance abuse. It is also clear that all of these issues are related in various ways. Until we can adequately describe the needs of families across these areas, we will not know whether family policy and service programs are meeting the needs of the population.

These findings were shared with policymakers and program administrators shortly after the initial data analysis was concluded in the late 2000s and have sparked conversations and interest across the intervening years through multiple administrations. However, it has proven difficult to implement programs and strategies to address the needs of these families.

Existing solutions are not simple and perhaps more local than at the state or national level (Corbett et al. 2005), although federal rules and regulations are often blamed for the problem at the local level. The problem in part stems from the continued operation of multiple programmatic and agency silos in government designed to deal with a limited set of problems and the inability of these agencies and programs to coordinate efforts, resulting in practitioners often not having the service resources or skills to access the array of interventions a family and its members might need.

As the demand for services changes and the perceived need for services has increased, considerable discussion and effort have focused on the notion of comprehensive service systems for children and families. Service providers often talk about how their cases are becoming more severe and how they lack the service armature to address child and family needs. This perception has led to many attempts at service reform, often without testing the magnitude of the population's needs. The goals of coordinated or integrated service systems are to weave together the programs and services that cut across service sectors and address the multiple needs that children and their families may present. Integration can occur at the financing, administrative, or casework level, but regardless of the particular strategies, the goals are to address the multiple problems of children and families in a comprehensive manner that increases the likelihood of improved well-being for the entire family.

The term *silo* has perhaps become overused, but probably because it is so apropos when talking about government services. The use of the term reflects a desire to make "the inability to share information and integrate system activity" more concrete (Roberts 2011, 677). The siloing begins with the federal government and the multitude of programs with similar goals across multiple agencies. These silos reflect and further reinforce federal policy in their own ways at the state and local levels through the separation of programs into separate agencies. They reflect the fragmentation that results from spreading the authority for programs across levels of government and across agencies within government (Farhang and Yaver 2016). Given what we have found, why would all resources related to the problems addressed in this study not be housed and integrated under one agency? Although some states do bring together multiple federal programs into a single agency, they often must still be managed separately and reported on separately, and the data belonging to each can often not be shared across these programs. For example, substance abuse and mental health professionals, child welfare caseworkers, counselors for ex-offenders, and parole officers all sit in separate agencies, often at different levels of government. Therefore, programmatic silos exist at all levels of government and these levels themselves are silos, preventing effective communication and collaboration across levels of government. To be sure, the private and advocacy sectors have their own silos (Civic Caucus 2009). Each condition or diagnosis has a special interest group devoted to competing with others to gather greater shares of the scarce resources.

Unfortunately, as mentioned, the data are also siloed, often under the rubric of privacy or confidentiality. Even with twenty-first-century technology, decades-old rules and regulations restrict data-sharing within the public sector, across agencies and levels of government, not to mention with researchers who are attempting to create better evidence on what works or simply a better understanding of what the problems are. Although computational advances have made it easier to do this work, significant challenges to anything approaching real-time implementation remain, including the resource investments necessary to build the infrastructure, the challenge of maintaining data quality, and the intensiveness of the required calculations. There are better ways to spend the resources involved than in building these large systems, especially given the challenge of implementing interventions to address these findings.

In short, integrated service delivery on a large scale is quite difficult. The technology and data needs to continually inform this work are complex, and the systems that manage these programs are not designed for integrated practice.

RECOMMENDATIONS FOR RESEARCH AND PRACTICE

Now that we better understand the scope and scale of the problem at a systemic level, we believe that further research can convert these findings into more actionable insights with a specific focus on unpacking patterns and subpopulations in the results. Our hope is that subsequent work will yield more tangible results that can help bridge the gap between data and action. The following list includes suggested areas of inquiry.

Timing of engagements. The results include engagements with the systems from as far back as 1990, and we do not consider temporal patterns in systems engagement—which engagements overlap or occur in close succession. We believe that each of the areas explored (mental health, substance abuse, incarceration, or child abuse or neglect) has a lasting impact on the family and the individuals in it. However, further analysis that looked at the relationships in these engagements over time could provide more insights about how and when challenges cluster. As mentioned, looking at timing more closely in the context of refining family definitions could also provide more detail about the types of families included in this analysis.

Individual versus family problems. This study aggregated engagements to the family level. Multisystem families in this study could have one individual in the family who engaged with services in all five areas or five individuals with one point of engagement each. More investigation could illuminate whether a few individuals within families account for a large number of the system engagements.

Magnitude of problems. The study counted multiple instances of engagement with the same system as a single engagement. For example, in a family with ten members, each family member could have received mental health treatment. In another family of ten, one member might have received mental health treatment. In this study, both examples would count as one point of engagement within a family. Similarly, one individual may have received a service once and another person may have received multiple services for the same problem over the course of years. Further research could discriminate among these cases.

Characterization of individual problems. Data are available that would allow for a more detailed picture of problems. For example, within records of mental health treatment are records of different diagnoses. The policy and program response to a family with an instance of clinical depression may be different than one with a schizophrenia diagnosis.

Networked service delivery. This research used familial networks rather than individuals as the unit of analysis. Are there implications for intervention design to consider service delivery via networks as well? Recognizing that families are themselves nodes within broad community networks, is it possible to move from serving even multisystem families to designing interventions for multisystem communities?

TECHNICAL RECOMMENDATIONS

Throughout this article, we note both the unique opportunities to conduct an analysis of this nature using administrative data and the unique challenges, resources, and limitations needed to do that analysis. We close with a few technical recommendations for improving the accessibility of administrative data and creating opportunities for further analyses of this type (see also Goerge 2018).

Develop secure data collections and the infrastructure to manage them. The kind of data preparation and record-linkage work that went into the development of our dataset was a high initial investment. Updating and expanding the data continues to be resource intensive, but the cost of maintaining and updating these kind of collections is much lower than the initial development. Developing infrastructure that allows data to be securely collected, integrated, and responsibly managed for research and analytic purposes will mean that the benefits to this sort of data preparation can be shared more broadly. This would also create opportunities to expand the rigor and complexity of data preparation. For example, having worked with these data as families, we now hypothesize that using family relationship to inform our record linkage might improve the original data integration process.

Train public-sector personnel in evaluation, research, and analysis. The effective use of data in the public sector, and the availability of data for ethical research, requires agency leaders who understand the value of evaluation and research. It also requires staff who are comfortable using and interpreting the results of research and comfortable using data in simple analyses to better understand programs.

Familiarize researchers with state information systems and databases. Many of the limitations and challenges of administrative data stem directly from the way data are collected and stored over time. Researchers who understand these systems can better interpret findings.

Encourage ongoing collaborations among state and local agencies and researchers. For investment value in administrative data to be maximized, program staff and researchers need to partner to bring a depth of understanding and interpretation to the data. Such a partnership will promote both better research and the translation of the research into better services to vulnerable families.

REFERENCES

Civic Caucus. 2009. "Summary of Discussion with Al Quie and Martin Sabo." Accessed October 22, 2018. http://www.civiccaucus.org/Interviews/2009/Quie-A_Sabo-M_12-11-09.htm.

Corbett, Thomas, James Dimas, James Fong, and Jennifer Noyes. 2005. "The Challenge of Institutional 'Milieu' to Cross-Systems Integration." *Focus* 24(1): 28–35. Accessed October 22, 2018. http://irp.wisc.edu/publications/focus/pdfs/foc241e.pdf.

Farhang, Sean, and Miranda Yaver. 2016. "Divided Government and the Fragmentation of American Law." *American Journal of Political Science* 60(2): 401–17. DOI: 10.1111/ajps.12188.

Fellegi, Ivan P., and Alan B. Sunter. 1969. "A Theory for Record Linkage." *Journal of the American Statistical Association* 64(328): 1183–210.

Goerge, Robert M. 2018. "Barriers to Accessing State Data and Approaches to Addressing Them." *Annals of the American Academy of Political and Social Science* 675(1): 122–37.

Goerge, Robert M., John van Voorhis, and Bong Joo Lee. 1994. "Illinois's Longitudinal and Relational Child and Family Research Database." *Social Science Computer Review* 12(3): 351–65. DOI: 10.1177/089443939401200302.

Grusky, David B., Michael Hout, Timothy M. Smeeding, and C. Matthew Snipp. 2019. "The American Opportunity Study: A New Infrastructure for Monitoring Outcomes, Evaluating Policy, and Advancing Basic Science." *RSF: The Russell Sage Foundation Journal of the Social Sciences* 5(2): 20–39. DOI: 10.7758/RSF.2019.5.2.02.

Hotz, V. Joseph, Robert M. Goerge, Julie Balzekas, and Francis Margolin, eds. 1998. *Administrative Data for Policy-Relevant Research: Assessment of Current Utility and Recommendations for Development*. Chicago: Northwestern University and the University of Chicago Joint Center for Poverty Research.

Jordan, B. Kathleen, Elizabeth B. Federman, Barbara J. Burns, William E. Schlenger, John A. Fairbank, and Juesta M. Caddell. 2002. "Lifetime Use of Mental Health and Substance Abuse Treatment Services by Incarcerated Women Felons." *Psychiatric Services* 53(3): 317–25.

Kitzmiller, Erika M. 2013. "IDS Case Study, Chapin Hall: Leveraging Chapin Hall's Mission to Enhance Child Well-Being." Philadelphia: University of Pennsylvania, Actionable Intelligence for Social Policy. Accessed November 27, 2018. http://www.aisp.upenn.edu/wp-content/uploads/2015/08/ChapinHall_CaseStudy.pdf.

Krumer-Nevo, Michal. 1998. "What's Your Story? Listening to the Stories of Mothers from Multi-Problem Families." *Clinical Social Work Journal* 26(2): 177–94.

Matos, Ana R., and Liliana M. Sousa. 2004. "How Multiproblem Families Try to Find Support in Social Services." *Journal of Social Work Practice* 18(1): 65–80. DOI: 10.1080/0265053042000180590.

Mazer, Milton. 1972. "Characteristics of Multi-Problem Households. A Study in Psychosocial Epidemiology." *American Journal of Orthopsychiatry* 42(5): 792–802.

Metzler, Marilyn, Melissa T. Merrick, Joanne Klevens, Katie A. Ports, and Derek C. Ford. 2017. "Adverse Childhood Experiences and Life Opportunities: Shifting the Narrative." *Children and Youth Services Review* 72 (January): 141–49. DOI: 10.1016/j.childyouth.2016.10.021.

Meyer, Bruce D., and Robert Goerge. 2011. "Errors in Survey Reporting and Imputation and Their Effects on Estimates of Food Stamp Program Participation." *US Census Bureau Center for Economic Studies* paper no. CES-WP-11-14. Washington: Government Printing Office.

National Association of State Budget Officers. 2009. *Fiscal Year 2008 State Expenditure Report*. Washington, D.C.: National Association of State Budget Officers. Accessed October 22, 2018. https://higherlogicdownload.s3.amazonaws.com/NASBO/9d2d2db1-c943-4f1b-b750-0fca152d64c2/UploadedImages/SER Archive/FY08 State Expenditure Report.pdf.

Newcombe, Howard B., James M. Kennedy, S. J. Axford, and A. P. James. 1959. "Automatic Linkage of Vital Records." *Science* 130(3381): 954–59.

Pecora, Peter J., Ronald C. Kessler, Kirk O'Brien, Catherine Roller White, Jason Williams, Eva

Hiripi, Diana English, James White, and Mary Anne Herrick. 2006. "Educational and Employment Outcomes of Adults Formerly Placed in Foster Care: Results from the Northwest Foster Care Alumni Study." *Children and Youth Services Review* 28(12): 1459–81. DOI: 10.1016/j.childyouth.2006.04.003.

Penner, Andrew M., and Kenneth A. Dodge. 2019. "Using Administrative Data for Social Science and Policy." *RSF: The Russell Sage Foundation Journal of the Social Sciences* 5(2): 1–18. DOI: 10.7758/RSF.2019.5.2.01.

Potter, Margaret A., Patricia Sweeney, Clarke Thomas, Theresa M. Miller, and Tyler Less Gourley. 2005. "Connecting Silos: The Legal Bases for Public Health Emergency Response in Pennsylvania." *Journal of Public Health Management and Practice*11(6): S50–S56. DOI: 10.1097/00124784-200511001-00009.

Roberts, Nancy C. 2011. "Beyond Smokestacks and Silos: Open-Source, Web-Enabled Coordination in Organizations and Networks." *Public Administration Review* 71(5): 677–93. DOI: 10.1111/j.1540-6210.2011.02406.x.

Sacco, Frank C., Stuart W. Twemlow, and Peter Fonagy. 2008. "Secure Attachment to Family and Community." *Smith College Studies in Social Work* 77(4): 31–51. DOI: 10.1300/J497v77n04_03.

Selig, Andrew L. 1976. "The Myth of the Multi-Problem Family." *American Journal of Orthopsychiatry* 46 (July): 526–32.

Sharlin, Shlomo A., and Michal Shamai. 1995. "Intervention with Families in Extreme Distress (FED)." *Marriage and Family Review* 21(1-2): 91–122. DOI: 10.1300/J002v21n01_06.

Shonkoff, Jack P., Andrew S. Garner, Benjamin S. Siegel, Mary I. Dobbins, Marian F. Earls, Andrew S. Garner, Laura McGuinn, John Pascoe, and David L. Wood. 2012. "The Lifelong Effects of Early Childhood Adversity and Toxic Stress." *Pediatrics* 129(1): e232–e246. DOI: 10.1542/peds.2011-2663.

Simon, Samuel E., Debra J. Lipson, and Christal M. Stone. 2010. "Mental Disorders Among Non-Elderly Nursing Home Residents." *Journal of Aging and Social Policy* 23(1): 58–72. DOI: 10.1080/08959420.2011.531989.

Sousa, Liliana, Cláudia Ribeiro, and Sofia Rodrigues. 2007. "Are Practitioners Incorporating a Strengths-Focused Approach When Working with Multi-Problem Poor Families?" *Journal of Community and Applied Social Psychology* 17(1): 53–66. DOI: 10.1002/casp.875.

Spratt, Trevor. 2011. "Families with Multiple Problems: Some Challenges in Identifying and Providing Services to Those Experiencing Adversities Across the Life Course." *Journal of Social Work* 11(4): 343–57. Accessed October 22, 2018. DOI: 10.1177/1468017310379256.

Stoltzfus, Kimberly, Cynthia Stohl, and David R. Seibold. 2011. "Managing Organizational Change: Paradoxical Problems, Solutions, and Consequences." *Journal of Organizational Change Management* 24(3): 349–37. DOI: 10.1108/09534811111132749.

Substance Abuse and Mental Health Services Administration. 2014. *Projections of National Expenditures for Treatment of Mental and Substance Use Disorders 2010–2020.* HHS Publication no. SMA-14-4883. Washington: U.S. Department of Health and Human Services.

Tausendfreund, Tim, Jana Knot-Dickscheit, Gisela C. Schulze, Erik J. Knorth, and Hans Grietens. 2016. "Families in Multi-Problem Situations: Backgrounds, Characteristics, and Care Services." *Child and Youth Services* 37(1): 4–22. DOI: 10.1080/0145935X.2015.1052133.

Teplin, Linda A. 1994. "Psychiatric and Substance Abuse Disorders Among Male Urban Jail Detainees." *American Journal of Public Health* 84(2): 290–93. Accessed October 22, 2018. http://ajph.aphapublications.org/doi/abs/10.2105/AJPH.84.2.290.

Wakefield, Sara, Hedwig Lee, and Christopher Wildeman. 2016. "Tough on Crime, Tough on Families? Criminal Justice and Family Life in America." *Annals of the American Academy of Political and Social Science* 665(1): 8–21. DOI: 10.1177/0002716216637048.

Wilkins, Carol. 2012. "Silos to Systems: Solutions for Vulnerable Families." Seattle, Wash.: Building Changes. Accessed October 22, 2018. http://www.buildingchanges.org/library-type/reports/item/472-silos-to-systems-solutions-for-vulnerable-families-summary-report.

Yong, Pierre L., Robert S. Saunders, and LeighAnne Olsen, eds. 2010. *The Healthcare Imperative: Lowering Costs and Improving Outcomes: Workshop Series Summary.* Washington, D.C.: National Academies Press. DOI: 10.17226/12750.

PART III
Neighborhoods and Housing

Poverty and Academic Achievement Across the Urban to Rural Landscape: Associations with Community Resources and Stressors

PORTIA MILLER, ELIZABETH VOTRUBA-DRZAL, AND REBEKAH LEVINE COLEY

Poor children begin school with fewer academic skills than their nonpoor peers, and these disparities translate into lower achievement, educational attainment, and economic stability in adulthood. Child poverty research traditionally focuses on urban or rural poor, but a shifting spatial orientation of poverty necessitates a richer examination of how urbanicity intersects with economic disadvantage. Combining geospatial administrative data with longitudinal survey data on poor children from kindergarten through second grade (N ≈ 2,950), this project explored how differences in community-level resources and stressors across urbanicity explain variation in achievement. Resources and stressors increased in more urbanized communities and were associated with academic achievement. Both mediated differences in poor children's achievement. Mediation was both direct and indirect, operating through cognitive stimulation and parental warmth.

Keywords: urbanicity, poverty, community context, achievement

Almost thirteen million children in the United States live in poverty according to the most recent estimates (Fontenot, Semega, and Kollar 2018). Poor children begin school almost a full school year behind their high-income peers on core academic skills (Garcia 2015). These disparities persist as they progress through school (Duncan and Magnuson 2011; Reardon 2011).

The hardships faced by poor children are often compounded because they are more likely than their advantaged counterparts to live in economically disadvantaged, chaotic, and under-resourced communities (Bischoff and Reardon 2014), and community disadvantage is linked to lower academic achievement (Sastry and Pebley 2010). Boosting poor children's achieve-

Portia Miller is a research scientist in the Learning Research and Development Center at the University of Pittsburgh. **Elizabeth Votruba-Drzal** is professor of psychology at the University of Pittsburgh and a research scientist in the Learning Research and Development Center at the University of Pittsburgh. **Rebekah Levine Coley** is department chair and professor in the Counseling, Developmental, and Educational Psychology Department at Boston College.

© 2019 Russell Sage Foundation. Miller, Portia, Elizabeth Votruba-Drzal, and Rebekah Levine Coley. 2019. "Poverty and Academic Achievement Across the Urban to Rural Landscape: Associations with Community Resources and Stressors." *RSF: The Russell Sage Foundation Journal of the Social Sciences* 5(2): 106–22. DOI: 10.7758/RSF.2019.5.2.06. This material is based on work supported by the Spencer Foundation (grant no. 201700117) and the National Science Foundation (grant no. 1650612). Any opinions, findings, and conclusions or recommendations expressed in this material are those of the authors and do not necessarily reflect the views of the Spencer Foundation or the National Science Foundation. Direct correspondence to: Portia Miller at plm11 @pitt.edu, 521 Learning Research and Development Center, 3939 O'Hara St., Pittsburgh, PA 15213.

Open Access Policy: *RSF: The Russell Sage Foundation Journal of the Social Sciences* is an open access journal. This article is published under a Creative Commons Attribution-NonCommercial-NoDerivs 3.0 Unported License.

ment is critical because gaps translate into diminished school success, lower educational attainment, and less economic stability in adulthood (Duncan et al. 2007; Magnuson and Votruba-Drzal 2009).

In addressing inequalities in poor children's development, it is important to consider the changing geography of poverty. Research on child poverty traditionally focuses on the urban poor, and a small literature considers the rural poor, but in recent years the spatial location of poor families has shifted dramatically (Allard 2017). Economically disadvantaged families have moved away from rural areas and inner cities toward suburbs and smaller towns. From 2000 to 2010, suburban poverty rose by 50 percent and grew at twice the rate of that in central cities. Suburbs are now home to the largest number of poor people (Kneebone and Berube 2013). Research finds that economic disparities in achievement differ for children living in urban, suburban, and rural communities, yet the contextual forces driving such disparities have not been systematically examined (Miller, Votruba-Drzal, and Setodji 2013).

One major reason researchers have not yet examined the intersection between poverty and place, and its implication for children and families, is that comprehensive data on community contexts are rarely included in longitudinal studies following children. Until recently, administrative data on community context have not been readily available at a national scale to combine with rich, longitudinal studies of children and families. Yet, with technological advances and the advent of geographic information systems (GIS) software, a wealth of administrative data is now publicly available at the zip code, census tract, and block level. These data can be used to create measures of key neighborhood and community processes, which can then be appended to longitudinal studies of children and families. This study uses these new methods and the burgeoning of publicly available geocoded administrative data, providing a unique example of how, even in the absence of data on community context at the individual level, researchers can leverage administrative data at the community level to study the lives of children and families.

This article attends to current gaps in the literature by combining administrative data with nationally representative longitudinal data on the well-being of children and families to examine whether community resources and stressors explain differences in poor children's achievement across urban, suburban, and rural areas. Using data from a broad array of publicly available administrative data sources on communities, geocoded and matched to children's addresses, we show that both resources and stressors were heightened in more urbanized communities. Moreover, differences in community context were pathways through which urbanicity was indirectly linked to children's achievement. Together, these results enhance understanding of how poverty and place intersect to predict children's early development (Galster and Sharkey 2017).

URBANICITY DIFFERENCES IN ECONOMIC DISPARITIES IN DEVELOPMENT

Recent evidence suggests that links between family income and child development may vary across urban, suburban, and rural areas. Studying a nationally representative sample of young children, Portia Miller, Elizabeth Votruba-Drzal, and Claude Messan Setodji find that for disadvantaged children, economic disparities in kindergarten reading and math skills were greatest in large urban cities, roughly 0.15 standard deviations (SD) per $10,000 increase in income, and smallest in rural areas, 0.05 SD (2013). In another study using parallel methods with nationally representative data on older children, family income had stronger relations with eighth-grade achievement in urban cities and weaker links in suburban and rural communities (Miller and Votruba-Drzal 2015). Although these studies provided evidence of urbanicity differences in income-achievement gaps, they did not identify the processes through which differences in children's development across urbanicity may be shaped.

Theoretical Framework

To understand how poverty shapes child development, we rely on two theories—resource and investment theory and stress theory. In brief, *resource and investment theory* posits that income dictates the resources available for investment in children, with poor children receiving fewer family and community investments, which hinders their early development (Becker 1981; Duncan and Brooks-Gunn 2000). Parents make a range of important investments in children by providing cognitive stimulation, educational activities, and warm and sensitive caregiving that promote young children's early cognitive development (Bassok et al. 2016; Kalil and Mayer 2016). Community contexts also provide opportunities for investments in children such as quality educational and cultural resources, social and health services, and recreational facilities that in turn provide enrichment directly to children and may also enhance parents' in-home investment behaviors. For example, access to nature and green spaces are linked to better attention skills (Wells and Evans 2003). Similarly, educational resources improve parenting (Brotman et al. 2011; Gutman and McLoyd 2000). Community-level socioeconomic advantage is another resource that has been tied to parental investments in children and to children's achievement (Kohen et al. 2008; Leventhal, Dupéré, and Shuey 2015).

The *family and environmental stress* model posits that poverty contributes to disparities in achievement by exposing children to stressors that impede healthy development. Within the home, economic pressure, coupled with other life stressors more commonly experienced by poor families, may lead to increased psychological distress and interparental conflict (Conger et al. 2002; McLoyd 1990). Financial stress also leads to harsher and less responsive parenting, in turn predicting numerous maladaptive outcomes for children like decreased cognitive and language skills (Chazan-Cohen et al. 2009; Farah et al. 2008). Beyond the family system, poor families face greater environmental stress at the community level in the forms of pollution, substandard housing, noise, lack of green space, and dangerous, dilapidated, and impoverished neighborhoods (Evans 2004). Such stressors hinder young children's cognitive development by triggering stress response systems and impeding children's self-regulatory skills (Kim et al. 2013; Shonkoff 2010). These in turn have implications for multiple domains of development including academic functioning (Evans and Kim 2013; Persico, Figlio, and Roth 2016). In addition to affecting children directly, neighborhood stressors shape children's development indirectly via parental functioning (Chung and Steinberg 2006; Coley, Lynch, and Kull 2015; Sharkey et al. 2012).

Last, bioecological theory also informs our conceptual framework. Bioecological theory argues that the processes that drive children's development transpire at multiple contextual levels, including the family and broader community level (Bronfenbrenner and Morris 2006). More specifically, it asserts that more distal contexts may shape children by influencing the quality of proximal processes within children's most immediate settings. Reflecting this framework, we assert that urbanicity is a macrocontext that may affect the proximal processes, such as access to resources and exposure to stressors, that drive children's development. This study tests how community resources and stressors vary across urban, suburban, and rural communities, and whether such variation is systematically associated with differences in parenting and, ultimately, poor children's achievement.

Differences in Resource and Stress Processes Across Urbanicity

Differences in resources and stressors across urbanicity may alter the way poverty shapes academic development. First, community resources such as museums, hospitals, libraries, and recreational centers are often more plentiful in urban cities than in suburbs and rural areas (Allard 2008; Gordon and Chase-Lansdale 2001; Lichter 2012). Beyond these broadly promotive community resources, the availability of resources that are particularly salient to disadvantaged populations, such as food banks and welfare offices, also appear lower in rural and suburban communities than in urban ones (Allard 2004, 2008; Murphy and Wallace 2010). That said, some research has shown that a strong sense of community in rural places may enhance access to limited resources for those in need (Tieken 2014). Breaking with this pattern, however, access to socioeconomically advantaged neighbors is limited in urban inner cities, where concentrated poverty and isolation of the poor are pervasive problems (Massey 1996; Wilson 1987). Suburban and rural areas, on the other hand, are generally more socioeconomically integrated (Evans and Kutcher 2011; Massey 1996).

Limited availability and accessibility of important resources in rural areas, and to a lesser extent suburban areas, may in turn impede the early development of poor rural and suburban children relative to urban peers. Rural and suburban children living in poverty may have fewer academic skills than their more urban counterparts because they receive fewer experiences, such as trips to cultural attractions and libraries, that have been linked to academic growth (Guo and Harris 2000; Duncan and Brooks-Gunn 2000). Lack of resources in rural and suburban areas may indirectly inhibit poor children's achievement if their parents are unable to draw from resources like libraries and social service organizations and hence are less able to provide stimulating, warm, and responsive parenting that enhances academic outcomes (Gutman and McLoyd 2000; Yeung, Linver, and Brooks-Gunn 2002).

Community stressors may also differ across urbanicity. Poor children in large cities and rural areas often experience chronic environmental risks that may be less prevalent in suburbs (see Evans 2004). Poor children are disproportionately exposed to environmental toxins and pollutants, though environmental justice research has not carefully compared differences in pollution exposure across the urban-rural continuum (Evans 2004). Urban areas have heightened prevalence of dangerous and dilapidated neighborhoods with relatively high rates of concentrated disadvantage (Amato and Zuo 1992). Heightened exposure to crime and violence has also been documented in large, inner-city communities (Amato and Zuo 1992; Burdick-Will 2016). These environmental risks may produce maladaptive physiological and psychological responses in urban children living in poverty (Evans and Kutcher 2011; Persico, Figlio, and Roth 2016; Shonkoff 2010). They may also inhibit disadvantaged urban children's academic functioning by increasing parental distress and, in turn, decreasing parenting quality (Evans and Saegert 2000; Linares et al. 2001; Wachs and Camli 1991). Although environmental risks are present in rural areas, rural children may enjoy relatively greater proximity to nature than their urban peers, which may buffer them from other sources of stress (Wells and Evans 2003). Consequently, the physical stressors of inner cities likely put poor urban children at a disadvantage relative to suburban and, to a lesser extent, rural peers.

RESEARCH AIMS

This study adds to the child poverty literature by examining differences in poor children's achievement across urban cities, suburbs, and rural areas. Second, it uses a range of administrative data to test whether poverty is differentially linked to children's achievement across urbanicity through differences in resources and stressors experienced by poor urban, suburban, and rural children. In so doing, it provides a comprehensive assessment of the mechanisms underlying urbanicity-related differences in poor children's academic development. Although pieces of the frameworks on which this article is based have been tested, extant work has not comprehensively compared the resources to which poor children have access or the stressors to which they are exposed across diverse urban, suburban, and rural communities. Research has drawn from contextual data such as the decennial census and American Community Survey (ACS) (Sastry and Pebley 2010) or data collected at a local level (Sharkey et al. 2012). It has not, however, fully exploited the rich array of national publicly available administrative data sources to compare and contrast the role of urbanicity in the lives of children living in poverty. This study is an exceptional example of how administrative data and rich, longitudinal data on children and families can be merged to create a fuller picture of the contexts in which child development unfolds.

METHOD

Data on children and families were drawn from the Early Childhood Longitudinal Study, Kindergarten Class of 2010–2011 (ECLS-K:2011), which followed a nationally representative cohort of more than eighteen thousand children entering kindergarten in the fall of 2010. This study analyzed data from the restricted use data files, which contain children's zip codes and census tracts of residence. Data were collected twice a year during the fall and spring of kindergarten, first grade, and second grade and annually thereafter from parents, teachers, school administrators, and direct child assessments.[1] The analytic sample includes the approximately 2,950 children who remained in the study through second grade and lived in families whose income to needs ratio was less than 100 percent of the federal poverty level at kindergarten or first grade.[2] Sampling weights were applied in all analyses to adjust for attrition and allow results to be generalized to a nationally representative kindergarten cohort. Missing data were imputed using multiple imputation in Mplus 6 to create ten imputed datasets (Asparouhov and Muthén 2010). Parameter estimates were averaged over the ten fitted models, and standard errors were computed using the average of the standard errors over the set of analyses and the between-imputation variation of parameter estimates (Rubin 1987).

Measures

Achievement. Children's knowledge and skills in reading, math, and science were measured with direct assessments at wave 6 (spring of second grade). The assessments drew items from several well-validated, standardized instruments to create highly reliable, age-appropriate composites of reading (α = 0.91), math (α = 0.94), and science (α = 0.83) skills scored using item response theory procedures (Tourangeau et al. 2017). An achievement composite was created by standardizing and averaging the reading, math, and science scores (α = 0.87).

Urbanicity. Urbanicity was delineated using rural-urban commuting area codes created by the Economic Research Service of the U.S. Department of Agriculture, which uses measures of population density, urbanization, and daily commuting. Urbanicity was categorized as large urban city (areas within the incorporated city limits of urbanized areas with populations of at least 750,000); small urban city (areas within incorporated city limits anchoring an area with between fifty thousand and 749,999 people); suburb (places inside urbanized areas but outside principal city limits); or rural area (places with fewer than fifty thousand residents). Children's urbanicity was measured at each wave, and more than 97 percent of children in the ECLS-K:2011 remained in the same urbanicity across all waves. Children who moved to a different urbanicity during the study were coded to the urbanicity where they lived a majority of waves. In the full sample, fewer than one hundred children spent equal time in different urbanicity categories and were excluded from our analytic sample.

Community characteristics. Seven measures of community resources and stressors were derived from national administrative data sources available at the zip code or census tract level. Using GIS software, we aggregated community measures to an appropriate geographic area determined on the basis of research and validation checks. This aggregation was done for two reasons. First, many community resources and stressors affect families beyond the specific zip code or census tract in which they live. For instance, families often access health care that is in a census tract and zip code outside their own (Wing and Reynolds 1988). Second, census tracts and zip codes vary widely in size across the United States, and aggregation by radius (such as a three-mile radius from the centroid of a zip or tract) helps make our community measures more uniform. We created and tested community measures at several different radii based on research, then used regression models to predict child or family measures to assess predictive validity in this sample (Miller et al. 2014). The radii tested ranged from the smallest geographic area measured, which was the census tract or zip code alone, to much larger areas, the largest being twenty-five miles from the zip or tract centroid. It is important to note that prior work by the authors showed that the most predictive radii does not differ across urbanicity (Votruba-Drzal et al. 2018). After the best measures were established, they were merged into the ECLS-K:2011 data via children's census tracts or zip codes of residence and averaged over the kindergarten and first grade waves.

Resources. Drawn from the 2010 U.S. Eco-

---

1. Response rates for waves 1 through 6 were 87 percent, 85 percent, 89 percent, 88 percent, 84 percent, and 87 percent, respectively.

2. The National Center for Education Statistics requires that all Ns be rounded to the nearest fifty.

nomic Census, *cultural resources* included counts of the number of important enriching resources such as museums, libraries, zoos, botanical gardens, and performing arts attractions within a twenty-mile radius of children's home zip codes, logged to increase normality. *Social service resources*, including services such as food banks, child and youth services, shelters, and family services drawn from the same data were also summed within a twenty-mile radius: because such services typically have limited capacity, the total was divided by the number of residents. A measure of *parks* was created using current data on the location of public parks and gardens from TomTom North America, Inc. published by ESRI. We used a dichotomous indicator for whether at least one park was available within a one-mile radius of children's home census tracts. This is a measure of public parks, not green space. Last, a measure of *socioeconomic advantage* was created with ACS data (2010–2014 five-year estimates) by standardizing and averaging the percentage of residents with college degrees, professional or managerial jobs, high incomes (greater than $100,000), and median income within a three-mile radius of children's census tracts ($\alpha = .95$).

Stressors. The Federal Bureau of Investigation's Uniform Crime Reporting database, which provides monthly reports on known criminal offenses and arrests by precinct zip code, was used to assess *violent crime*. Counts of murder, manslaughter, assault, rape, and robbery in 2010 were summed across a five-mile radius of each child's zip code. *Pollution* was assessed using data from the 2011 Environmental Protection Agency's (EPA) Toxic Release Inventory (TRI), aggregating the amount of chemicals hazardous to human development as designated by the EPA, released within a one-mile radius of children's home zip code. *Neighborhood disadvantage* was assessed with a composite of ACS data (2010–2014 five-year estimates) delineating percentage of individuals in poverty, receiving public assistance, unemployed, without a high school degree, and in female-headed households within three miles of children's census tracts ($\alpha = 0.92$).

Parenting. Parenting measures were drawn from the ECLS-K:2011. *Cognitive stimulation* in the home environment was reported by parents at waves 1 through 4, capturing activities such as reading books, participating in lessons or programs, and taking trips to the zoo or museum, with kindergarten (sixteen items; $\alpha = 0.80$) and first grade (ten items; $\alpha = 0.56$) measures averaged. *Parental warmth* was assessed at wave 2 via parent report (for example, parent and child "have warm, close times together"; parent "shows child love even when in bad mood"; parent expresses affection by "hugging, kissing, and holding"; 8 items; $\alpha = .56$). *Parental harshness* was also assessed via wave 2 parent reports of corporal punishment which, due to skewedness was dichotomized to indicate whether the parent spanked the child in the past week.

Child and family demographic characteristics. Numerous child and family demographic factors were included as covariates. Child characteristics include age in months at assessment, child gender, race-ethnicity (white, African American, Hispanic, Asian, Native American, or multiracial), and primary language. We also included measures of children's language skills, twenty items, $\alpha = 0.91$ (PreLAS) (Duncan and DeAvila 2000) and executive functioning skills, the average of dimensional change card sort (Zelazo 2006) and numbers reversed subtest of the Woodcock-Johnson III Tests of Cognitive Abilities (Woodcock, McGrew, and Mather 2001), assessed at kindergarten entry. These measures were included to control for unmeasured, time-invariant differences in children and families that affect children's achievement and behavior (Duncan and NICHD SECC 2003), thus helping reduce concerns of omitted variable bias.

Family characteristics that are correlated with family income, urbanicity, and child development also served as covariates, including highest level of parental education (less than a high school degree, high school degree or GED, some college or vocational school, or a bachelor's degree or greater), stable marital status, stable maternal employment, and the number of children under the age of eighteen in the household (averaged across wave).

Data Analysis

Structural equation models (SEM) were run in Mplus Version 6 software using maximum likelihood estimation (Muthén and Muthén 2008). Several community characteristics were rescaled so that their variances were of similar scale to other variable variances, which is necessary when using maximum likelihood estimation. Specifically, social service availability was multiplied by a factor of ten, toxic releases divided by one hundred, and crime divided by one thousand.

Three sets of models were estimated. First, to test the hypothesis of urbanicity-related differences in the achievement of poor children, we predicted achievement with urbanicity, controlling for all demographic covariates including kindergarten language and executive functioning skills. Next, we tested urbanicity-related differences in community characteristics in a similar manner, using freely estimated covariances among community characteristics. Finally, we assessed whether community and parenting characteristics mediated associations between urbanicity and children's functioning, testing the full model presented in figure 1 and allowing freely estimated covariances between community characteristics and between parenting measures. To account for nesting of children within schools and communities, cluster adjustments were made at the school level for all analyses (Preacher, Zyphur, and Zhang 2010).

Overall fit of each model was assessed using chi-square values, the root mean square error of approximation (RMSEA), a measure of relative fit better suited for larger sample sizes, the comparative fit index (CFI), and the Tucker-Lewis index (TLI). RMSEA values below 0.06 and CFI and TLI values above 0.95 support good model fit (Hu and Bentler 1999). Nonsignificant paths were eliminated from the models (with the exception of covariates) to improve model fit. Once the most parsimonious model was established, estimates of indirect effects were calculated using the model indirect command in Mplus to test whether community and family characteristics mediated links between urbanicity and child outcomes (Preacher, Zyphur, and Zhang 2010). Throughout this article, we use the term *effect* in the statistical sense to describe indirect effects (associations between predictor and outcome operating through another variable), direct effects (associations between predictor and outcome without a mediating variable), and effect sizes (size of associations). These terms do not imply causality.

RESULTS

Descriptive statistics for the analytic sample and for each urbanicity group separately are presented in the online appendix (table A). To understand the context of poverty across urbanicity, it is vital to consider the varying demographic profiles of poor families living in different urbanicities. For instance, low-income African American families disproportionally resided in urban areas, and the majority of poor families in rural areas were white. Conversely, poor Latino families tended to live in large cities or suburbs, and these places had relatively more English-language learners. Parental education was also lower in more urbanized communities.

After adjusting for these differences in child and family demographics as well as for children's skills in kindergarten, we found that poor children in suburbs had 0.13 of a standard deviation higher academic skills than those in rural areas (table 1). Notably, although few differences in child achievement across urbanicity emerged, urbanicity may operate through contrasting resource and stress processes to shape children's development, a hypothesis tested through our second research aim.

Indeed, as standardized estimates show in table 2, differences in community resources and stressors across urbanicity were stark. Considering community resources, poor children living in large urban cities had the most cultural resources and park availability in their communities and poor rural children had the fewest. Small city and suburban children living in poverty fell in the middle, with suburbs having more cultural resources. Poor children living in large urban settings also had the greatest social service availability, significantly greater than poor children in small cities and suburbs. In contrast, suburban children had the highest levels of neighborhood socioeconomic advantage and rural children had the lowest.

Differences were marked in community stressors as well. Violent crime and neighborhood disadvantage both showed the highest rates in large urban settings and lowest in rural areas. On the other hand, children in small ur-

Table 1. Relations Between Urbanicity and Child Achievement

	Unadjusted Coefficient	Adjusted Coefficient
Small urban	0.10	-0.03
	(0.07)	(0.06)
Suburban	0.09	0.04[a]
	(0.06)	(0.05)
Rural	0.07	-0.08[a]
	(0.07)	(0.06)

Source: Authors' calculations.
Note: N ≈ 2,950. Standard errors in parentheses. Urbanicity groups are compared with large urban areas. Post hoc analyses tested the significance of differences between other urbanicity groups. Within each column, coefficients with shared superscript letters are different from each other at the $p < .05$ level. Adjusted models controlled for the following covariates: race, gender, age, English language status, kindergarten language skills, kindergarten executive functioning, highest level of parental education, number of children in the house, maternal employment, and maternal marital status.

ban cities were exposed to the most pollutants, followed by suburban children; pollution rates were lower in large urban and rural communities.

RESOURCE AND STRESS PROCESSES MEDIATING URBANICITY DIFFERENCES IN ACHIEVEMENT

Figure 1 presents the standardized coefficients in the final path model testing mediation of urbanicity's links to poor children's achievement, with small urban, suburban, and rural children relative to their large urban counterparts. Arrows represent significant paths, with dashed arrows signaling associations significant at $p < .10$. In initial model specifications, we freely estimated all paths from urbanicity to community variables, parenting, and child outcomes. Notably, urbanicity did not have direct effects on parenting or child achievement. Non-significant paths were eliminated from the model, resulting in excellent fit: $\chi^2(30) = 61.22$, RMSEA = 0.02, CFI = 1.00, TLI = 0.96.

Holding all else constant, including kindergarten language and executive functioning skills, parental cognitive stimulation and warmth were

Table 2. Adjusted Differences in Community Characteristics

	Resources				Stressors		
	Cultural Resources β	Social Services Availability β	Park Availability β	Neighborhood Advantage β	Violent Crimes β	Toxic Releases β	Neighborhood Disadvantage β
Small urban	-1.17***ab	-0.23*	-0.51***a	-0.06ab	-0.59***a	0.43**a	-0.27*ab
	(0.07)	(0.11)	(0.08)	(0.10)	(0.12)	(0.13)	(0.11)
Suburban	-0.50***ac	-0.26***	-0.54***b	0.32**ac	-0.68***b	0.11*	-0.55***a
	(0.07)	(0.08)	(0.07)	(0.09)	(0.10)	(0.06)	(0.09)
Rural	-1.84***bc	-0.10	-1.44***ab	-0.33**bc	-0.91***ab	0.03a	-0.64***b
	(0.06)	(0.16)	(0.08)	(0.10)	(0.10)	(0.04)	(0.11)

Source: Authors' calculations.
Note: N ≈ 2,950. Standard errors in parentheses. Urbanicity groups are compared with large urban areas. Post hoc analyses tested the significance of differences between other urbanicity groups. Within each column, coefficients with shared superscript letters are different from each other at the $p < .05$ level. Controls included in models are race, gender, age, English language status, kindergarten language skills, kindergarten executive functioning, highest level of parental education, number of children in the house, maternal employment, and maternal marital status.
*$p < .05$; **$p < .01$; ***$p < .001$

Figure 1. Full Path Model of Urbanicity's Links to Achievement

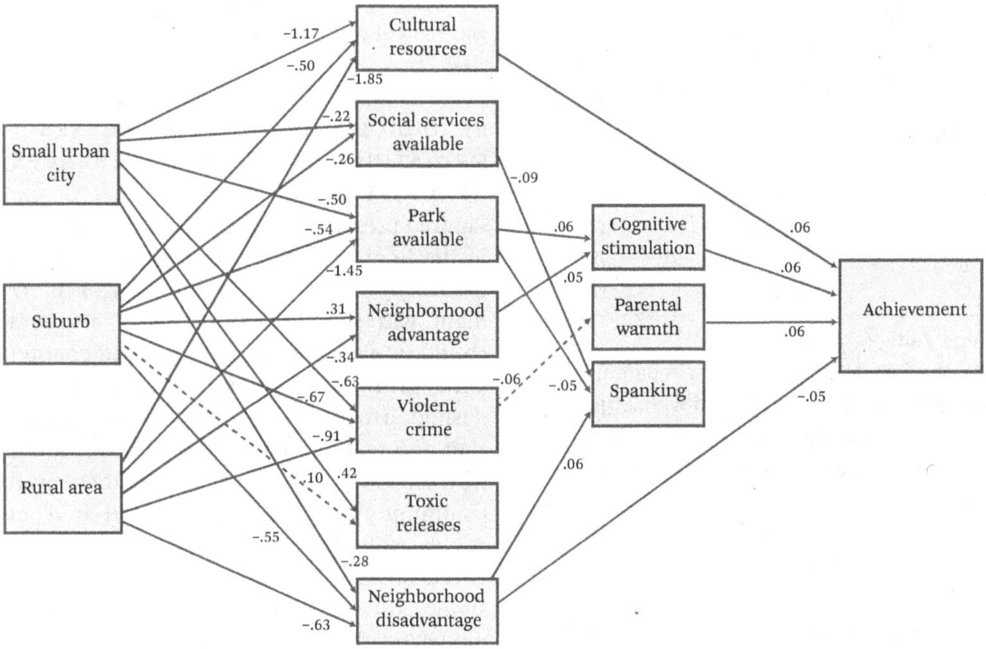

Source: Authors' calculations.
Note: N ≈ 2,950. Arrows illustrate significant paths in model ($p < .05$ or $p < .10$ if dashed line). Standardized path coefficients presented within figure. Urbanicity groups are compared with large urban cities. $\chi^2(30) = 61.22$, RMSEA = 0.02, CFI = 1.00, TLI = 0.96.

associated with greater child achievement, both with small effect sizes (0.06 SD units). Considering community contexts, cultural resources were directly positively associated with children's achievement, whereas neighborhood disadvantage showed a direct negative relation, again with small effect sizes (0.06 and 0.05 SD, respectively). Park availability and neighborhood advantage were positively associated with achievement through parental cognitive stimulation. In contrast, violent crime in the neighborhood was indirectly associated with achievement through lower levels of parental warmth. Although several community resources and stressors (social service availability, parks, and neighborhood disadvantage) were associated with parental spanking, spanking did not show significant associations with children's achievement. All highlighted associations were small in size, averaging less than 0.10 of a standard deviation after a broad array of covariates and children's earlier skills were taken into account.

Community and family processes helped explain associations between urbanicity contexts and children's achievement. Figure 2 highlights numerous significant indirect effects from urbanicity to poor children's achievement. Relative to residence in a large city, living in a small city, suburb, or rural area was negatively associated with achievement through decreased cultural resources (−0.5 SD, −0.02 SD, −0.08 SD, per urbanicity, respectively) as well as through decreased park availability (−0.002 SD, −0.002 SD, −0.01 SD, respectively) and in turn lower home cognitive stimulation. However, there were positive indirect effects of residence in small cities, suburbs, or rural areas, relative to large cities operating through lower neighborhood disadvantage (0.01 SD, 0.03 SD, 0.03 SD, respectively) as well as through less violent crime and in turn greater parental warmth (0.003 SD, 0.003 SD, 0.004 SD, respectively).

Urbanicity also had indirect effects on poor children's achievement when comparing small cities, suburbs, and rural areas (see online appendix, figures A and B). The suburbs where

Figure 2. Indirect Effects of Urbanicity on Achievement

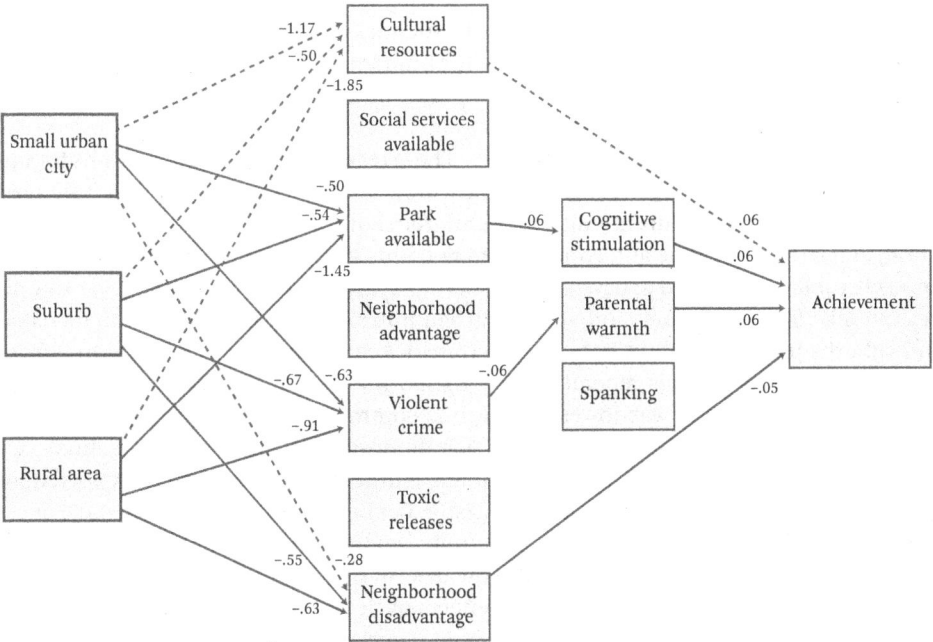

Source: Authors' calculations.
Note: N ≈ 2,950. Arrows illustrate significant indirect effects ($p < .05$ or $p < .10$ if dashed line). Standardized path coefficients presented within figure. Urbanicity groups are compared with large urban cities. $\chi2(30) = 61.22$, RMSEA = 0.02, CFI = 1.00, TLI = 0.96.

poor children lived had more cultural resources and less concentrated disadvantage than small cities, which resulted in significant positive indirect effects (0.03 SD and 0.01 SD, respectively) on suburban children's achievement. Relative to their peers in small cities, poor rural children had fewer cultural resources (–0.03 SD) and parks (–0.003 SD), but also less violent crime (0.002 SD) and disadvantage (0.02 SD), resulting in counteracting indirect effects of rural residence. Last, living in a rural area had negative indirect effects compared to a suburban area that stemmed from reduced access to cultural resources (–0.06 SD), parks (–0.003 SD), and socioeconomically advantaged neighbors (–0.002 SD). This was only partially counteracted by a positive indirect effect stemming from decreased violent crime in the rural areas (0.001 SD).

DISCUSSION

The academic skills that children have in their early school years set the stage for future success in life. Research has consistently shown that children living in poverty tend to have deficits in these early skills (Duncan and Magnuson 2011). Yet studies have not explored whether poor children's early skills differ across urban, suburban, and rural areas, despite increasing evidence that urbanicity is an important developmental context (Miller, Votruba-Drzal, and Setodji 2013; Rudolph et al. 2014). Using a nationally representative sample of poor children starting kindergarten in 2010 linked with a broad array of administrative data on both resources and stressors within communities, this study finds that although children's levels of achievement look mostly similar across large urban cities, small urban cities, suburbs, and rural areas, the processes by which economic disadvantage is associated with poor children's development vary notably depending on place. These identified processes have important implications for efforts to improve contextual supports for disadvantaged children and target scarce public resources.

Differences in Community Context Across Urbanicity and Their Links to Achievement

Using a wealth of data characterizing various aspects of communities, this study uncovered several systematic differences in the neighborhoods of poor children across urbanicity. Much as hypothesized, the urban inner-city neighborhoods that disadvantaged children resided in tended to be flush with both resources (cultural and natural) and stressors (crime and concentrated poverty); rural areas tended to have fewer resources but also fewer stressors; and small cities and suburbs tended to fall in between. There were some exceptions to this general pattern. Social service availability was lowest in small cities and suburban communities, and neighborhood socioeconomic advantage was highest in suburbs. These findings are consistent with the literature on suburbs (Massey 1996; Murphy and Wallace 2010). Another exception was surprising. Pollution in small cities and suburbs was, on average, greater than in large cities or rural areas. This is probably due to the measure of pollution used, which captures toxic releases from businesses and industries but misses other sources of pollution, such as automobiles or residential buildings. Because this measure taps into pollution most associated with manufacturing, our results are consistent with where manufacturing is currently taking place in the United States—small Rust Belt cities and suburbs (Hollander et al. 2009; Lewis 2008). To our knowledge, these findings are the first attempt to characterize the differences in community contexts of poor children across the urban-rural continuum using multiple indicators and nationally representative data.

Further, as hypothesized, these community characteristics were related to poor children's academic development. The quantity of community cultural resources such as zoos, libraries, and museums were directly and positively related to achievement. Meanwhile, the level of concentrated disadvantage in neighborhoods had direct negative links to achievement. Community resources and stressors also related to poor children's achievement through their links with several aspects of parenting; resources such as social services, parks, and socioeconomically advantaged neighbors were associated with more stimulating and warm parenting and less harsh parenting, and stressors such as violent crime and concentrated disadvantage were linked to less warm parenting and more physical punishment, respectively.

These results may have implications for improving academic outcomes for disadvantaged children. Policies targeted to community type may be most effective at narrowing achievement disparities. Our results suggest that in urban inner cities it is important to focus on strategies that reduce or buffer children from neighborhood stressors. For instance, in high crime communities, successful policies may include programs that decrease school violence and foster feelings of safety in school (Astor, Benbenishty, and Estrada 2009). For example, evidence from a study in this issue indicates that safe schools buffer the negative effects of neighborhood violence on achievement (Laurito et al. 2019). Similarly, programs like Chicago's Safe Passage Program, which employs community members to watch streets and routes children use to travel to and from school, has been linked to decreased crime and increased school attendance (Chicago Public Schools 2018). On the other hand, effective policies to improve poor children's achievement in underresourced suburbs and rural areas may involve providing important resources to children and families. For instance, library outreach programs such as bookmobiles have been successfully used to provide services to rural populations (Boyce and Boyce 1995). Expanding these programs, as well as using this model to deliver other cultural resources to poor rural families could have positive impacts on the academic development of poor rural children. Similarly, increasing social service availability in suburbs where poverty is burgeoning may help decrease parental stress and improve parenting quality, leading to improvements in poor children's achievement.

Implications for Research on Children, Families, and Communities

A striking lesson from this research is that the adequate and complete study of the macrosystems in which children develop requires a simultaneous examination of multiple forces shaping development. Simply looking at mean differences by urbanicity or differences adjusted by demographic characteristics obscured a more complex picture of the role of urbanicity in children's achievement, in which neighborhood processes can be simultaneously supportive of and detrimental for children's development. For instance, positive links between increased cultural and natural resources and child achievement in large cities were countered by negative associations between violence and disadvantage and achievement. Moreover, the community context measures were intercorrelated. This further highlights the importance of accounting for various aspects of children's communities and the biases likely to underlie studies assessing the effect of one characteristic in isolation.

What does this imply for existing research on neighborhood effects? Extant studies of links between community characteristics and child development have generally assessed a single aspect or a group of similar indicators of community in isolation. For instance, several studies examining neighborhood socioeconomic disadvantage or advantage do not consider these factors in conjunction (Sastry and Pebley 2010; Xue et al. 2005). Results of this study suggest that neighborhood advantage and disadvantage may play distinct roles, through different mechanisms, in the development of children's academic skills. Moreover, given that these aspects of neighborhoods are correlated with other community characteristics such as pollution, violence, and cultural resources, it is hard to know whether prior studies were identifying true associations between neighborhood socioeconomic status and outcomes, or whether results are biased due to the failure to consider other key neighborhood characteristics. In this respect, this study improves on past literature by examining several aspects of communities simultaneously to reveal which features of children's neighborhoods are most predictive of subsequent development. Future research using methods allowing causal conclusions is necessary to expand knowledge on the causal roles of individual community resource and stress characteristics.

Role of Administrative Data in Studies of Children and Families

This study is a prime example of how administrative geospatial data from various agencies can be leveraged to create measures of community characteristics that can inform and expand studies of children's development. Studies of neighborhood effects on children and families often use data on neighborhoods reported by the families, and studies that use independent administrative data have overwhelmingly been limited to the use of data from the decennial census (Chung and Steinberg 2006; Sastry and Pebley 2010). Although census data have several strengths, many aspects of community context—such as crime rates, pollution, and resource availability—are not available via decennial censuses. This study provides a unique example of how administrative data from a variety of sources can be combined with nationally representative data on children and families to gain a more complete understanding of how multiple aspects of communities simultaneously operate in relation to parenting practices and children's achievement.

Other research has richly studied targeted aspects of communities at local levels. For instance, using data from the Chicago School Readiness Project and the Chicago Police Department, Patrick Sharkey and his colleagues geocoded all homicides in the city of Chicago to pinpoint the exact date and location and then determined whether a homicide occurred close to children's homes prior to children's assessment (2012). This study is an excellent examination of considering both the spatial and temporal aspects of children's contexts. Future research of this nature in other cities and communities across the United States is needed to explore the generalizability of findings. To do so, we need more data of this richness to be collected at a national level to expand the breadth of our research on neighborhood contexts.

This study makes clear that, although additional work is needed to create valid and comprehensive data on children's communities, currently available administrative data serve a useful purpose in the study of child development. All community resources and stressors explored here, with the exception of pollution, relate to child and family functioning in some way. Moreover, these indicators generally operated in accordance with research and our hypotheses, which lends credence to their worth. For instance, having a park within a mile of children's homes positively predicted cognitive stimulation—a variable that includes activities such as playing outside, discussing nature, and exercising that we may expect to increase when parks are easily accessible (Wells and Evans 2003). Neighborhood violent crime was linked to decreased parental warmth, as documented in smaller studies (Pinderhughes et al. 2001), though this study replicates the association using administrative as opposed to parent-reported data on neighborhood danger. The presence of cultural resources such as libraries, museums, and zoos had a direct relation to children's learning; the availability of social services that are often vital to poor families predicted better parenting. These associations between community factors and children and families have long been conjectured but not until now empirically demonstrated on a national scale.

Although administrative data were immensely useful for characterizing differences in poor children's communities, this study would not be possible without rich, longitudinal data with measures of child and family processes and information (through secure data agreements) on children's census tract or zip code. Administrative data are unlikely to include measures of processes occurring within children's microsystem, such as parenting quality or home learning environment, or validated measures of children's physical, behavioral, or cognitive development (Bronfenbrenner and Morris 2006). To the extent that researchers can use administrative data in conjunction with survey and observational data containing measures of processes and individual functioning, we can propose and test more contextually rich conceptual models of multiple forces affecting child development. Indeed, efforts currently under way in the American Opportunity Study will make such linkages between administrative data and rich longitudinal data on children and families much easier and, it stands to reason, more common in the literature (Grusky et al. 2019).

Limitations

Limitations to this study must be acknowledged. First, these results are correlational and, hence, must be interpreted with caution. Accordingly, although the correlational design of this study provides a rich description of the community and family contexts of poor children across urbanicity, it is possible that the observed associations between urbanicity, community characteristics, parenting, and achievement were caused by some unmeasured features of the parents or children in our sample. Notably, attempts were made to limit endogeneity bias by controlling for children's kindergarten language and executive functioning skills, as well as for characteristics of parents and families when predicting children's second-grade achievement scores. Nonetheless, future work in this area should try to leverage experimental and quasi-experimental designs to better address selection effects.

Second, despite the overall strengths and comprehensiveness of data used in this study, measurement weaknesses were also apparent. For instance, the pollution variable did not capture sources of pollution other than that associated with business. Moreover, the TRI is not a direct measure but instead is self-reported by businesses, which could certainly lead to underreporting. Similarly, the FBI's Uniform Crime Reporting is a voluntary program, and many jurisdictions do not make these reports. This leads to a great deal of missing data on crime, which had to be imputed. In addition, these data are reported at the precinct level and do not pinpoint the precise location of the crimes that were committed. Last, the administrative data varied in terms of the geographic level available, and though census tract data are preferable because tracts are smaller than zip codes, several indicators were available only at the zip code level. Thus, our community measures created using zip code data—cultural resources, social service availability, pollution, and crime—were less precise than the other measures available at the tract level. Given these notable measurement limitations, it is somewhat remarkable that the majority of our community measures showed reliable associations with child and family functioning and their use marks an advancement to prior literature on poverty and place.

We must also note that the effect sizes obtained from our results were consistently small. Although moderate to large differences emerged in community resources and stressors across urbanicity contexts, links with family processes and child achievement were small. We argue that results still have practical importance. First, estimates may be deflated because of high levels of measurement error, particularly in community characteristics. As noted, administrative data on communities currently available at a national scale have drawbacks that may weaken the signal when examining links to child and family functioning. Second, estimates may be conservative because we controlled for language skills and executive functioning in kindergarten when predicting second-grade skills. To the extent that urbanicity's associations with achievement stem from connections with cognitive and behavioral skills that children acquire prior to school entry, our estimates will be downwardly biased.

CONCLUSION

Research is beginning to explore how the lived experiences of economic disadvantage differ depending on place. Links between poverty and children's development differ depending on whether they live in cities, suburbs, or rural areas, but no studies had examined what aspects of communities contribute to these differences. This study contributes to the literature by systematically exploring differences in community processes across the large urban cities, small urban cities, suburbs, and rural areas in which poor children reside, and by assessing whether such differences explain variation in children's achievement. Results show that children in poverty experience very different community contexts depending on urbanicity, which are associated with differences in children's achievement both directly and through parenting. Moreover, results suggest that the most effective policies aimed at improving poor children's academic skills may differ across the rural-urban continuum. Policies buffering poor children and families from neighborhood stressors may be the best way to narrow achievement gaps in large inner cities, and increasing resources in resource-deprived rural areas may be most helpful in improving the achievement of disadvantaged rural children.

REFERENCES

Allard, Scott W. 2004. "Access to Social Services: The Changing Urban Geography of Poverty and Service Provision." Washington, D.C.: The Brookings Institution.

———. 2008. "Accessibility and Stability of Nonprofit Service Providers: Faith-Based and Community-Based Organizations in Urban and Rural America." In *Innovations in Effective Compassion*, edited by Pamela Joshi, Stephanie Hawkins, and Jeffrey Novey. Washington: U.S. Department of Health and Human Services.

———. 2017. *Places in Need: The Changing Geography of Poverty*. New York: Russell Sage Foundation.

Amato, Paul R., and Jiping Zuo. 1992. "Rural Poverty, Urban Poverty, and Psychological Well-Being." *Sociological Quarterly* 33(2): 229–40.

Asparouhov, Tihomir, and Bengt Muthén. 2010. "Multiple Imputation with Mplus." Version 2. September 29. Accessed October 25, 2018. http://statmodel2.com/download/Imputations7.pdf.

Astor, Ron Avi, Rami Benbenishty, and Jose Nuñez Estrada. 2009. "School Violence and Theoretically Atypical Schools: The Principal's Centrality in Orchestrating Safe Schools." *American Educational Research Journal* 46(2): 423–61.

Bassok, Daphna, Jenna E. Finch, RaeHyuck Lee, Sean F. Reardon, and Jane Waldfogel. 2016. "Socioeconomic Gaps in Early Childhood Experiences: 1998 to 2010." *AERA Open* 2(3): 1–22. DOI: 10.1177/2332858416653924.

Becker, Gary S. 1981. *A Treatise on the Family*. Cambridge, Mass.: Harvard University Press.

Bischoff, Kendra, and Sean Reardon. 2014. "Residential Segregation by Income, 1970–2009." In *Diversity and Disparities: America Enters a New Century*, edited by John R. Logan. New York: Russell Sage Foundation.

Boyce, Judith I., and Bert R. Boyce. 1995. "Library Outreach Programs in Rural Areas." *Library Trends* 44(1): 112–28.

Bronfenbrenner, Urie, and Pamela A. Morris. 2006. "The Bioecological Model of Human Development." In *Handbook of Child Psychology*, vol. 1, edited by Richard M. Lerner. Hoboken, N.J.: John Wiley & Sons.

Brotman, Laurie Miller, Esther Calzada, Keng-Yen Huang, Sharon Kingston, Spring Dawson-McClure, Dimitra Kamboukos, Amanda Rosenfelt, Amihai Schwab, and Eva Petkova. 2011. "Promoting Effective Parenting Practices and Preventing Child Behavior Problems in School Among Ethnically Diverse Families from Underserved, Urban Communities." *Child Development* 82(1): 258–76.

Burdick-Will, Julia. 2016. "Neighborhood Violent Crime and Academic Growth in Chicago: Lasting Effects of Early Exposure." *Social Forces* (95)1: 133–58.

Chazan-Cohen, Rachel, Helen Raikes, Jeanne Brooks-Gunn, Catherine Ayoub, Barbara Alexander Pan, Ellen E. Kisker, Lori Roggman, and Allison Sidle Fuligni. 2009. "Low-Income Children's School Readiness: Parent Contributions over the First Five Years." *Early Education and Development* 20(6): 958–77.

Chicago Public Schools. 2018. "Safe Passage Routes." Last modified August 30, 2018. Accessed January 24, 2019. https://cps.edu/Pages/safepassage.aspx.

Chung, Hen Len, and Laurence Steinberg. 2006. "Relations Between Neighborhood Factors, Parenting Behaviors, Peer Deviance, and Delinquency Among Serious Juvenile Offenders." *Developmental Psychology* 42(2): 319–31.

Coley, Rebekah Levine, Alicia Doyle Lynch, and Melissa Kull. 2015. "Early Exposure to Environmental Chaos and Children's Physical and Mental Health." *Early Childhood Research Quarterly* 32 (2015): 94–104.

Conger, Rand D., Lora Ebert Wallace, Yumei Sun, Ronald L. Simons, Vonnie C. McLoyd, and Gene H. Brody. 2002. "Economic Pressure in African American Families: A Replication and Extension of the Family Stress Model." *Developmental Psychology* 38(2): 179–93.

Duncan, Greg J., and Jeanne Brooks-Gunn. 2000. "Family Poverty, Welfare Reform, and Child Development." *Child Development* 71(1): 188–96.

Duncan, Greg J., Chantelle J. Dowsett, Amy Claessens, Katherine Magnuson, Aletha C. Huston, Pamela Klebanov, Linda S. Pagani, Leon Feinstein, Mimi Engel, Jeanne Brooks-Gunn, Holly Sexton, and Kathryn Duckworth. 2007. "School Readiness and Later Achievement." *Developmental Psychology* 43(6): 1428–46.

Duncan, Greg J., and Katherine Magnuson. 2011. "The Nature and Impact of Early Achievement Skills, Attention Skills, and Behavior Problems." In *Whither Opportunity?: Rising Inequality, Schools, and Children's Life Chances*, edited by Greg J. Duncan and Richard J. Murnane. New York: Russell Sage Foundation.

Duncan, Greg J., and the National Institute of Child Health and Human Development Study of Early Child Care (NICHD SECC). 2003. "Modeling the Impacts of Child Care Quality on Children's Preschool Cognitive Development." *Child Development* 74(5): 1454–75.

Duncan, Sharon, and Edward DeAvila. 2002. *Pre-Language Assessment Scales [PreLAS 2000]*. Monterey, Calif.: CTB-McGraw Hill.

Evans, Gary W. 2004. "The Environment of Childhood Poverty." *American Psychologist* 59(2): 77–92.

Evans, Gary W., and Pilyoung Kim. 2013. "Childhood Poverty, Chronic Stress, Self-Regulation, and Coping." *Child Development Perspectives* 7(1): 43–48.

Evans, Gary W., and Rachel Kutcher. 2011. "Loosening the Link Between Childhood Poverty and Adolescent Smoking and Obesity: The Protective Effects of Social Capital." *Psychological Science* 22(1): 3–7.

Evans, Gary W., and Susan Saegert. 2000. "Residential Crowding in the Context of Inner City Poverty." In *Theoretical Perspectives in Environment-Behavior Research: Underlying Assumptions, Research Problems, and Relationships*, edited by Seymour Wapner, Jack Demick, and C. Takiji Yamamoto. New York: Plenum.

Farah, Martha J., Laura Betancourt, David M. Shera, Jessica H. Savage, Joan M. Giannetta, Nancy L. Brodsky, Elsa K. Malmud, and Hallam Hurt. 2008. "Environmental Stimulation, Parental Nurturance and Cognitive Development in Humans." *Developmental Science* 11(5): 793–801.

Fontenot, Kayla, Jessica Semega, and Melissa Kollar. 2018. "Income and Poverty in the United States." *Current Populations Reports*, series P60, no. 263. Washington: U.S. Census Bureau.

Galster, George, and Patrick Sharkey. 2017. "Spatial Foundations of Inequality: A Conceptual Model and Empirical Overview." *RSF: The Russell Sage Journal of the Social Sciences* 3(2): 1–33.

Garcia, Emma. 2015. *Inequalities at the Starting Gate: Cognitive and Noncognitive Skills Gaps Between 2010–2011 Kindergarten Classmates*. Washington, D.C.: Economic Policy Institute.

Gordon, Rachel A., and P. Lindsay Chase-Lansdale.

2001. "Availability of Child Care in the United States: A Description and Analysis of Data Sources." *Demography* 38(2): 299–316.

Grusky, David B., Michael Hout, Timothy M. Smeeding, and C. Matthew Snipp. 2019. "The American Opportunity Study: A New Infrastructure for Monitoring Outcomes, Evaluating Policy, and Advancing Basic Science." *RSF: The Russell Sage Foundation Journal of the Social Sciences* 5(2): 20–39. DOI: 10.7758/RSF.2019.5.2.02.

Guo, Guang, and Kathleen Mullan Harris. 2000. "The Mechanisms Mediating the Effects of Poverty on Children's Intellectual Development." *Demography* 37(4): 431–47.

Gutman, Leslie Morrison, and Vonnie C. McLoyd. 2000. "Parents' Management of Their Children's Education Within the Home, at School, and in the Community: An Examination of African-American Families Living in Poverty." *Urban Review* 32(1): 1–24.

Hollander, Justin B., Karina Pallagst, Terry Schwarz, and Frank Popper. 2009. "Planning Shrinking Cities." *Progress in Planning* 72(4): 223–32.

Hu, Li-tze, and Peter M. Bentler. 1999. "Cutoff Criteria for Fit Indexes in Covariance Structure Analysis: Conventional Criteria Versus New Alternatives." *Structural Equation Modeling: A Multidisciplinary Journal* 6(1): 1–55.

Kalil, Ariel, and Susan E. Mayer. 2016. "Understanding the Importance of Parental Time with Children: Comment on Milkie, Nomaguchi, and Denny (2015)." *Journal of Marriage and Family* 78(1): 262–65.

Kim, Pilyoung, Gary W. Evans, Michael Angstadt, S. Shaun Ho, Chandra S. Sripada, James E. Swain, Israel Liberzon, and K. Luan Phan. 2013. "Effects of Childhood Poverty and Chronic Stress on Emotion Regulating Brain Function in Adulthood." *Proceedings of the National Academy of Sciences* 110(46): 18442–47.

Kneebone, Elizabeth, and Alan Berube. 2013. *Confronting Suburban Poverty in America*. Washington, D.C.: Brookings Institution Press.

Kohen, Dafna E., Tama Leventhal, V. Susan Dahinten, and Cameron N. McIntosh. 2008. "Neighborhood Disadvantage: Pathways of Effects for Young Children." *Child Development* 79(1): 156–69.

Laurito, Agustina, Johanna Lacoe, Amy Ellen Schwartz, Patrick Sharkey, and Ingrid Gould Ellen. 2019. "School Climate and the Impact of Neighborhood Crime on Test Scores." *RSF: The Russell Sage Foundation Journal of the Social Sciences* 5(2): 141–66. DOI: 10.7758/RSF.2019.5.2.08.

Leventhal, Tama, Véronique Dupéré, and Elizabeth A. Shuey. 2015. "Children in Neighborhoods." In *Handbook of Child Psychology and Developmental Science*, vol. 4, edited by Marc H. Bornstein and Tama Leventhal. Hoboken, N.J.: John Wiley & Sons.

Lewis, Robert D. 2008. *Manufacturing Suburbs: Building Work and Home on the Metropolitan Fringe*. Philadelphia, Pa.: Temple University Press.

Lichter, Daniel T. 2012. "Immigration and the New Racial Diversity in Rural America." *Rural Sociology* 77(1): 3–35.

Linares, L. Oriana, Timothy Heeren, Elisa Bronfman, Barry Zuckerman, Marilyn Augustyn, and Edward Tronick. 2001. "A Mediational Model for the Impact of Exposure to Community Violence on Early Child Behavior Problems." *Child Development* 72(2): 639–52.

Magnuson, Katherine A., and Elizabeth Votruba-Drzal. 2009. "Enduring Influences of Childhood Poverty." In *Changing Poverty, Changing Policies*, edited by Marcia Cancian and Sheldon Danziger. New York: Russell Sage Foundation.

Massey, Douglas S. 1996. "The Age of Extremes: Concentrated Affluence and Poverty in the Twenty-First Century." *Demography* 33(4): 395–412.

McLoyd, Vonnie C. 1990. "The Impact of Economic Hardship on Black Families and Children: Psychological Distress, Parenting, and Socioemotional Development." *Child Development* 61(2): 311–46.

Miller, Portia, and Elizabeth Votruba-Drzal. 2015. "Urbanicity Moderates Associations Between Family Income and Adolescent Academic Achievement." *Rural Sociology* 80(3): 362–86.

Miller, Portia, Elizabeth Votruba-Drzal, and Claude Messan Setodji. 2013. "Family Income and Early Achievement Across the Urban-Rural Continuum." *Developmental Psychology* 49(8): 1452–65.

Miller, Portia, Elizabeth Votruba-Drzal, Rebekah Levine Coley, and Amanda S. Koury. 2014. "Immigrant Families' Use of Early Childcare: Predictors of Care Type." *Early Childhood Research Quarterly* 29(4): 484–98.

Murphy, Alexandra K., and Danielle Wallace. 2010. "Opportunities for Making Ends Meet and Upward Mobility: Differences in Organizational Deprivation across Urban and Suburban Poor

Neighborhoods." *Social Science Quarterly* 91(5): 1164–86.

Muthén, Linda K., and Bengt O. Muthén. 2008. Mplus. Version 5.1. Los Angeles, Calif.: Muthén & Muthén.

Persico, Claudia, David Figlio, and Jeffrey Roth. 2016. "Inequality Before Birth: The Developmental Consequences of Environmental Toxicants." NBER working paper no. w22263. Cambridge, Mass.: National Bureau of Economic Research.

Pinderhughes, Ellen E., Robert Nix, E. Michael Foster, and Damon Jones. 2001. "Parenting in Context: Impact of Neighborhood Poverty, Residential Stability, Public Services, Social Networks, and Danger on Parental Behaviors." *Journal of Marriage and Family* 63(4): 941–53.

Preacher, Kristopher J., Michael J. Zyphur, and Zhen Zhang. 2010. "A General Multilevel SEM Framework for Assessing Multilevel Mediation." *Psychological Methods* 15(3): 209–33.

Reardon, Sean F. 2011. "The Widening Academic Achievement Gap Between the Rich and the Poor: New Evidence and Possible Explanations." In *Whither Opportunity?: Rising Inequality, Schools, and Children's Life Chances*, edited by Greg J. Duncan and Richard J. Murnane. New York: Russell Sage Foundation.

Rubin, Donald B. 1987. "Comment." *Journal of the American Statistical Association* 82(398): 543–46.

Rudolph, Kara E., Elizabeth A. Stuart, Thomas A. Glass, and Kathleen R. Merikangas. 2014. "Neighborhood Disadvantage in Context: The Influence of Urbanicity on the Association Between Neighborhood Disadvantage and Adolescent Emotional Disorders." *Social Psychiatry and Psychiatric Epidemiology* 49(3): 467–75.

Sastry, Narayan, and Anne R. Pebley. 2010. "Family and Neighborhood Sources of Socioeconomic Inequality in Children's Achievement." *Demography* 47(3): 777–800.

Sharkey, Patrick T., Nicole Tirado-Strayer, Andrew V. Papachristos, and C. Cybele Raver. 2012. "The Effect of Local Violence on Children's Attention and Impulse Control." *American Journal of Public Health* 102(12): 2287–93.

Shonkoff, Jack P. 2010. "Building a New Biodevelopmental Framework to Guide the Future of Early Childhood Policy." *Child Development* 81(1): 357–67.

Tieken, Mara Casey. 2014. *Why Rural Schools Matter*. Chapel Hill: University of North Carolina Press.

Tourangeau, Karen, Christine Nord, Thanh Lê, Kathleen Wallner-Allen, Nancy Vaden-Kiernan, Lisa Blaker, and Michelle Najarian. 2017. *User's Manual for the* ECLS-K:2011 *Kindergarten–Second Grade Data File and Electronic Codebook, Public Version*. NCES 2017-285. Washington, D.C.: National Center for Education Statistics.

Votruba-Drzal, Elizabeth, Portia Miller, Rebekah Levine Coley, and Bryn Spielvogel. 2018. "Using National Survey Data, Administrative Data, and GIS to Determine Community Boundaries Across Cities, Suburbs, and Rural Areas." Conference paper. Washington, D.C.: Society for Research in Child Development.

Wachs, Theodore D., and Ozlem Camli. 1991. "Do Ecological or Individual Characteristics Mediate the Influence of the Physical Environment upon Maternal Behavior." *Journal of Environmental Psychology* 11(3): 249–64.

Wells, Nancy M., and Gary W. Evans. 2003. "Nearby Nature: A Buffer of Life Stress Among Rural Children." *Environment and Behavior* 35(3): 311–30.

Wilson, William Julius. 1987. *The Truly Disadvantaged: The Inner City, The Underclass, and Public Policy*. Chicago: University of Chicago Press.

Wing, Paul, and Christopher Reynolds. 1988. "The Availability of Physician Services: A Geographic Analysis." *Health Services Research* 23(5): 649–67.

Woodcock, Richard W., Kevin S. McGrew, and Nancy Mather. 2001. *Woodcock-Johnson Tests of Achievement*. Itasca, Ill.: Riverside Publishing.

Xue, Yange, Tama Leventhal, Jeanne Brooks-Gunn, and Felton J. Earls. 2005. "Neighborhood Residence and Mental Health Problems of 5- to 11-Year-Olds." *Archives of General Psychiatry* 62(5): 554–63.

Yeung, W. Jean, Miriam R. Linver, and Jeanne Brooks-Gunn. 2002. "How Money Matters for Young Children's Development: Parental Investment and Family Processes." *Child Development* 73(6): 1861–79.

Zelazo, Philip David. 2006. "The Dimensional Change Card Sort (DCCS): A Method of Assessing Executive Function in Children." *Nature Protocols* 1 (June): 297–301. Accessed October 25, 2018. https://www.nature.com/articles/nprot.2006.46.

Subprime Babies: The Foreclosure Crisis and Initial Health Endowments

JANELLE DOWNING AND TIM BRUCKNER

The subprime mortgage crisis was a devastating financial shock for many homeowners. This research uses a probabilistic matching strategy to link foreclosure records with birth certificate records from 2006 to 2010 in California to identify birth parents who experienced a foreclosure. Among mothers who did, those issued a loan during the peak of subprime lending from 2005 to 2007 were more Hispanic and socioeconomically disadvantaged than mothers with loans originating before 2005. We use a mother fixed-effects analyses of ever-foreclosed mothers issued a loan during 2006 and 2007 and find that infants in gestation during or after the foreclosure had a lower birth weight for gestational age than those born earlier, suggesting that the foreclosure crisis was a plausible contributor to disparities in initial health endowments.

Keywords: foreclosure, perinatal epidemiology, birth certificate, stress, administrative

The subprime mortgage crisis was characterized by an unprecedented rise in mortgage delinquencies and foreclosures (Duca 2013). At the national peak month of the crisis in January of 2011, foreclosures numbered 1.56 million (CoreLogic 2017). Between 2007 and 2010, homeownership rates fell most dramatically for minorities and households with incomes of $20,000 or less (CoreLogic 2017). In response to the crisis and to protect Americans from predatory lending practices in the future, policies such as Dodd-Frank Wall Street Reform were implemented, establishing regulatory entities, including the Consumer Financial Protection Bureau. Yet, in June 2017, the House passed the Financial CHOICE Act, which is designed to repeal certain provisions of Dodd-Frank and loosen regulatory policies.[1] Given the contemporaneous nature of this policy and the ongoing debate about financial regulatory policies, the period in our recent history prior to the financial regulatory reform—the subprime mort-

Janelle Downing is assistant professor in the OHSU-PSU School of Public Health. **Tim Bruckner** is associate professor of public health at the University of California, Irvine.

© 2019 Russell Sage Foundation. Downing, Janelle, and Tim Bruckner. 2019. "Subprime Babies: The Foreclosure Crisis and Initial Health Endowments." *RSF: The Russell Sage Foundation Journal of the Social Sciences* 5(2): 123–40. DOI: 10.7758/RSF.2019.5.2.07. This study was approved by the Committee for the Protection of Human Subjects of the California Health and Human Services Agency and the Institutional Review Board of the University of California, Irvine (IRB #2013–9716). Direct correspondence to: Janelle Downing at downingj@ohsu.edu, 3181 SW Sam Jackson Park Rd., Portland, OR 97239; and Tim Bruckner at tim.bruckner@uci.edu, 653 East Peltason Dr., Irvine, CA 92697.

Open Access Policy: RSF: The Russell Sage Foundation Journal of the Social Sciences is an open access journal. This article is published under a Creative Commons Attribution-NonCommercial-NoDerivs 3.0 Unported License.

1. H.R. 10—Financial CHOICE Act of 2017, 115th Congress, 1st session.

gage crisis—can help us to predict how a less regulated financial environment might affect society in the future.

The economic causes and consequences of the subprime crisis have been well studied (Been et al. 2011; Financial Crisis Inquiry Commission 2011; Foote, Gerardi, and Willen 2012). The financial regulatory environment and cascade of events influenced a set of complex adaptive responses which included not only banks and government entities—but also communities, households, and individuals. Less is known about the unintended (spillover) effects of the subprime crisis.

Some evidence indicates that the foreclosure crisis contributed to increased racial segregation (Hall, Crowder, and Spring 2015a; Rugh and Massey 2010) and neighborhood crime (Ellen, Lacoe, and Sharygin 2013), and had negative effects on education (Bradbury, Burke, and Triest 2014). More recently, scholars have explored the effect of the foreclosure crisis on health (Downing 2016; Downing et al. 2017, 2016; Currie and Tekin 2015). Evidence from a small set of studies suggests that homeowners who experienced a foreclosure had more anxiety and depression, whereas population-level studies—which measure, for example, the relationship between health and the foreclosure rate in a given census tract—showed an increase in violent behavior and urgent unscheduled health-care visits (Downing 2016; Currie and Tekin 2015).

Research on the foreclosure crisis and health, though distinct from other work on the health effects of financial shocks, shares an underlying aim of quantifying unintentional effects of a phenomenon that plausibly served as an unexpected population-level stressor. A vast body of work has been undertaken on the effects of a coincident financial shock—the Great Recession—on health and health behaviors (Margerison-Zilko et al. 2016; Catalano et al. 2011; Margerison-Zilko, Li, and Luo 2017). Although the evidence does not converge across all areas of health, studies on the effect of economic shocks on a highly sensitive period of development—pregnancy—have shown particularly compelling evidence that fetal exposure to unexpected job loss reduced birth weight for gestational age and increased male fetal death (Margerison-Zilko et al. 2011; Catalano and Bruckner 2005). Although both the foreclosure crisis and the Great Recession serve as population-level stressors, we know of no research that examines whether the sensitive period of pregnancy responded to the foreclosure crisis.

MERIT OF LINKING ADMINISTRATIVE DATA

Use of administrative data to answer policy-relevant questions has become increasingly important (Harris-Kojetin and Groves 2017). Despite technical, legal, and perceptual challenges associated with its use, administrative data enable researchers to answer questions that were previously unanswerable (Penner and Dodge 2019). One type of administrative data, vital statistics, has been collected since the early 1900s, although use of birth certificates for population-level perinatal research was not feasible until the 1990s, when some states began to keep these in digital format (Buescher et al. 1993). The advantages of these data, such as their comprehensiveness (all births in a state), large sample sizes, and wealth of birth-related and socioeconomic variables, have made vital records increasingly attractive for research in the last decade (Schoendorf and Branum 2006). Although birth certificate data were collected for administrative rather than research purposes, their reuse for research has been beneficial because it allows a minimum set of questions to be answered without placing additional burdens of further data collection on vulnerable populations, pregnant women, and infants.

Linkage of birth certificate data with other sources of administrative data is the next frontier of perinatal epidemiology. The United States lags behind other countries in linking data for perinatal health (Delnord et al. 2016). For example, Denmark maintains a civil registration system that has allowed researchers to link all administrative data with birth certificate data by unique identifiers (Pedersen 2011). Although several studies in the United States have demonstrated feasibility of linking birth certificate records with hospital records (Barfield et al. 2008; Herrchen, Gould, and Nesbitt 1997; Hall et al. 2014), far fewer have linked birth certificate records with other sources of administrative data at the individual level (Autor et al. 2016; Coulton et al. 2016; Putnam-Hornstein et al. 2013).

This article fills an important gap by demonstrating feasibility of linking birth certificates with another source of public administrative data, foreclosure deed records. In the absence of unique identifiers, we use a probabilistic matching technique (Gliklich, Dreyer, and Leavy 2014). The linkage of the data allows us to answer two policy-relevant questions unanswerable without this approach. We describe each of these questions and how we leveraged this unique source of linked data to address key content and methodological gaps in the literature.

> What are the demographics of families affected by the foreclosure crisis?

Family formation and homeownership are important goals of many Americans, and the transition to either tenet can be delayed or disrupted by changes in lending policies. The demographics of who was affected by the foreclosure crisis is still not yet well understood (Reid et al. 2017). The majority of studies have focused on specific cities or types of loans, or showed the impact on neighborhoods of varying demographics (Hall, Crowder, and Spring 2015a, 2015b; Bocian et al. 2011). Even one of the most comprehensive studies on demographics of lending during the subprime crisis was unable to include the complete universe of lenders because of data limitations (Reid et al. 2017). The Home Mortgage Disclosure Act data are considered one of the most comprehensive sources of mortgage and demographic data, yet do not cover all home loans nationwide.

Research on California finds that African American and Hispanic borrowers were more likely to have a subprime loan and more likely to default during the crisis, even after accounting for underwriting risk factors and neighborhood characteristics (Reid and Laderman 2009). These findings are troubling because the unequal distribution of foreclosures can contribute to social stratification by widening the racial wealth gap (Reid et al. 2017). It is then critical to understand its impact on young families, who are often in the process of transitioning to homeownership.

Young families often access family wealth to transition to homeownership, yet discriminatory institutional polices have reproduced racial differences in wealth and increased barriers for Hispanic and black young families to purchase a first home (Krivo and Kaufman 2004). Subprime loans provided an opportunity for households with less wealth to purchase their first home. Hispanic and black young families are then most at risk to be affected by the subprime mortgage crisis.

This is the first study we are aware of to examine population-level characteristics of families who went through foreclosure during the crisis. Differential responses to foreclosure, for instance, may affect the sociodemographic composition of who selects into, or postpones, fertility.

> How might exposure to foreclosure affect birth outcomes?

Through this data linkage, we also investigate the repercussion on fetal development of experiencing a foreclosure during pregnancy. The maternal stress response, when activated by an external stressor such as job loss or another catastrophic event, reportedly perturbs timing of parturition, fetal growth, or both processes (Hobel, Goldstein, and Barrett 2008). This study investigates whether in utero exposure to foreclosure affected gestations by examining differences in birth weight for gestational age, which is sensitive to the maternal stress response and precedes adverse health and lower human capital development over the life course.

Acute and chronic psychosocial stressors have reportedly slowed fetal growth or accelerated the timing of delivery. Stress, smoking, and low socioeconomic status over the life course have been shown to increase risk of preterm birth (delivery before thirty-seven weeks) and reduced birth weight (Lu and Halfon 2003). Although some of the consequences of these risk factors are observable at birth, others are latent and appear much later in life. Adults who showed preterm delivery or slower fetal growth had increased morbidity, lower educational attainment, and even lower labor market outcomes (Almond and Currie 2011; Strauss 2000; Currie and Moretti 2007; Hack, Klein, and Taylor 1995; Black, Devereux, and Salvanes 2007; Goldenberg et al. 2008).

Homeownership has been portrayed as the American Dream and ideologically as a political right (Flood et al. 2015). Many who defaulted on their loans during the subprime crisis experienced feelings of anxiety, stress, and personal failure (Ross and Squires 2011). Mothers who defaulted on their loan and were undergoing foreclosure may also increase maladaptive coping behaviors such as smoking and alcohol use. Any of these exposures may adversely affect fetal growth and development.

A foreclosure can lead to a loss in time, wealth, and energy of a household. Mothers who manage paperwork and the cognitive burden of the foreclosure process may inadvertently place a lower priority or less time on receiving antenatal care and engaging in health-promoting behaviors (Mullainathan and Shafir 2013; Bruckner 2008). In addition, a foreclosure can reduce wealth and the amount of resources available to purchase healthy food and pay for health care. Finally, some households who lost a home to foreclosure experienced high levels of fear, shame, and guilt, which could reduce the degree to which mothers rely on others for social support (Ross and Squires 2011). Prior studies have found strong social support to be a contributor to normal fetal growth and term birth (Feldman et al. 2000).

METHODOLOGICAL CONCERNS AND INNOVATIONS

Pregnancy responses to adverse events are typically reported only among those that end in a live birth. Research, however, finds that stressful events may also increase the likelihood of fetal mortality. Specifically, stressful experiences reduce the chances that pregnant women will deliver males (Hansen, Møller, and Olsen 1999). A decline in the human secondary sex ratio (of male to female live births) has been reported following population stressors such as man-made disasters (Bruckner, Catalano, and Ahern 2010; Fukuda et al. 1998) and economic recessions (Catalano et al. 2011; Catalano and Bruckner 2005). Therefore, mothers who have the most stressful foreclosure may experience an early spontaneous loss, such that only "hardier" births are positively selected to live birth.

Furthermore, another concern is that there might be selection into treatment (being in utero during the foreclosure process). People with loans in default may be more likely to delay fertility. We suspect that only couples who were aware that a foreclosure was imminent would be able to delay fertility. However, individual decisions to take out a mortgage, refinance, or default implicitly reflect knowledge about current and future expectations of health, fertility, and economic status. For example, individuals who are sick might lose their job or take out a lien on their house to pay for medical bills, which could lead to foreclosure. In addition, relatively healthier persons who experienced an economic setback in advance of a foreclosure may have chosen to delay fertility until prospects improve.

The issue of selection into treatment is mitigated in part when studying the effect of foreclosure on health during the height of the foreclosure crisis. A majority of foreclosures during this period were caused by the loan characteristics (that is, the subprime structure) or declines in home equity rather than individual job loss or medical bills (Palmer 2015). The increase in the default rate of subprime mortgages during the crisis accounted for more than half of all the foreclosures at its peak (Palmer 2015). The year in which the mortgage originated plays a role in the likelihood of default. Subprime mortgages originating in 2006 and 2007 were more likely to default within three years than those originating in 2003 and 2004 (Palmer 2015). Therefore, borrowers with loans originating between 2006 and 2007 were less likely to be subject to selection into treatment than those borrowing at other times because of their lack of knowledge about riskiness of the loan.

To further address the issue of selection into treatment, we compare outcomes of siblings born to the same mother. Linkage of sibling births for the entire population base of live births in a state is relatively novel in perinatal epidemiology (Kramer, Dunlop, and Hogue 2014). Increasingly, scholars have recognized that mothers experience a dynamic socioeconomic trajectory during adulthood. This dynamism calls for innovative data linkage approaches to capture information about mothers and their pregnancies over a longer life course.

Our research aims to understand how fetal exposure to a loan that results in foreclosure relates to poor birth outcomes. To address this question while minimizing the risk of selection into pregnancy during stressful times, we compare birth outcomes within mothers (that is, across siblings) who ultimately experienced a foreclosure. In addition, consistent with the notion that loans in 2006 and 2007 are a plausibly exogenous stressor, we assess whether results appear stronger among those who took out a loan during 2006 and 2007 rather than before or after this period.

METHODS

We obtained birth certificate records for all live births in California (2005 to 2010, n = 3,278,847) from the California Department of Health Services. We selected California as our study population because it was one of the hardest hit states by the foreclosure crisis (CoreLogic 2017). California also shows substantial within-state geographic variation in the foreclosure rate and yielded the highest number of live annual births of any state in the country (Martin et al. 2017). Mother's address was geocoded using ArcGIS and a census tract was assigned to each record. Births to mothers with at least one multiple birth between 2005 and 2010 were excluded (n = 106,755) because birth outcomes for singleton and multiple births have different etiologies.

We retrieved foreclosure records on all residential properties in California that were subject to at least one completed foreclosure between 2006 and 2015 (n = 1,058,311). These records are publicly available from the clerk in each county. Because of the time cost of contacting each of the fifty-eight counties, we purchased the assembled and cleaned data of all records in California from CoreLogic. The foreclosure records were then geocoded using ArcGIS, and census tracts were assigned to each record.

Matching

To match foreclosure records to the birth file, we preprocessed all address and name data to ensure consistency in formatting across the two sources of data (Wasi and Flaaen 2015). Of these, 0.25 percent of birth records (n = 8,130) had missing addresses and thus were excluded. Given that some mothers had multiple births at the same address, we allowed for multiple matches as the father name might vary over time. Of the foreclosure data, 0.3 percent (n = 3,300) did not have an address and 2.1 percent (n = 22,143) did not list the mortgage-holder name and were therefore excluded. We reformatted the foreclosure data to include one unique address and lender for each row by collapsing multiple loans at the same property to the same borrower and retaining the earliest notice of default date and summing the loan amount and balance for each.

We used a deterministic matching technique in Stata to link foreclosure record data to the master birth certificate data by mother's address. Because we wanted exact matches only and data were preprocessed, this method optimized speed without compromising accuracy. Next, we used a probabilistic matching technique in Stata (reclink) to link foreclosure record data to the master birth certificate data by first and last names of parents listed on the birth certificate. This technique used a bigram string comparator to assess imperfect string matches. We reviewed the output for quality of match and separated falsely matched files.

We created a variable, exact match, which was defined as matching on address and mother or father full name. Next, we reran the matching procedure with an exact match of an address and last name of mother or father using the same procedure. We created two partial match variables. First, relative match, which was defined as matching on address and mother and father last name (excluding exact matches). Second, address match, which was defined as matching on address only and not name (not exact match or relative match).

Figure 1. Illustration of Gestations in Utero

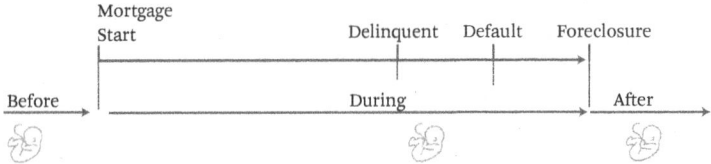

Source: Authors' calculations.
Note: Based on the conception, delivery, and foreclosure dates, we created a match timing variable for each pregnancy according to whether it occurred before, during, or after the foreclosure process.

We link births for the same mother, creating a unique identifier based on her first name, last name, birthdate, and mother's birthplace. A categorical variable, match type (0 = not matched, 1 = exact, 2 = relative, and 3 = address), and a binary variable, matched, (0 = not matched, 1 = exact, relative, or address) were developed from the above measures for each mother. Next, we created variables based on timing of the foreclosure process and gestational period. The variable, match timing, was a categorical variable (0 = not matched, 1 (before loan) = birth date < mortgage start date, 2 (during loan) = birth date > = mortgage start date & conception date < = foreclosure date, 3 (after foreclosure) = foreclosure date < conception date). For a visual explanation, see figure 1.

Because we matched administrative records that likely contained legal last names (and maiden names for mothers on the birth certificates), we might have classified some mortgage-holders as *address-only* matches if they changed their last names or had variations in spellings of their name. Common reasons for changing one's name include divorce or simplification. Therefore, we likely underestimated foreign-born mortgage holders and women, particularly those in unstable partnerships. In addition, our matching process relied on exact matching of addresses because a substantial number of foreclosures were condominiums or apartment buildings with multiple units. Although we preprocessed these addresses to standardize them, we likely did not match some people living in condominiums or apartment buildings if the number or letter of the unit was different or missing. Our matching process was conservative, and thus we avoided falsely matching at the cost of excluding some true matches.

Key Variables

Birth-related

Our dependent variable of interest is birth weight for gestational age percentile (BWGA). BWGA measures fetal growth and, unlike birth weight (in grams), separates being born light from being born early. Fetal growth and timing of delivery reportedly have distinct causes, and for this reason BWGA is preferred in perinatal epidemiology over the general measure of birth weight (Kramer et al. 2001; Oken et al. 2003). BWGA takes into account continuous birth weight conditional on gestational age. We calculated BWGA using the Oken method from the sex-specific birth tables after using the Alexander method to remove implausible birth weight for gestational age combinations (Oken et al. 2003; Alexander et al. 1996). We excluded all births that were missing BWGA (n = 141,099). In addition, we included sex of neonate (1 = female, 0 = male), and parity (1 = first birth, 2 = 1 or more prior births) as control variables.

Mother-related

The mother-related variables of interest include age at delivery, race-ethnicity (non-Hispanic white, non-Hispanic black, non-Hispanic Asian, Hispanic, non-Hispanic other), educational attainment, health insurance (Medicaid, private or self-pay, no insurance, other), and no father (had at least one birth with no father listed). We also used body mass index (BMI) (continuous kg/m^2) and smoking status (never smoker, smoked prior to pregnancy only, smoked before

Table 1. Mean Characteristics of Mothers by Foreclosure Match Status

	Exact Match	Relative	Address Only	Not Matched
Age thirty-five in 2010	0.43	0.17	0.22	0.34
Non-Hispanic white	0.32	0.14	0.21	0.27
Hispanic	0.49	0.66	0.62	0.53
Non-Hispanic black	0.04	0.04	0.06	0.05
Non-Hispanic Asian	0.13	0.13	0.08	0.13
Non-Hispanic other	0.03	0.03	0.03	0.03
Less than high school	0.16	0.31	0.35	0.28
High school graduate	0.26	0.34	0.28	0.25
Some college	0.32	0.26	0.22	0.22
Bachelor's+	0.26	0.09	0.15	0.25
Medicaid ever	0.26	0.63	0.60	0.49
Obese ever	0.23	0.24	0.23	0.20
Smoked ever	0.03	0.05	0.05	0.04
1+ prior birth	0.80	0.65	0.68	0.63
No father (1+ birth)	0.02	0.12	0.13	0.10
Total births 2005–2010	1.36	1.39	1.38	1.23
Observations	60,611	31,374	155,611	2,179,690

Source: Authors' calculations based on data from linked California foreclosure records and birth certificates.
Note: Mothers with 1+ single birth from 2005 to 2010 in California.

and during pregnancy) for 2007 through 2010; data for 2005 and 2006 on BMI and smoking were not collected on the birth file.

Foreclosure-related
The foreclosure-related variables of interest include property address, mortgage-holder names, mortgage issue date, notice of default date, and deed transfer date (when the foreclosure was completed). We created a categorical variable for all matched births, borrower cohort, which was set to the calendar year in which the loan was originated (1 = before 2005, 2 = 2005, 3 = 2006, 4 = 2007, and 5 = after 2007).

Statistical Approach
We summarized the mean characteristics of all unique mothers (table 1) from 2005 to 2010 who had at least one birth. Mothers were separated into four groups based on the match type, which include exact, relative, address, and not matched.

Next, we restricted our sample to exact match only (mothers who have ever experienced a foreclosure, for example). We created a descriptive table of mothers ever foreclosed with within- and between-mother standard deviations for each of our key variables (see table 2). Mother-invariant characteristics included race-ethnicity, educational attainment, borrower cohort, and borrower type. Characteristics that varied within-mother (for mothers with more than one birth during the test period) included BWGA, infant sex, parity, health insurance, and mother's age. In addition, we summarized the mean characteristics of all unique mothers ever foreclosed by loan cohort (table 3).

To understand how foreclosure rates for various matched groups vary over time, we created a series of descriptive monthly time series plots. We used the total universe of foreclosures in California as our denominator. Figure 2 presents the total monthly count of all foreclosures in California and the total monthly count of all foreclosures that matched at least one birth from 2005 to 2010 (foreclosures to exact or partial matches). Figure 3 presents the proportion

Table 2. Descriptive Statistics of Mothers Ever Foreclosed, 2005–2010

	Mean	Standard Deviation	Between-Person Standard Deviation	Within-Person Standard Deviation
BWGA percentile	48.32	28.40	27.26	10.44
Gestational age (weeks)	39.26	2.02	1.92	0.86
Mother's age (years)	29.89	5.07	5.07	0.95
Before loan[a]	0.24	0.43	0.39	0.23
Zero to two years of loan[a]	0.57	0.50	0.43	0.29
Two years to end[a]	0.15	0.36	0.31	0.20
After foreclosure[a]	0.03	0.18	0.11	0.13
Less than high school[a]	0.15	0.36	0.36	0.10
High school graduate[a]	0.26	0.44	0.42	0.15
Some college[a]	0.32	0.47	0.45	0.15
Bachelor's+[a]	0.26	0.44	0.43	0.09
Medicaid[a]	0.23	0.42	0.41	0.14
Male[a]	0.51	0.50	0.46	0.25
First birth[a]	0.27	0.45	0.40	0.25
Non-Hispanic white[a]	0.32	0.47	0.47	0.00
Hispanic[a]	0.48	0.50	0.50	0.00
Non-Hispanic black[a]	0.04	0.19	0.19	0.00
Non-Hispanic Asian[a]	0.13	0.34	0.34	0.00
Non-Hispanic other[a]	0.03	0.18	0.17	0.00
Before 2005[a]	0.08	0.27	0.27	0.00
2005[a]	0.30	0.46	0.46	0.00
2006[a]	0.38	0.49	0.48	0.00
2007[a]	0.21	0.40	0.40	0.00
After 2007[a]	0.04	0.21	0.20	0.00
Number of newborns	80,131			
Number of mothers	60,354			
Infants per mother	1.328			

Source: Authors' calculations based on data from linked California foreclosure records and birth certificates.
Note: Nonmissing observations only.
[a]Expressed as a proportion.

of all foreclosures in that month that were to exact, relative, and address, and figure 4 presents the proportion of all exact match foreclosures by race-ethnicity with all foreclosures as the denominator. Given that the foreclosures could have happened after the birth, the time axis extends through 2015. Next, to show how conception cohorts changed over time, we used the total universe of births in California as our denominator. Figure 5 presents trends in the proportion of conceptions resulting in a live birth to parents who experienced a foreclosure.

Modeling Approach

All Births We treat all births as statistically independent of one another and fit an ordinary least squares model to estimate the association between BWGA and match type (exact, relative, address) where the reference group is unmatched, adjusting for *infant sex, parity*, and *health insurance, mother's age, mother's race, mother's educational attainment* (model 1).

Births to Matched Next, we keep only births to exact or partial (exact, relative, address) matches.

Table 3. Mean Characteristics of Mothers with a Foreclosure by Loan Cohort

	Before 2005	2005	2006	2007	After 2007
Mother's age (years)	31.11	30.35	30.20	30.38	30.10
White	0.41	0.33	0.28	0.31	0.41
Black	0.04	0.04	0.04	0.04	0.03
Asian	0.16	0.15	0.12	0.12	0.12
Hispanic	0.37	0.46	0.53	0.50	0.42
Less than high school	0.11	0.15	0.18	0.17	0.10
High school graduate	0.23	0.26	0.27	0.26	0.25
Some college	0.34	0.33	0.32	0.31	0.35
Bachelor's+	0.32	0.26	0.23	0.26	0.29
Medicaid ever	0.18	0.22	0.28	0.25	0.22
Obese ever	0.23	0.23	0.24	0.22	0.23
Smoked ever	0.03	0.03	0.03	0.03	0.04
1+ prior birth	0.80	0.80	0.79	0.75	0.69
No father (1+ birth)	0.02	0.02	0.02	0.02	0.02
Observations	4,715	16,975	20,473	10,853	2,153

Source: Authors' calculations based on data from linked California foreclosure records and birth certificates.

Figure 2. Total Foreclosures and Matched Foreclosures

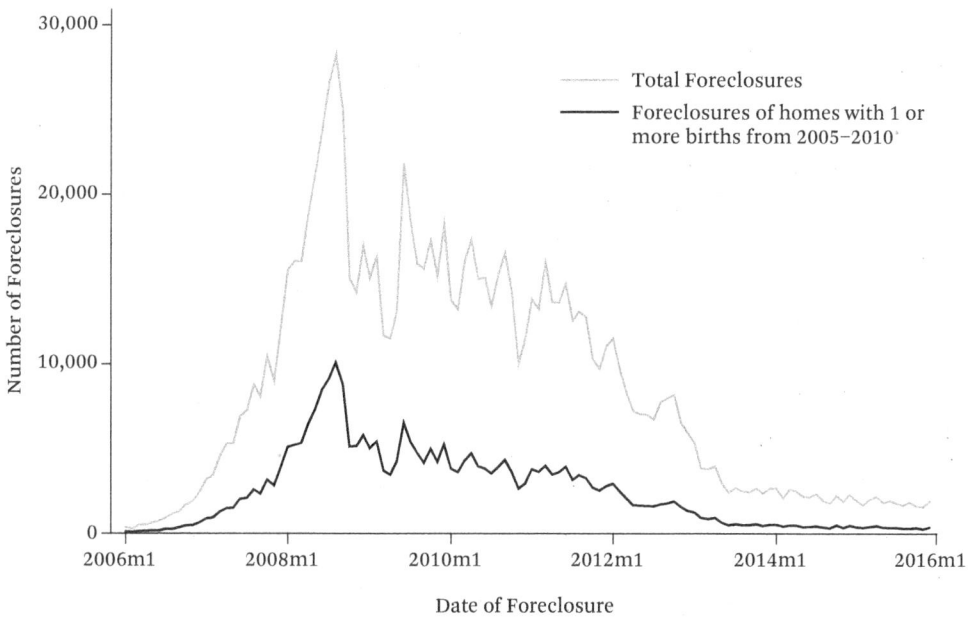

Source: Authors' calculations based on data from linked California foreclosure records and birth certificates.

Figure 3. Proportion of All Foreclosures by Match Type

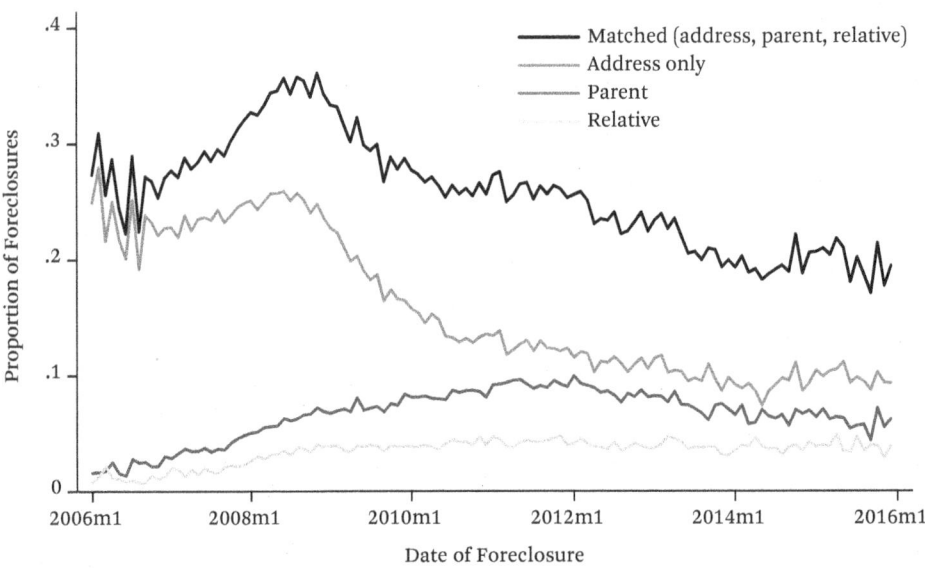

Source: Authors' calculations based on data from linked California foreclosure records and birth certificates.

Figure 4. Proportion of Parent Foreclosures by Race

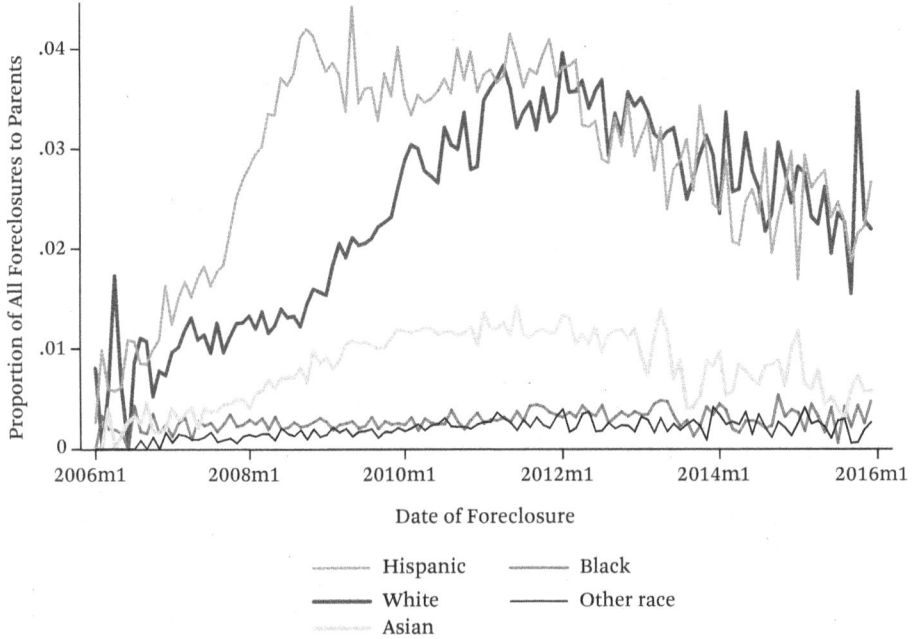

Source: Authors' calculations based on data from linked California foreclosure records and birth certificates.

Figure 5. Proportion of Conceptions to Foreclosed Parents by Date of Foreclosure

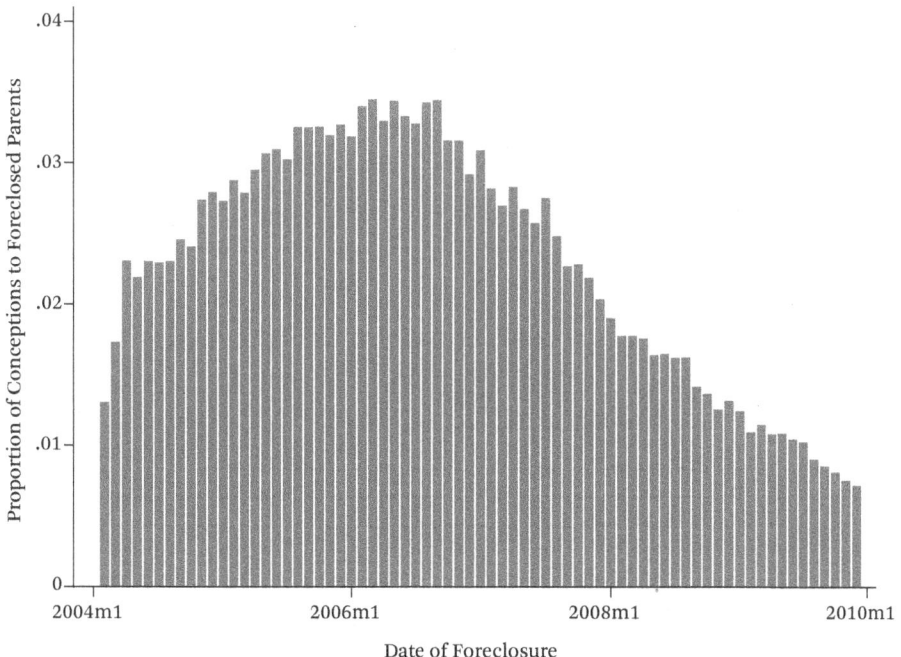

Source: Authors' calculations based on data from linked California foreclosure records and birth certificates.

We compare the match timing across all groups (model 2). Given that higher order births are typically heavier than first births, we use the earliest period (before loan) as our reference group with the expectation that our results would be biased toward the null if foreclosure stress corresponded with lower BWGA. We then include a mother fixed effect (that is, sibling comparison) to compare differences in BWGA within each mother's pair of singleton siblings (model 3).

The use of mother-fixed-effects strategy, though useful in minimizing unobserved confounding between mothers, may introduce selection bias (Kaufman 2013). The strategy relies on observing only a select population of mothers with a specific sequence of events—namely, she had an infant, later took out a loan that resulted in foreclosure, and then had yet another infant. This approach likely biased our results toward the null, given that mothers who were able to detect that foreclosure was imminent were likely to delay pregnancy. In addition, all second births in this sibling pair occurred to an older mother of higher parity, both of which tend to increase BWGA. The fixed-effects approach cannot statistically control for these influences on BWGA when estimating the foreclosure–BWGA relation. Thus, we interpret the mother-fixed-effects coefficients as a lower bound estimate of the true effect.

Births to Mothers Ever-Foreclosed (Exact Match)
In model 4, we restrict our sample to births to mothers who have ever been foreclosed (exact match) and apply the same approach as in model 2. Finally, we investigate how BWGA varies within-mother (model 5). Given the increased probability that foreclosures among those who took out a subprime loan in 2006 or 2007 was plausibly exogenous, we then restrict the sample to parents who took out their loan in 2006 or 2007. This loan cohort group may have been less likely to delay foreclosure due to the nature of their loan, and therefore may have exhibited more acutely the stress of foreclosure. All analyses were conducted using Stata 14.

Figure 6. Matching Birth Certificate and Foreclosure Records by Address and Parents' Names

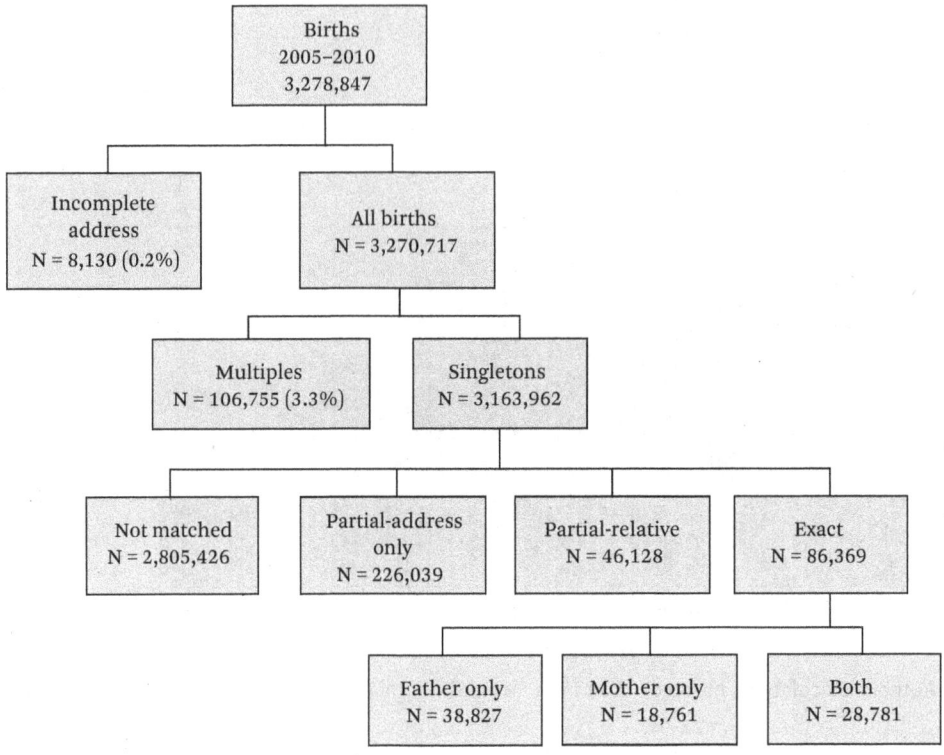

Source: Authors' calculations based on data from linked California foreclosure records and birth certificates.

RESULTS

Figure 6 shows the inclusion criteria and number of births (not unique mothers) classified by the foreclosure matching algorithm. Table 1 shows the mean characteristics of unique mothers by match status: 60,611 mothers were classified as an exact match, 31,374 as a relative match, 155,611 as address-only match, and 2,179,690 as not matched.

Compared with non–mortgage holders, mothers who were mortgage holders or had a child with a mortgage holder (exact match) were older, more likely to be non-Hispanic white, highly educated, had a prior birth, and listed the father on the birth certificate (table 1). In addition, they were less likely to have ever used Medicaid for a birth. Mothers who were residing with a relative who experienced a foreclosure (relative match) were younger and more likely to be Hispanic, less educated, use Medicaid, and be obese (BMI higher than 30) than the other groups.

Table 2 presents the mean characteristics of the mothers with nonmissing data who experienced a foreclosure and the within- and between-standard deviations of the key variables. Mean BWGA was 48.3 with a within-mother standard deviation of 10.4. The mean BWGA is lower than 50 percent because California has a greater proportion of Asian (lighter) births than the United States as a whole does.

Table 3 presents the mean characteristics by loan cohort of mothers who experienced a foreclosure. More than a third of mothers were part of the 2006 cohort. Among mothers who were in the 2006 cohort, there was the lowest proportion of non-Hispanic white mothers, highest proportion of black and Hispanic mothers, highest proportion of Medicaid ever mothers, highest proportion of no father, and lowest proportion with a bachelor's degree.

At the peak in late 2008, ten thousand homes where newborns lived were foreclosed (figure 2), which represents roughly 35 percent of all foreclosures (figure 3). Yet the proportion of all foreclosures of parents (mortgage holders) peaked in 2012 at about 10 percent. The trend in proportion of foreclosures of parents varied widely by race-ethnicity (figure 4), the rate of foreclosed Hispanic parents rising earlier and faster than that of white parents.

Figure 5 plots the monthly proportion of conceptions resulting in live births of foreclosed parents (exact matched). This proportion rose from 1 percent in 2004 to more than 3 percent in 2007, and then returned to its pre-crisis rate.

Main Results

Table 4 presents the results for change in BWGA based on match type and foreclosure timing. Model 1 shows that births to parents with a mortgage that ultimately foreclosed have a 0.93 percentage point higher BWGA than those not matched to a foreclosed home. There was no difference in the relative and address-only matches relative to the unmatched group.

Model 2 includes only those matched to a foreclosed property (n = 339,620). Despite the fact that advancing parity and maternal age is typically associated with heavier infants, births before the loan period are heavier for gestational age than those during and after the foreclosure period. When we include mother fixed effects (model 3), our results cannot reject the null. We find no evidence of within-mother difference in BWGA across various timing of exposure to the foreclosure process.

Model 4 includes only parents of exact matches (n = 82,058), and as in model 2, births before the loan period are heavier for gestational age compared to those before the loan. Inclusion of mother fixed effects attenuates these results and makes the coefficients statistically insignificant (model 5). Restricting our sample further, only to mothers who took out their loan in 2006 and 2007 and including mother fixed effects, we find that relative to before the loan, BWGA was 1.3 percentage points less during the foreclosure and 6.9 points less after it (model 6). Given the within-mother standard deviation of BWGA percentile is 10.4 percentage points, these results represent 13 percent and 66 percent of the average change in BWGA for each mother.

DISCUSSION

Our study indicates strong feasibility of linking birth vital statistics records to foreclosure deed records to examine perinatal outcomes before, during, and after foreclosures. Using the universe of administrative data from both birth certificates and foreclosure records in California, we find that the proportion of foreclosures in California among parents increased from 2 percent in 2006 to 10 percent in 2012. This suggests that families with newborns—particularly Hispanic and white mothers—faced challenges to transitioning to homeownership during this period.

We find that a higher proportion of non-Hispanic white and college-educated mothers had ever gone through foreclosure than those who had not. This finding is not surprising given that the population not exposed to foreclosure contained—in addition to secure homeowners—a large population of renters. However, among mothers who had ever gone through foreclosure, those who received their loan from 2005 to 2007 were more likely to be Hispanic, less educated, and to use Medicaid to pay for their birth than those who received their loans before 2005. Given that our study consists of all foreclosures and births in California, these descriptive statistics provide compelling evidence that the foreclosure crisis disproportionately impacted more marginalized families. Our results are consistent with other work using a subpopulation of adult mortgage holders, demonstrating racial-ethnic disparities in lending and foreclosure in California (Reid and Laderman 2009).

Next, we find that—among all infants with a mother who had a birth while residing in foreclosed home as the owner, relative, or renter—those who were in gestation during the loan period or resided in the home after the foreclosure were worse off than those who were born prior to the mortgage. It remains possible that unobserved factors correlate with both BWGA and a mother's decision to conceive before (rather than after) the initiation of a home loan that ultimately leads to foreclosure. We, however, controlled for maternal race-ethnicity, maternal age, and socioeconomic status in the full sample (model 2); rival explanations of confounding would have to invoke an unmeasured variable

Table 4. Differences in Birthweight for Gestational Age Percentile

	Model 1 Coef./SE	Model 2 Coef./SE	Model 3 Coef./SE	Model 4 Coef./SE	Model 5 Coef./SE	Model 6 Coef./SE
During loan		-0.523***	-0.105	-0.475*	-0.454	-1.331+
		0.12	0.226	0.232	0.436	0.868
After foreclosure		-1.189***	-0.447	-0.287	-0.922	-6.960*
		0.159	0.376	0.569	0.853	2.881
Exact match	0.933***					
	0.0993					
Relative	0.154					
	0.135					
Address only	0.0644					
	0.0628					
First birth	-6.109***	-5.735***	-4.333***	-6.422***	-4.686***	-4.464***
	0.036	0.11	0.183	0.233	0.377	0.763
Male	-0.710***	-0.893***	-0.300*	-0.644***	-0.122	-0.315
	0.0321	0.096	0.143	0.195	0.29	0.586
Age	0.207***	0.280***	0.515***	0.178***	0.634***	0.999***
	0.00307	0.00945	0.0679	0.0206	0.132	0.286
Medicaid	-1.273***	-1.290***	-0.22	-1.361***	-1.202*	-0.829
	0.0399	0.113	0.239	0.258	0.533	1.218
High school graduate	0.567***	0.258+	-0.430+	-0.764*	-0.458	
	0.0465	0.132	0.281	0.334	0.734	
Some college	1.104***	0.902***	-0.439	-0.0957	-0.186	
	0.0518	0.147	0.354	0.338	0.835	
Bachelor's+	0.856***	0.988***	-0.64	-0.2	-0.828	
	0.06	0.183	0.544	0.37	1.078	
Hispanic	-2.501***	-2.822***		-2.764***		
	0.0439	0.131		0.242		
Non-Hispanic black	-9.933***	-10.54***		-7.910***		
	0.0786	0.233		0.54		
Non-Hispanic Asian	-12.20***	-12.52***		-12.27***		
	0.0565	0.185		0.325		
Non-Hispanic other	-2.194***	-2.164***		-3.171***		
	0.1	0.285		0.576		
Observations	3,022,862	339,620	339,620	82,058	82,058	40,164
Fixed effects	No	No	Yes	No	Yes	Yes
Sample	All	Matched	Matched	Parent	Parent	Parent (06/07)

Source: Authors' calculations based on data from linked California foreclosure records and birth certificates.
Note: Coef. (coefficient), SE (standard error). Adjusted for sex, parity, Medicaid, age, education, and race.
+$p < .10$; *$p < .05$; **$p < .01$; ***$p < .001$

not strongly correlated with these covariates but which strongly predicts later timing of fertility and causes a reduction BWGA. We know of no such variable in the perinatal epidemiology literature. When we compare sibling's outcomes of each mother in the fixed-effects approach which controls for unobserved, time-invariant maternal characteristics (model 3), we cannot reject the null, although the direction of this foreclosure effect on BWGA remains negative.

Infants with a mother who had a birth while residing in a foreclosed home as the mortgage holder show lower BWGA than infants who were born prior to the mortgage (model 4). As in the full test, these coefficients are attenuated in the mother-fixed-effects approach (model 5). We suspect that this pattern of results arises from a circumstance in which healthier mothers who were aware of the upcoming foreclosure delayed fertility, but those who were worse off (either unaware or faced other circumstances) gave birth during the loan period.

Finally, our results are particularly compelling when we restrict our sample of all infants with a mother who took out a loan during the peak of the subprime boom (2006–2007) and later had a birth while living in a foreclosed home. In the maternal fixed-effects model, those who were born during the mortgage had a 1.3 percentage point lower BWGA than their siblings in gestation before the mortgage. Those conceived after the foreclosure showed a 7 percentage point lower BWGA than their siblings conceived before the mortgage. These coefficients are substantially large and statistically detectable, accounting for 10 to 70 percent of a within-mother standard deviation.

Our results go against the tide to show that—although advancing maternal age and increasing parity correlate with higher BWGA—infants born during the foreclosure process and after the foreclosure had a lower BWGA relative to their siblings born earlier (before the mortgage). The results, taken in combination with the finding that Hispanic, socioeconomically disadvantaged families were disproportionately represented in the loan cohorts of 2005–2007, suggest that the foreclosure crisis may have contributed to disparities in initial health endowments.

This study has several limitations. Our findings rest on the assumption that different periods of the loan elicited stress and anxiety, yet the magnitude and qualitative experience of this stress was not directly measured. Additionally, we assume that those born prior to the loan are less likely to be exposed to the financial stress. This circumstance may not hold if parents decide to take out a second lien on their home after the birth of their child because they are stressed. We suspect that additional administrative data on finances and loan characteristics may elucidate a nuanced picture of finance-related stress in this population.

Finally, absent routinized data collection on pregnancy loss, we cannot know the extent to which pregnancy loss induced by foreclosure may affect our findings. It remains possible that, consistent with the literature, the most at-risk gestations may be less likely to survive until birth (Bruckner, Mortensen, and Catalano 2016). Such selection in utero may have attenuated the foreclosure coefficient toward the null.

The feasibility of linking public foreclosure records to individual-level vital statistics holds promise for future research applications. The literature examining social and economic stressors before and during the perinatal period tends to rely on mother's self-report of stressors (Hogue et al. 2013), which can introduce strong measurement error (Kesmodel 2018). By contrast, linkage to administrative datasets which records key social and economic setbacks to a family have the potential to minimize measurement error of these important exposures. In addition, the use of linked siblings for perinatal health studies remains an underused strategy to minimize confounding that arises from unmeasured differences in maternal health (Kramer, Dunlop, and Hogue 2014).

Population-level work such as this could complement existing small (and relatively expensive) cohort studies that rely on sampling. For instance, identification of economic (such as credit constraints) and neighborhood stressors experienced at multiple time points among adults of childbearing age could inform basic research on fertility timing, family formation, and migration patterns. In addition, to the extent that the timing, dose, and duration of family stressors can be measured from administrative data, such work has the potential to identify economic and social antecedents of endowments at birth.

REFERENCES

Alexander, Greg R., John H. Himes, Rajni B. Kaufman, Joanne Mor, and Michael Kogan. 1996. "A United States National Reference for Fetal Growth." *Obstetrics and Gynecology* 87(2): 163–68. DOI:10.1016/0029-7844(95)00386-X.

Almond, Douglas, and Janet Currie. 2011. "Killing Me Softly: The Fetal Origins Hypothesis." *Journal of Economic Perspectives* 25(3): 153–72.

Autor, David H., David N. Figlio, Krzysztof Karbownik, Jeffrey Roth, and Melanie Wasserman. 2016. "School Quality and the Gender Gap in Educational Achievement." *American Economic Review* 106(5): 289–95. DOI:10.1177/0003122412440802.

Barfield, Wanda D., Karen M. Clements, Kimberly G. Lee, Milton Kotelchuck, Nancy Wilber, and Paul H. Wise. 2008. "Using Linked Data to Assess Patterns of Early Intervention (EI) Referral Among Very Low Birth Weight Infants." *Maternal and Child Health Journal* 12(1): 24–33.

Been, Vicki, Sewin Chan, Ingrid Gould Ellen, and Josiah R. Madar. 2011. "Decoding the Foreclosure Crisis: Causes, Responses, and Consequences." *Journal of Policy Analysis and Management* 30(2): 388–96.

Black, Sandra E., Paul J. Devereux, and Kjell G. Salvanes. 2007. "From the Cradle to the Labor Market? The Effect of Birth Weight on Adult Outcomes." *Quarterly Journal of Economics* 122(1): 409–39.

Bocian, Debbie Gruenstein, Wei Li, Carolina Reid, and Roberto G. Quercia. 2011. "Lost Ground, 2011: Disparities in Mortgage Lending and Foreclosures." Durham, N.C.: Center for Responsible Lending.

Bradbury, Katharine, Mary A. Burke, and Robert K. Triest. 2014. "Within-School Spillover Effects of Foreclosures and Student Mobility on Student Academic Performance." 2015 Series working paper no. 15-6. Boston, Mass.: Federal Reserve Bank of Boston.

Bruckner, Tim A. 2008. "Metropolitan Economic Decline and Infant Mortality Due to Unintentional Injury." *Accident Analysis and Prevention* 40(6): 1797–803. DOI:10.1016/j.aap.2008.07.011.

Bruckner, Tim A., Ralph Catalano, and Jennifer Ahern. 2010. "Male Fetal Loss in the US Following the Terrorist Attacks of September 11, 2001." *BMC Public Health* 10(1): 273. DOI: 10.1186/1471-2458-10-273.

Bruckner, Tim A., Laust H. Mortensen, and Ralph A. Catalano. 2016. "Spontaneous Pregnancy Loss in Denmark Following Economic Downturns." *American Journal of Epidemiology* 183(8): 701–08.

Buescher, Paul A., Karen P. Taylor, Mary H. Davis, and J. Michael Bowling. 1993. "The Quality of the New Birth Certificate Data: A Validation Study in North Carolina." *American Journal of Public Health* 83(8): 1163–65.

Catalano, Ralph A., and Tim Bruckner. 2005. "Economic Antecedents of the Swedish Sex Ratio." *Social Science & Medicine* 60(3): 537–43.

Catalano, Ralph A., Sidra Goldman-Mellor, Katherine Saxton, Claire Margerison-Zilko, Meenakshi Subbaraman, Kaja LeWinn, and Elizabeth Anderson. 2011. "The Health Effects of Economic Decline." *Annual Review of Public Health* 32(1): 431–50.

CoreLogic. 2017. "United States Residential Foreclosure Crisis: Ten Years Later." Irving, Calif.: CoreLogic. Accessed October 25, 2018. https://www.corelogic.com/research/foreclosure-report/national-foreclosure-report-10-year.pdf.

Coulton, Claudia J., Francisca Richter, Seok-Joo Kim, Robert Fischer, and Youngmin Cho. 2016. "Temporal Effects of Distressed Housing on Early Childhood Risk Factors and Kindergarten Readiness." *Children and Youth Services Review* 68 (September): 59–72.

Currie, Janet, and Enrico Moretti. 2007. "Biology as Destiny? Short- and Long-Run Determinants of Intergenerational Transmission of Birth Weight." *Journal of Labor Economics* 25(2): 231–64.

Currie, Janet, and Erdal Tekin. 2015. "Is There a Link Between Foreclosure and Health?" *American Economic Journal: Economic Policy* 7(1): 63–94. DOI:10.1257/pol.20120325.

Delnord, Marie, Katarzyna Szamotulska, A. D. Hindori-Mohangoo, Béatrice Blondel, A. J. Macfarlane, Nirupa Dattani, Carmen Barona, Sylvie Berrut, Irisa Zile, Rachel H. Wood. Luule Sakkeus, Mika Gissler, and Jennifer Zeitlin. 2016. "Linking Databases on Perinatal Health: A Review of the Literature and Current Practices in Europe." *European Journal of Public Health* 26(3): 422–30.

Downing, Janelle. 2016. "The Health Effects of the Foreclosure Crisis and Unaffordable Housing: A Systematic Review and Explanation of Evidence." *Social Science and Medicine* 162 (August): 88–96. DOI:10.1016/j.socscimed.2016.06.014.

Downing, Janelle, Andrew Karter, Hector Rodriguez, William H. Dow, Nancy Adler, Dean Schillinger, Margaret Warton, and Barbara Laraia. 2016. "No Spillover Effect of the Foreclosure Crisis on Weight Change: The Diabetes Study of Northern California (DISTANCE)." *PloS One* 11(3): e0151334. DOI:10.1371/journal.pone.0151334.

Downing, Janelle, Barbara Laraia, Hector Rodriguez,

William H. Dow, Nancy Adler, Dean Schillinger, E. Margaret Warton, and Andrew J. Karter. 2017. "Beyond the Great Recession: Was the Foreclosure Crisis Harmful to the Health of Individuals with Diabetes?" *American Journal of Epidemiology* 185(6): 429–35. DOI:10.1093/aje/kww171.

Duca, John V. 2013. "Subprime Mortgage Crisis." *Federal Reserve History*, November 23. Accessed October 25, 2018. http://www.federalreservehistory.org/events/detailview/55.

Ellen, Ingrid Gould, Johanna Lacoe, and Claudia Ayanna Sharygin. 2013. "Do Foreclosures Cause Crime?" *Journal of Urban Economics* 74 (March): 59–70.

Feldman, Pamela J., Christine Dunkel-Schetter, Curt A. Sandman, and Pathik D. Wadhwa. 2000. "Maternal Social Support Predicts Birth Weight and Fetal Growth in Human Pregnancy." *Psychosomatic Medicine* 62(5): 715–25.

Financial Crisis Inquiry Commission. 2011. *The Financial Crisis Inquiry Report*. Washington: Government Printing Office.

Flood, Sarah, Miriam King, Steven Ruggles, and J. Robert Warren. 2015. Integrated Public Use Microdata Series, Current Population Survey. Version 4.0 [dataset]. Minnesota: University of Minnesota.

Foote, Christopher L., Kristopher S. Gerardi, and Paul S. Willen. 2012. "Why Did So Many People Make so Many Ex Post Bad Decisions? The Causes of the Foreclosure Crisis." NBER working paper no. 18082. Cambridge, Mass.: National Bureau of Economic Research.

Fukuda, Misao, Kyomi Fukuda, Takashi Shimizu, and Henrik Møller. 1998. "Decline in Sex Ratio at Birth After Kobe Earthquake." *Human Reproduction* 13(8): 2321–22.

Gliklich, Richard E., Nancy A. Dreyer, and Michelle B. Leavy. 2014. "Linking Registry Data with Other Data Sources to Support New Studies." In *Registries for Evaluating Patient Outcomes*, 3rd ed., edited by Richard E. Gliklich and Nancy A. Dreyer. Rockville, Md.: Agency for Healthcare Research and Quality.

Goldenberg, Robert L., Jennifer F. Culhane, Jay D. Iams, and Roberto Romero. 2008. "Epidemiology and Causes of Preterm Birth." *The Lancet* 371(9606): 75–84.

Hack, Maureen, Nancy K. Klein, and H. Gerry Taylor. 1995. "Long-Term Developmental Outcomes of Low Birth Weight Infants." *The Future of Children* 5(1): 176–96.

Hall, Eric S., Neera K. Goyal, Robert T. Ammerman, Megan M. Miller, David E. Jones, Jodie A. Short, and Judith B. Van Ginkel. 2014. "Development of a Linked Perinatal Data Resource from State Administrative and Community-Based Program Data." *Maternal and Child Health Journal* 18(1): 316–25.

Hall, Matthew, Kyle Crowder, and Amy Spring. 2015a. "Neighborhood Foreclosures, Racial/Ethnic Transitions, and Residential Segregation." *American Sociological Review* 80(3): 526–49.

———. 2015b. "Variations in Housing Foreclosures by Race and Place, 2005–2012." *Annals of the American Academy of Political and Social Science* 660(1): 217–37. DOI: 10.1177/0002716215576907.

Hansen, Dorthe, Henrik Møller, and Jørn Olsen. 1999. "Severe Periconceptional Life Events and the Sex Ratio in Offspring: Follow Up Study Based on Five National Registers." *British Medical Journal* 319(7209): 548–49.

Harris-Kojetin, Brian A., and Robert M. Groves. 2017. "Using Government Administrative and Other Data for Federal Statistics." In *Innovations in Federal Statistics: Combining Data Sources While Protecting Privacy*, edited by Brian Harris-Kojetin and Robert Groves. Washington, D.C.: National Academies Press.

Herrchen, Beate, Jeffrey B. Gould, and Thomas S. Nesbitt. 1997. "Vital Statistics Linked Birth/Infant Death and Hospital Discharge Record Linkage for Epidemiological Studies." *Computers and Biomedical Research* 30(4): 290–305.

Hobel, Calvin J., Amy Goldstein, and Emily S. Barrett. 2008. "Psychosocial Stress and Pregnancy Outcome." *Clinical Obstetrics and Gynecology* 51(2): 333–48.

Hogue, Carol J. R., Corette B. Parker, Marian Willinger, Jeff R. Temple, Carla M. Bann, Robert M. Silver, Donald J. Dudley, Matthew A. Koch, Donald R. Coustan, and Barbara J. Stoll. 2013. "A Population-Based Case-Control Study of Stillbirth: The Relationship of Significant Life Events to the Racial Disparity for African Americans." *American Journal of Epidemiology* 177(8): 755–67.

Kaufman, Jay S. 2013. "Some Models Just Can't Be Fixed. A Commentary on Mortensen." *Social Science & Medicine* 76(1): 8–11.

Kesmodel, Ulrik S. 2018. "Information Bias in Epidemiological Studies with a Special Focus on Obstetrics and Gynecology." *Acta Obstetricia et Gynecologica Scandinavica* 97(4): 417–23.

Kramer, Michael R., Anne L. Dunlop, and Carol J. R.

Hogue. 2014. "Measuring Women's Cumulative Neighborhood Deprivation Exposure Using Longitudinally Linked Vital Records: A Method for Life Course MCH Research." *Maternal and Child Health Journal* 18(2): 478–87.

Kramer, Michael S., Lise Goulet, John Lydon, Louise Seguin, Helen McNamara, Clement Dassa, Robert W. Platt, Moy Fong Chen, Henriette Gauthier, Jacques Genest, Susan R. Kahn, Michael Libman, Rima Rozen, André Masse, Louise Milner, Guylaine Asselin, Alice Benjamin, Julia Klein, Gideon Koren. 2001. "Socio-Economic Disparities in Preterm Birth: Causal Pathways and Mechanisms." *Paediatric and Perinatal Epidemiology* 15(S2): 104–23. DOI: 10.1046/j.1365-3016.2001.00012.x.

Krivo, Lauren J., and Robert L. Kaufman. 2004. "Housing and Wealth Inequality: Racial-Ethnic Differences in Home Equity in the United States." *Demography* 41(3): 585–605.

Lu, Michael C., and Neal Halfon. 2003. "Racial and Ethnic Disparities in Birth Outcomes: A Life-Course Perspective." *Maternal and Child Health Journal* 7(1): 13–30.

Margerison-Zilko, Claire E., Ralph Catalano, Alan Hubbard, and Jennifer Ahern. 2011. "Maternal Exposure to Unexpected Economic Contraction and Birth Weight for Gestational Age." *Epidemiology* 22(6): 855–58.

Margerison-Zilko, Claire E., Yu Li, and Zhehui Luo. 2017. "Economic Conditions During Pregnancy and Adverse Birth Outcomes Among Singleton Live Births in the United States, 1990–2013." *American Journal of Epidemiology* 186(10): 1131–39.

Margerison-Zilko, Claire, Sidra Goldman-Mellor, April Falconi, and Janelle Downing. 2016. "Health Impacts of the Great Recession: A Critical Review." *Current Epidemiology Reports* 3(1): 81–91. DOI:10.1007/s40471-016-0068-6.

Martin, Joyce A., Brady E. Hamilton, M. J. Osterman, Anne K. Driscoll, and T. J. Mathews. 2017. "Births: Final Data for 2015." *National Vital Statistics Reports* 66(1): 1–69.

Mullainathan, Sendhil, and Eldar Shafir. 2013. *Scarcity: Why Having Too Little Means So Much*. London: Macmillan.

Oken, Emily, Ken P. Kleinman, Janet Rich-Edwards, and Matthew W. Gillman. 2003. "A Nearly Continuous Measure of Birth Weight for Gestational Age Using a United States National Reference." *BMC Pediatrics* 3(1): 6.

Palmer, Christopher. 2015. "Why Did So Many Subprime Borrowers Default During the Crisis: Loose Credit or Plummeting Prices?" *SSRN Electronic Journal*. DOI: 10.2139/ssrn.2665762.

Pedersen, Carsten Bøcker. 2011. "The Danish Civil Registration System." *Scandinavian Journal of Public Health* 39(S7): 22–25.

Penner, Andrew M., and Kenneth A. Dodge. 2019. "Using Administrative Data for Social Science and Policy." *RSF: The Russell Sage Foundation Journal of the Social Sciences* 5(2): 1–18. DOI: 10.7758/RSF.2019.5.2.01.

Putnam-Hornstein, Emily, Julie A. Cederbaum, Bryn King, and Barbara Needell. 2013. "California's Most Vulnerable Parents: When Maltreated Children Have Children." Agoura Hills, Calif.: Conrad N. Hilton Foundation. Accessed October 25, 2018. http://www.chhs.ca.gov/Child%20Welfare/7California's%20Most%20Vulnerable_Parents_Full_Report_11-11-13.pdf.

Reid, Carolina K., Debbie Bocian, Wei Li, and Roberto G. Quercia. 2017. "Revisiting the Subprime Crisis: The Dual Mortgage Market and Mortgage Defaults by Race and Ethnicity." *Journal of Urban Affairs* 39(4): 469–87.

Reid, Carolina K., and Elizabeth Laderman. 2009. "The Untold Costs of Subprime Lending: Examining the Links Among Higher-Priced Lending, Foreclosures, and Race in California." San Francisco: Federal Reserve Bank of San Francisco.

Ross, Lauren M., and Gregory D. Squires. 2011. "The Personal Costs of Subprime Lending and the Foreclosure Crisis: A Matter of Trust, Insecurity, and Institutional Deception." *Social Science Quarterly* 92(1): 140–63.

Rugh, Jacob S., and Douglas S. Massey. 2010. "Racial Segregation and the American Foreclosure Crisis." *American Sociological Review* 75(5): 629–51.

Schoendorf, Kenneth C., and Amy M. Branum. 2006. "The Use of United States Vital Statistics in Perinatal and Obstetric Research." *American Journal of Obstetrics & Gynecology* 194(4): 911–15.

Strauss, Richard S. 2000. "Adult Functional Outcome of Those Born Small for Gestational Age: Twenty-Six-Year Follow-Up of the 1970 British Birth Cohort." *Journal of the American Medical Association* 283(5): 625–32.

Wasi, Nada, and Aaron Flaaen. 2015. "Record Linkage Using Stata: Pre-Processing, Linking and Reviewing Utilities." *Stata Journal* 15(3): 672–97.

School Climate and the Impact of Neighborhood Crime on Test Scores

AGUSTINA LAURITO, JOHANNA LACOE, AMY ELLEN SCHWARTZ, PATRICK SHARKEY, AND INGRID GOULD ELLEN

Does school climate ameliorate or exacerbate the impact of neighborhood violent crime on test scores? Using administrative data from the New York City Department of Education and the New York City Police Department, we find that exposure to violence in the residential neighborhood and an unsafe climate at school lead to substantial test score losses in English language arts (ELA). Middle school students exposed to neighborhood violent crime before the ELA exam who attend schools perceived to be less safe or to have a weak sense of community score 0.06 and 0.03 standard deviations lower, respectively. We find the largest negative effects for boys and Hispanic students in the least safe schools, and no effect of neighborhood crime for students attending schools with better climates.

Keywords: neighborhood violence, test scores, school climate and environment

Despite the well-documented drop in violent crime in American cities, violence is part of daily life for many children. A growing body of research shows that exposure to neighborhood violence negatively affects academic performance, particularly among children living in high crime neighborhoods (Burdick-Will et al. 2011; Sharkey 2010; Sharkey et al. 2014; Schwartz et al. 2016). Whereas police, government officials, and civic organizations seek to reduce crime, schools can play a role in mitigating the negative effect of exposure to violence on stu-

Agustina Laurito is assistant professor in the Department of Public Administration at the University of Illinois Chicago. **Johanna Lacoe** is researcher at Mathematica Policy Research. **Amy Ellen Schwartz** is Daniel Patrick Moynihan Chair in Public Affairs and professor of economics, public administration, and international affairs in the Maxwell School of Citizenship and Public Affairs at Syracuse University. **Patrick Sharkey** is professor of sociology at New York University. **Ingrid Gould Ellen** is Paulette Goddard Professor of Urban Policy and Planning in the Robert F. Wagner Graduate School of Public Service at New York University.

© 2019 Russell Sage Foundation. Laurito, Agustina, Johanna Lacoe, Amy Ellen Schwartz, Patrick Sharkey, and Ingrid Gould Ellen. 2019. "School Climate and the Impact of Neighborhood Crime on Test Scores." *RSF: The Russell Sage Foundation Journal of the Social Sciences* 5(2): 141–66. DOI: 10.7758/RSF.2019.5.2.08. We gratefully acknowledge the support of the W. T. Grant Foundation. We thank participants at the Russell Sage Foundation conference on Using Administrative Data for Science and Policy for their comments. We also thank the *RSF* editors of this issue and three anonymous reviewers for their feedback. Direct correspondence to: Agustina Laurito at malaurit@uic.edu, 400 S. Peoria St., Room 2113 AEH (MC 278), Chicago, IL 60607; Johanna Lacoe at jlacoe@mathematica-mpr.com, 505 14th St., Suite 800, Oakland, CA 94612–1475; Amy Ellen Schwartz at amyschwartz@syr.edu, 426 Eggers Hall, Syracuse, NY 13244; Patrick Sharkey at patrick.sharkey@nyu.edu, 295 Lafayette St., Fourth Floor, New York, NY 10012; and Ingrid Gould Ellen at ingrid.ellen@nyu.edu, 295 Lafayette St., Second Floor, New York, NY 10012.

Open Access Policy: *RSF: The Russell Sage Foundation Journal of the Social Sciences* is an open access journal. This article is published under a Creative Commons Attribution-NonCommercial-NoDerivs 3.0 Unported License.

dents. Schools vary along many dimensions, including academic quality, student body characteristics, and school climate and environment. In some schools, disorder and conflict may contribute to feelings of fear and vulnerability among students; in other schools, students feel safe and supported. As reported in an article about New York City schools in the *New York Times*, "[school name] is more than just a place to learn algebra and history. A public middle school, it is seen by many families as a safe zone in a crime-plagued neighborhood" (Hu 2014). School climate, including how safe, orderly, and welcoming a school is perceived to be, may affect how youth are able to cope with traumatic events at home or in the residential community. Factors outside of school influence student success, yet little is known about whether school climate moderates the effects of these external events. In this article, we focus on the relationship between school climate and neighborhood crime and answer the question of whether school climate ameliorates or exacerbates the impact of neighborhood crime on academic performance.

To answer this question, we combine detailed administrative and survey data on neighborhood violent crime, student achievement, and student perceptions of school climate. Administrative data are key to our analysis. First, student-level data from the New York City Department of Education allow us to track test scores for the universe of public middle school students in New York City over time and observe their demographic characteristics and residential addresses. Second, incident-level crime data from the New York City Police Department (NYPD), which we geocode to individual street segments throughout the city, provide us with a daily measure of violence occurring on the blockfaces where those students reside. Finally, we use responses to an annual survey that the New York City Department of Education administers to all middle and high school students to construct measures of school climate that we link with students' school records. This linkage provides us a unique look at how the impact of violence varies depending on school climate.

Our empirical approach capitalizes on the exogenous exposure of students to violent events in their neighborhood relative to the timing of standardized exams to estimate the causal acute effect of exposure to neighborhood violence on student outcomes (see Sharkey 2010; Sharkey et al. 2014). Within this framework, we examine how the acute effect of neighborhood crime varies with school climate, measured in different ways. We use factor analysis to combine middle school (grades six to eight) student responses to the New York City Learning Environment Survey and create three school-level scales that capture key constructs of school climate: school safety, disorder, and sense of community. We divide schools into quartiles for each of these dimensions, and estimate how the acute effect of neighborhood violence on English language arts (ELA) and mathematics test scores differs across schools with different climates.

To summarize our findings: students suffer declines in standardized test scores following exposure to a violent crime if they attend schools perceived as unsafe or having a weak sense of community. Specifically, middle school students exposed to violent crime before the test who attend schools that are less safe or have a weak sense of community score 0.06 and 0.03 standard deviations lower in the ELA exam, respectively. Students attending the schools perceived as being the safest, the least disorderly, or having the strongest sense of community suffer no visible reduction in test performance when exposed to violent crime, suggesting that schools with stronger climates might insulate students from the negative effects of neighborhood violence.

LITERATURE REVIEW
Living in a disadvantaged and dangerous neighborhood affects the lives of young people along multiple dimensions, including their health, education, and employment. A growing body of research highlights the effect of exposure to neighborhood violence on the academic attainment and achievement of students (Burdick-Will et al. 2011; Harding 2009; Rendón 2014; Sharkey 2010). In New York City, exposure to a violent assault or homicide in the week before a standardized exam decreases achievement in ELA relative to students who are exposed in the week after the exam (Sharkey et al. 2014).

School climate may also affect the academic performance of students (Thapa et al. 2013). Exposure to violence at school reduces attendance, decreases test scores, increases misbehavior, and reduces the likelihood of high school graduation and college attendance (Bowen and Bowen 1999; Burdick-Will 2013; Grogger 1997). Being the victim of an attack at school is associated with increased student misbehavior and declines in grades (Patton, Woolley, and Hong 2012). Even witnessing violence at school has consequences for student conduct, attitudes about school, and attendance (Janosz et al. 2008). School violence does not have to be extreme to have negative effects on students. Exposure to disorder in school, such as bullying, is negatively related to achievement and is also associated with more serious school violence (Arseneault, Bowes, and Shakoor 2006; Chen 2007; Juvonen, Wang, and Espinoza 2011). Schools may also be able to insulate students from violent neighborhoods by becoming a safe haven from the surrounding violence and disorder (Patton, Woolley, and Hong 2012).

The evidence suggests that four primary dimensions of school climate are likely to influence student performance: school-based violence and disorder, school safety, school discipline, and sense of community within the school. Specifically, in New York City, feeling unsafe at school decreases the academic achievement of middle school students, and the largest effects are found in schools with the most school-based violence (Lacoe 2016).

School disciplinary policy and student perceptions of the fairness of school discipline may also affect achievement. At the school level, the suspension rate is correlated with the share of students who pass competency exams (Raush and Skiba 2004). Youth who are suspended struggle to make academic progress over time and are more likely to drop out of high school than their peers who are not suspended (Arcia 2006; Lacoe and Steinberg 2018). Research has yielded mixed evidence of the efficacy of school security measures, such as metal detectors or police in schools. Some studies find these measures improve perceptions of school climate (Bhatt and Davis 2016). Others find decreases in perceived safety among students and increased involvement with the juvenile justice system (Theriot 2009). Therefore, school disciplinary policies that take zero tolerance approaches emphasizing out-of-school suspensions, or school security measures, may also affect student achievement if they make students feel less safe. Finally, the degree to which students feel connected to their school and a sense of belonging at school can affect their academic achievement. For instance, characteristics of the school environment influence students' level of engagement and participation in school, which in turn may affect their academic achievement (Wang and Holcombe 2010).

These dimensions of school climate may affect youth differently depending on their racial and ethnic background or gender. Johanna Lacoe finds that African American and Hispanic middle school students are more likely to report feeling unsafe in the classroom and on school grounds than white and Asian peers who attend the same schools (2015). Patrick Sharkey and his colleagues find that neighborhood violence has the most pronounced effect on the achievement of black students, with little effect on Hispanic students, despite similar rates of exposure to neighborhood violence between the two groups (2014). Studies also suggest that boys and girls respond differently to school climate and neighborhood violence as well (Harding 2009).

In sum, the literature shows that community violence can be detrimental to students' academic success. Further, research also suggests that the climate within a school (including safety, disorder and support levels) can shape students' academic performance. This article bridges these two literatures to investigate whether and to what extent school climate moderates the effect of neighborhood crime on middle school students' test scores.

THEORY

Several theorists have put forth models and frameworks to describe how multiple environments affect youth outcomes (Bronfenbrenner 2004; Eccles and Roeser 2011; Kirk 2009). In particular, Jacquelynne Eccles and Robert Roeser describe schools as prime developmental contexts for youth during adolescence. Schools are organizations with customs, norms, and rules that influence student interactions, learning, and development on a daily basis (Eccles and Roeser 2011). Schools, however, are not located in a vacuum, but instead are intimately connected to the surrounding neighborhoods, which for most middle school students are where they live. "By attending to the social structure of community conflict, whatever its spatial form, schools can understand, and possibly anticipate, the development of violent confrontations and possibly intervene to redirect the conflict to some other outcome" (Mateu-Gelabert and Lune 2003, 366). School climate may dictate how successfully schools manage youth responses to violence, distinguishing some schools as safe havens.

Building on this literature, our theoretical model in figure 1 describes how schools may play a moderating role in the relationship between exposure to community violence and educational outcomes. Schools may moderate this relationship if school factors change the magnitude or direction of the impact of violent crime on test scores (that is, insulate students from the full effect of exposure, or exacerbate the response to violence).

The primary school climate factors that may affect the relationship between neighborhood violent crime and academic outcomes are school-based violence and disorder, perceptions of safety, discipline, and school supports. The direction of the relationship, however, is unknown. Exposure to violence everywhere (at school and at home) may desensitize students and lessen the effects of neighborhood violence on outcomes. That is, for example, the effects of exposure to neighborhood crime on children attending schools that are perceived as unsafe or disorderly may be smaller or nonexistent. Alternatively, exposure to violence or disorder at school may compound the effect of violence in students' home neighborhoods, causing them to perform poorly on exams, so that we would observe the largest test score losses after exposure to violent crime for children who feel unsafe at school. In contrast, if the school represents a safe haven from a violent home neighborhood, the effect of exposure to violence may be smaller.

Other aspects of the environment can also shape effects of neighborhood violence. If the disciplinary environment is strong and effective, it may support students who feel at risk in their home neighborhood. Likewise, a supportive, inclusive, and friendly school environment may insulate students from the negative effects of exposure to violence in their neighborhood. Conversely, if students feel little sense of community at the school or view the disciplinary environment as unfair or biased, then their academic performance may be more affected by violence they observe or experience outside of the school.

DATA AND MEASURES

We exploit three detailed sources of administrative data. First, we use point-specific crime data from the NYPD on daily violent crime—homicide and aggravated assault—occurrences in New York City from 2004 to 2010.[1] The data contain the spatial coordinates of the crimes that we geocode to the blockface, a street segment between the two closest cross streets (figure A1), using ArcGIS.

Second, we use longitudinal student administrative records from the city's Department of Education. This dataset contains a wide range of student demographic characteristics including student race-ethnicity, gender, participation in special education, and receipt of free or reduced-price meals. It includes test scores on the ELA and mathematics standardized tests, as well as the school students attend and their residential address in each academic year (as of October). Our measure of exposure to neighborhood violence captures the number of violent crimes that occur on students' residential blockface each year they remain enrolled in New York City public schools.[2] Students who

---

1. The data also have information about robberies (excluded from our measure), property crime including burglary, larceny, motor vehicle theft, and arson. The data include other less serious crimes such as drug sales or use, weapons, simple assault, prostitution, gambling, graffiti, trespassing, disturbing the peace, and moving vehicle violations.

2. Our annual address data allow us to track students' exposure to violent crime even when they move. Approximately 85 percent of students never move. These numbers are similar if we use the high poverty sample

Figure 1. Conceptual Model of the Role of School Climate

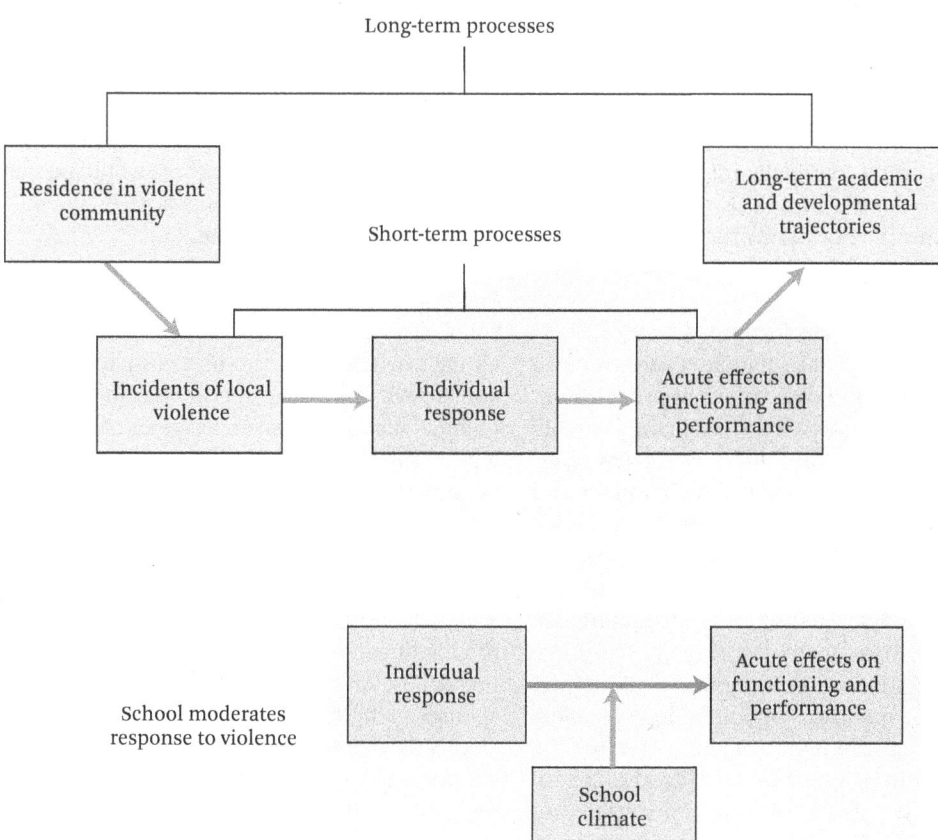

Source: Authors' compilation.

live on the same blockface are considered to be exposed to the same crimes. Note that we do not know if the child actually witnessed the crime. However, because the blockface is such a small geographic unit and homicides and violent assaults are serious offenses, it is likely that students will have either direct or indirect knowledge of the crime.

Third, to obtain measures of school climate we use student answers to the Learning Environment Survey collected by the New York City Department of Education. The survey is administered annually to students, parents and teachers in grades six to twelve during the spring semester (between mid-February and mid-March). In this article, we focus on all middle school students' responses to the survey. The survey started in 2007, the first year of our panel.

Our analytic sample contains 16,146 students in 533 schools in grades six to eight from academic years 2006–2007 to 2009–2010. We restrict the sample to students living in high poverty census tracts who are exposed to violent crime within one week—seven days—of the ELA test.[3] We focus on high poverty census tracts because it allows us to exclude sections

---

or the full sample of students. Of those who move, about 13 percent move only once, and 1.2 percent move more than once during the sample period. Results reported in the article are not sensitive to using a sample of non-movers (table B8).

3. High poverty census tracts are those with a child poverty rate above the citywide median in 2000. We focus on this sample because most of the analyses that follow examine effects on ELA. Note that we also conduct

of the city that have high crime rates but that are relatively wealthy, such as midtown Manhattan.[4] Further, as prior work shows (Sharkey et al. 2014), exposure to violence has larger effects on these students, and thus understanding the role of school climate for these more vulnerable students seems especially important. We also exclude students in charter schools, in ungraded special education, and those exposed to crime both before and after the test.

Constructing School Climate Measures

To construct school climate measures we take both a theory- and data-driven approach similar to that of Matthew Kraft, William Marinell, and Darrick Yee (2016). First, we review questions in the Learning Environment Survey and select those that capture the four dimensions of school climate identified in the literature as important determinants of student outcomes: safety, disorder, sense of community, and disciplinary environment. We identify seventeen survey questions in these domains. For example, we use questions about feelings of safety in classrooms, in hallways and locker rooms, and on school grounds outside the school building. We also select questions related to bullying, fighting, substance use, gangs, perceptions of disciplinary fairness, conflict resolution, and the presence of safety agents. Finally, we also use questions about whether students feel welcome at school, treat each other with respect, or just look out for themselves. All responses consist of a scale from one to four.[5] We code all responses so that an answer of one in the survey would be the best outcome, an answer of two would be the second best outcome, an answer of three would be the third best outcome, and an answer of four would be the worst outcome.

We use exploratory principal components factor analysis to identify whether student responses capture one overall measure of school climate or map into distinct climate dimensions. We rotate the factor loadings using oblique rotation because it assumes correlation among the factors instead of treating them as exogenous, and we expect the different climate measures to be correlated with one another.[6] For example, a school that students perceive as highly disorderly is also likely to be perceived as unsafe. Rotating factor loadings maximizes the loadings for each factor, facilitating interpretability. After rotation, we find that the responses to the survey questions map onto three factors that capture three dimensions of school climate: safety, sense of community, and disorder and conflict.[7] Contrary to expectations, there is no separate dimension for the disciplinary environment. The first factor (safety) explains 28 percent of the item variance, the second factor (sense of community) approxi-

---

analyses using math test scores as the outcome. These analyses use a sample of students exposed within seven days of the mathematics test. This sample contains 16,676 student-year observations in 535 schools for students living in high poverty census tracts. Testing dates vary by year and grade. The ELA test was administered between January and early February from 2007 to 2009, and in April in 2010. The math test was administered later in the spring (between March and May depending on the year).

4. Students in high poverty census tracts make up 67 percent of the overall sample of students in grades six through eight and thus are representative of a significant portion of the public school population in the city. This number is roughly 89 percent when we restrict the sample to students exposed within one week of the ELA test. By restricting the sample in this way we reduce the potential for results to be overly influenced by anomalous sections of New York City, such as midtown Manhattan, which is a very wealthy area but also contains a high crime rate because of its density of commercial and tourist activity and very high daytime population. That said, results are largely unchanged when estimating our models on the full sample of students.

5. Some questions include responses such as: all of the time, most of the time, some of the time, never. Other questions include responses: strongly agree, agree, disagree, and strongly disagree.

6. We created climate scales using exogenous rotation as well. These measures are highly correlated with the ones used in this article. Exogenous rotation is preferred when measures are used as predictors in the same model to avoid multicollinearity (Kraft, Marinell, and Yee 2016).

7. These three factors have eigenvalues greater than one (Kaiser-Guttman stopping criterion).

Table 1. Rotated Factor Loadings, School Climate Measures

	Factor 1: Safety	Factor 2: Sense of Community	Factor 3: Disorder-Conflict
I am safe on school property outside my school.	0.65		
I am safe in the hallways, bathrooms, and locker rooms at my school.	0.68		
I am safe in my classes.	0.76		
Discipline in my school is fair.	0.62		
There is a person or program in my school that helps students resolve conflicts.	0.71		
The presence and actions of school safety agents help promote a safe and respectful learning environment.	0.50		
I feel welcome at school.	0.58		
Students threaten or bully other students at school.		0.51	
Students get into physical fights at my school.		0.55	
Most students in my school help and care about each other.		0.65	
Most students in my school just look out for themselves.		0.66	
Most students in my school treat each other with respect.		0.65	
I stay home because I don't feel safe at school.			0.67
Students use alcohol or illegal drugs while at school.			0.80
There is gang activity in my school.			0.71
Adults at my school yell at students.			0.51
There is conflict in my school based on race, culture, religion, sexual orientation, gender, or disabilities.			0.58

Source: Authors' calculations using data from the New York City Learning Environment Survey.
Note: Results from factor analyses. Table shows factor loadings after oblique rotation. Loadings less than 0.4 are omitted.

mately 23 percent, and the third factor (disorder) 22 percent. Table 1 presents the relevant survey questions in each factor with the corresponding factor loadings. Consistent with the literature, we show those with factor loadings of 0.4 or greater.[8]

To create school safety, disorder, and sense of community scales we compute factor scores for each student answering the surveys.[9] To obtain school-level measures we follow Kraft, Marinell, and Yee and average those scores for each school across years to obtain time invariant school climate scales or indices (2016).[10] The resulting scales are centered on zero. Higher

---

8. To further check the robustness of these measures, we calculated Cronbach's alpha for the three constructs separately, including all relevant questions we identified for each construct. Overall, we find that the three school climate measures are highly reliable, having a Cronbach's alpha reliability value of 0.7 or greater.

9. Weighted sums of standardized versions of the questions, with the factor loadings used as weights.

10. Despite some variation over time in school climate measures, perceptions of school climate do not appear to change substantially over time. When we divide the three scales into quartiles, the majority of schools always stay in the same quartile (32 to 37 percent, depending on the measure) or experience small changes (move up or down one quartile, 35 to 38 percent of schools). Less than 2 percent of schools move three or more quartiles from one year to the next (for example, move from an unsafe (Q4) school to a safe (Q1) school). Thus, a minority of schools experience large changes in perceptions of school climate. Further, the direction of the changes in perceptions of school climate over time is not always consistent. In some schools, perceptions of climate improve

Figure 2. Distribution of School Climate Measures Across Schools

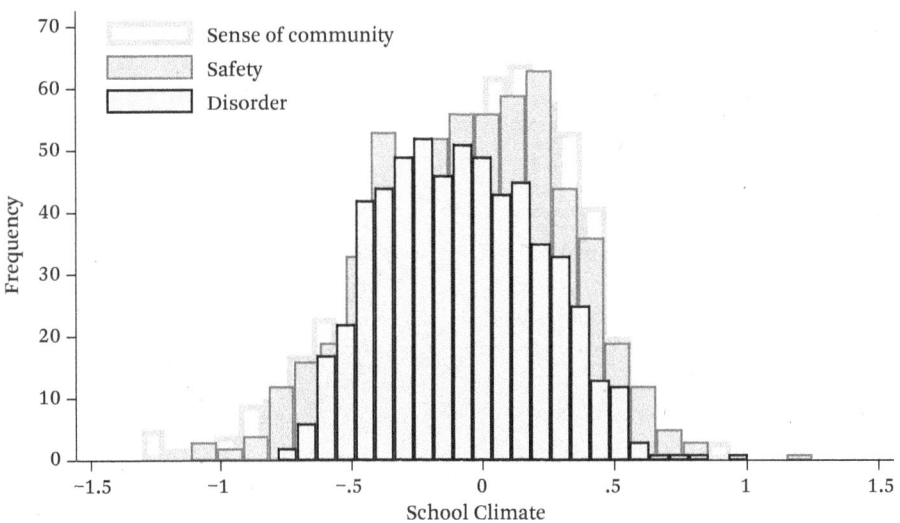

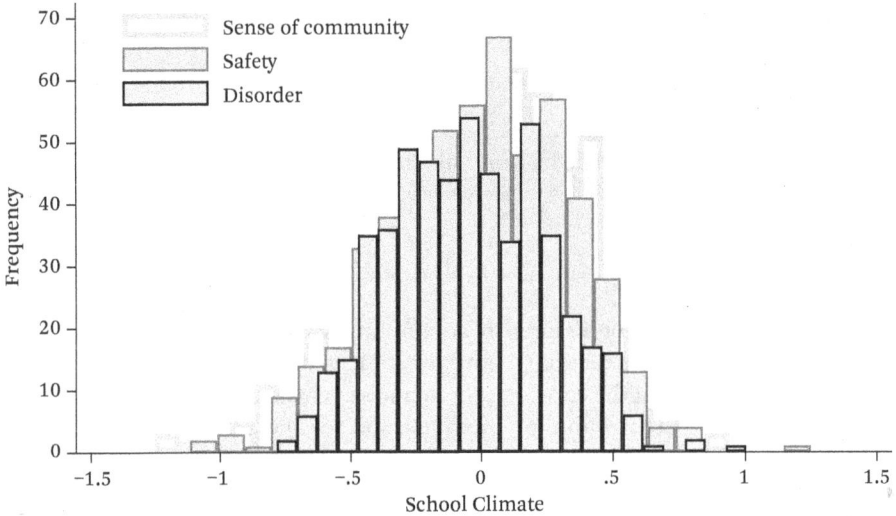

Source: Authors' calculations using data from the New York City Learning Environment Survey.
Note: Panel A sample consists of 593 schools. Panel B sample is restricted to 533 schools in the high poverty sample of students exposed to violent crime both before or after the ELA test.

one year, but decline in the next. It is unclear if these movements reflect meaningful variations in the school environment students face each year. Exploiting this annual variation to estimate our effects may just leave measurement error as the source of variation. Using time invariant measures minimizes this problem while still allowing us to extract meaningful conclusions about the relationship between the school environment and neighborhood crime. Not all students answer the surveys. Table A1 shows the percentage of students who answered all seventeen questions in our measures. Response rates are low on the first year of the survey but significantly increase after that (reaching about 80 percent).

values indicate weaker climates and lower values indicate stronger climates. Panel A of figure 2 plots the distribution of these scales across all the 593 schools in our data (including those not in high poverty census tracts). Overall, the disorder scale shows less variation: most values are concentrated around zero and below (less disorder) and no schools are perceived as having either very high levels or very low levels of disorder. Variation is greater in the sense of community measure, and the distribution is more skewed. Most schools are perceived to have a lower than average sense of community (indicated by positive values on the scale), but more schools are perceived as having very strong sense of community than as having a very weak sense. We observe a similar pattern for the school safety scale.

The school climate in the schools the students in our sample attend might differ from the full sample of schools, but we find they look fairly similar. Panel B of figure 2 shows the distribution of school climate measures for the 533 schools in the analytical sample and demonstrates that these distributions do not look substantially different from the full sample.[11]

EMPIRICAL STRATEGY

Our empirical strategy compares students exposed to violent crime within a one-week window around standardized testing dates. Specifically, we compare the test performance of students exposed to violent crime in the week before a standardized test with that of otherwise similar students exposed in the week after. The identifying assumption is that the occurrence of a violent crime on a student's residential blockface one week before or after the test is conditionally random within this window. This strategy yields causal estimates of the acute effect of violent crime on test scores.

The empirical strategy relies on the assumption that students exposed to violent crime within a week of the ELA or math exam are very similar to each other. Students exposed to violent crime one week before and after the tests are quite similar demographically (see table A2). Hispanics make up the majority of students in all four samples (more than 50 percent), and black students represent approximately 40 percent. The samples are all evenly distributed between male and female students, and students receiving free or reduced-price lunch are overrepresented, as are students whose language at home is not English. To further test the assumption that students exposed to neighborhood crime before and after the test are similar, we estimate a regression model predicting exposure in the week before the ELA and math tests as a function of individual demographic characteristics. These models also include grade, year, and borough fixed effects. Results from a joint-F test on the demographic controls confirm that our sample is balanced, supporting the appropriateness of the identification assumption (table A2).[12]

We begin by estimating a baseline specification as shown in equation (1)

$$Test_{it} = \alpha_t + \beta Crime_{it} + X'_{it}\theta + \gamma_g + \varepsilon_{it}. \quad (1)$$

In this model, Test represents student i's test score on the ELA or math exam, measured as a z-score standardized for each grade citywide with a mean of zero and a standard deviation of one. Crime takes a value of one if a student was exposed to a homicide or aggravated assault on their block in the week before the ELA test, and is zero if they were exposed in the week after the test. The coefficient of interest is β, and it can be interpreted as a causal estimate of the acute effect of exposure to violent crime. The model also includes a vector (X') of student demographic controls: gender, race-ethnicity, eligibility for free or reduced-price lunch, special education, limited English proficiency, foreign born, home language not English, and over age for grade. Grade fixed effects are γ_g, year fixed effects are α_t, and ε_{it} is the usual error term. We follow this baseline specification by adding student i's test scores lagged one year, thus controlling for a student's prior performance.

To estimate whether school climate moder-

---

11. For additional details on these distributions see table B1 in the online appendix, available at https://www.rsfjournal.org/content/5/2/141/tab-supplemental.

12. Regression results of the balance test are available in table B2 of the online appendix.

ates the acute effect of neighborhood crime, we first divide schools into quartiles based on their scores on the three climate perception measures: safety, disorder, and sense of community. Schools in the first quartile are those with stronger climates (perceived as safe) and those in the fourth quartile are those with weaker climates (perceived as unsafe). Then, for each climate measure, we estimate our baseline model stratified by climate quartile. In this way, we compare the test performance of students exposed to violent crime on their block in the week before the test with those exposed in the week after attending schools that have similar climates. Specifically, we estimate as follows:

$$Test_{it} = \alpha_t + \beta Crime_{it} * Climate_i^{q1-4} + \rho Climate_i^{q1-4} + X'_{it}\theta + \gamma_g + \varepsilon_{it}.$$

We extend our baseline specification by adding a set of interactions between the crime exposure indicator and each of the four climate quartiles. In this model, β yields estimates of the acute effect for each climate quartile by comparing students exposed before the test with those exposed after attending schools in the same quartile. For example, we compare the test performance of a student exposed to violent crime in the week before the ELA test with a similar student exposed in the week after, who both attend schools perceived as being the least safe (quartile four). If schools that are perceived as safer, or less disorderly, or with a stronger sense of community act as safe havens for students living in violent neighborhoods, we may see no difference in test performance between children exposed to homicides and violent assaults in the week before the test or after. Conversely, if schools with weaker climates (safety, disorder, and sense of community) exacerbate the effect of living in violent neighborhoods, we may see a decrease in performance after exposure to violent crime.

Schools with different climates may vary on a number of other characteristics that can influence both school climate and student performance. We examine the robustness of our main results through a series of tests. First, we add school-level, time-varying spending data, teacher-pupil ratio, and reported incidents of school violence to control for other school characteristics that might be correlated with student achievement or contribute to school climate. Second, we also estimate models with school fixed effects to control for time-invariant school characteristics that might be correlated both with perceptions of school climate and student achievement. Third, we conduct a falsification test using exposure to property crimes as our main crime exposure indicator. If students are, indeed, affected by neighborhood violent crime then we should see no effect of exposure to less serious property crimes on test scores. Finally, we test the robustness of our results using the full sample of students instead of the high poverty sample.

RESULTS

We begin by examining the demographic composition of schools with stronger and weaker climates for the three climate measures: safety, disorder, and sense of community. The most striking differences across quartiles concern the racial-ethnic composition of the students (figure 3, panel A). Black students are overrepresented in schools with weak climates (quartile four) across the three climate scales. Indeed, more than 50 percent of black students attend schools in quartile four across the three climate dimensions. In contrast, schools in quartile one are more than 60 percent Hispanic. We observe a similar pattern in schools with more mixed climates (quartiles two and three). Students who are white or Asian are the smallest group in the sample, and are also more likely to attend schools that are safer, less disorderly, and more community-oriented. As for gender, differences across quartiles are relatively small but girls are more likely to attend schools in the first quartile. This is a high poverty sample, thus more than 90 percent of students are eligible for free or reduced-price lunch, however, the percentage of poor students is slightly higher in quartile four schools than in the other three quartiles. Students whose home language is not English are less likely to attend schools with the weakest climates. In contrast, students who are over age for grade are overrepresented in quartile four

Figure 3. Student Characteristics, High Poverty Sample

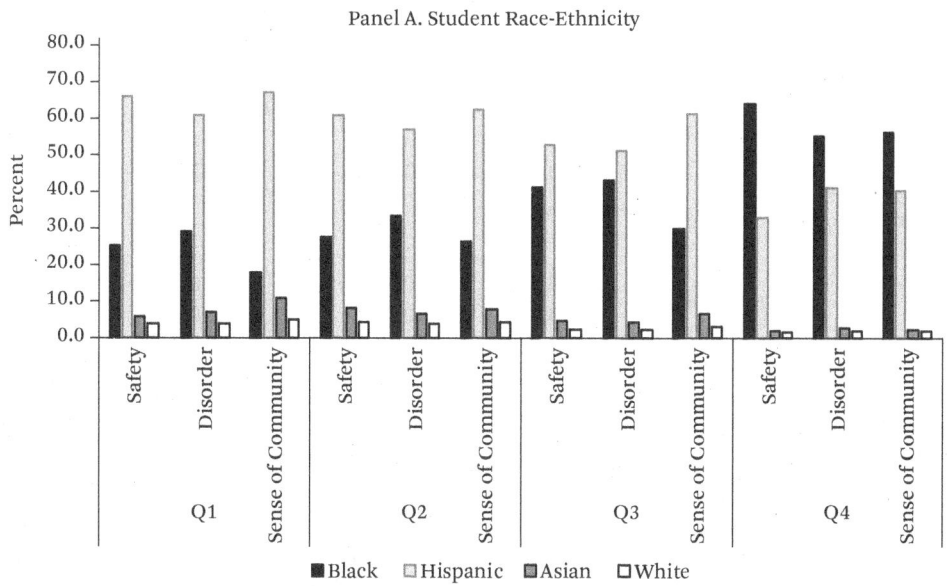

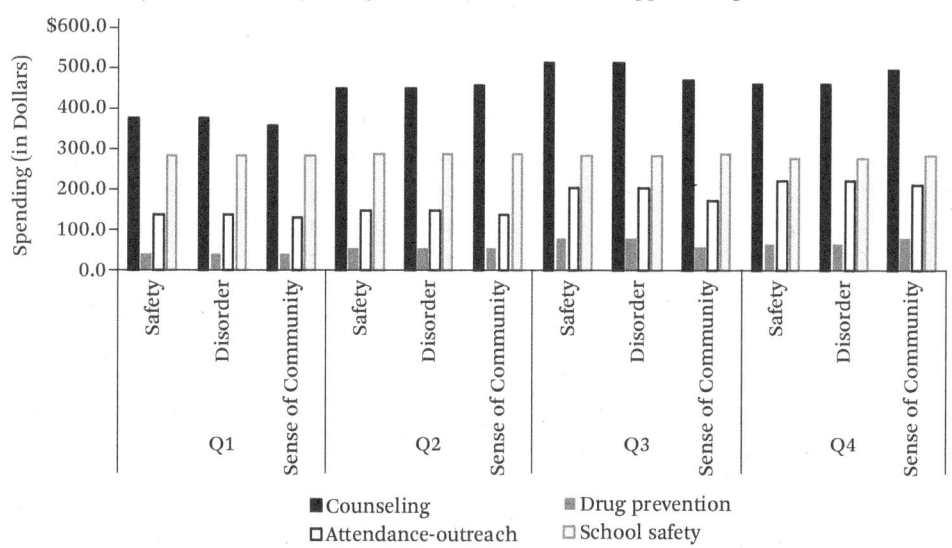

Source: Authors' calculations using data from the New York City Learning Environment Survey. Panel A: New York City public schools, student-level administrative data, provided to New York University and Syracuse University by the New York City Department of Education. Panel B: School-based expenditure reports, New York City Department of Education.
Note: Sample restricted to students living in high poverty census tracts and exposed to a violent crime on their block in the week before the ELA test or in the week after. Students exposed both before and after the test are excluded. Sample includes students in grades six to eight between academic years 2006–2007 and 2009–2010.

Table 2. Regression Results: Exposure to Neighborhood Violent Crime and Test Scores, One-Week Window, High Poverty Sample

	ELA		Math	
DV: z-score	(1)	(2)	(3)	(4)
Crime	−0.015	−0.005	−0.015	−0.001
	(0.014)	(0.010)	(0.017)	(0.012)
Student controls	Y	Y	Y	Y
Lagged test scores	N	Y	N	Y
Observations	16,146	16,146	16,676	16,676
R^2	0.229	0.459	0.193	0.532

Source: Authors' calculations using NYPD complaint data and New York City public schools student-level administrative data, provided to New York University and Syracuse University by the New York City Department of Education.
Note: Standard errors in parentheses (clustered at the school level). Student controls include female, black, Hispanic, Asian, free lunch, reduced-price lunch, special education, limited English proficiency, foreign born, home language not English, over age for grade. All models include grade, year, fixed effects, and an indicator for missing lagged test scores. Sample includes students in grades six to eight between 2006–2007 and 2009–2010.

schools across the three dimensions. Across all climate measures, schools are fairly similar in the percent of students with limited English proficiency, the share of foreign born, and those in special education.[13]

Panel B of figure 3 shows differences for school spending categories: counseling, drug prevention programs, attendance and outreach, and school safety.[14] Climate quartiles show no large differences for these school resources. In general, spending in counseling and attendance-outreach is lower in quartile one schools than in the other quartiles. As for other school resources (not shown), per pupil spending on classroom instruction is slightly higher in quartile three and four schools; pupil-teacher ratios and spending on school leadership are fairly similar across quartiles. Perhaps not surprisingly, school violence increases as we move from quartile one to quartile four schools across all dimensions.[15]

Does the Acute Effect of Violent Crime on Test Scores Vary with the School Climate?

In the regression results that follow we show models with demographic controls, and with lagged test scores. In most cases these results are very similar to each other and we show all of them for completeness. In the discussion, however, we focus on those that account for a student's prior performance as the preferred specification. Results from our baseline regression (table 2) show no overall average acute effect of exposure to violent crime on ELA test scores for middle school students (grades six and seven). That is, middle school students exposed to violent crime in the week before the ELA test perform no differently on average than comparable students exposed after.[16] This average effect, however, masks significant variation across schools as figure 4 shows, suggesting that school-level factors might play a role in

---

13. This information is available in tabular form in the online appendix (panel A, tables B3–B5).

14. These are selected budget items under the instructional support spending category.

15. Detailed information in tabular form is available in the online appendix (panels B and C, tables B2–B4).

16. In prior work, the acute effect on ELA test scores is driven by students in elementary school grades (for more details, see Sharkey et al. 2014).

Figure 4. School-Specific Random Slopes, Violent Crime

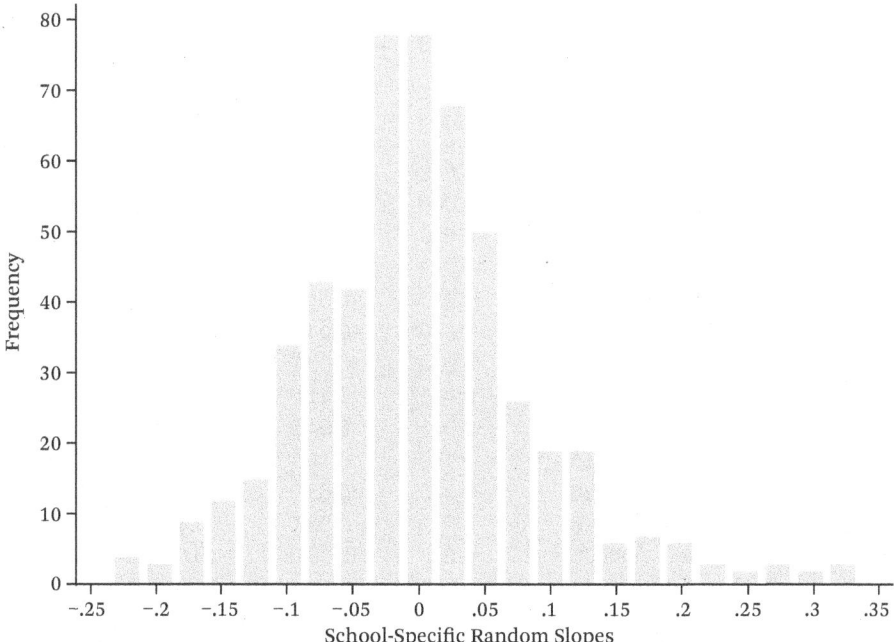

Source: Authors' calculations using NYPD complaint data and New York City public schools student-level administrative data, provided to New York University and Syracuse University by the New York City Department of Education.
Note: Results from estimating the baseline regression in our paper as an HLM model with school random intercepts and slopes. Graph shows best linear unbiased predictions.

ameliorating or exacerbating the acute effect. Indeed, when we explore whether results vary across school climate quartiles, we find that the average estimate conceals significant heterogeneity by school climate.

Table 3 shows that exposure to violence affects students in schools with the weakest climates (quartile four). Students attending schools deemed the least safe (quartile four) score 0.06 standard deviations lower as a result of exposure to violent crime one week before testing (column 2). Similarly, column 6 shows students in schools that have the weakest sense of community (quartile four) score 0.03 standard deviations lower after exposure to violent crime in the week before the test (significant at the 10 percent level). We do not find strong evidence of an acute effect for students attending more disorderly schools. In models not accounting for prior performance (column 3), students exposed to violent crime prior to the ELA test attending schools perceived as the most disorderly (quartile four) score 0.08 standard deviations lower (significant at the 10 percent level). Once we control for prior performance, this coefficient drops to –0.04 and is no longer statistically significant.[17]

Results in this section indicate that safety and sense of community are the most critical elements of school climate in moderating the effects of violence. Our findings suggest that schools have the potential to insulate students from the negative effects of exposure to neighborhood violence on academic performance, shown by the absence of any negative effect on test scores for students attending schools with

---

17. Note that this quartile has the least number of observations (1,013) relative to quartile four for the other scales (2,550 for safety and 6,016 for sense of community).

Table 3. Regression Results: ELA, Exposure to Neighborhood Violent Crime, and School Climate Quartile

	Safety		Disorder		Sense of Community	
DV: z-score ELA	(1)	(2)	(3)	(4)	(5)	(6)
Crime*Q1	−0.055	−0.032	−0.051	−0.002	−0.073	−0.019
	(0.038)	(0.029)	(0.039)	(0.031)	(0.055)	(0.050)
Crime*Q2	0.015	0.021	−0.006	−0.000	0.014	0.019
	(0.025)	(0.019)	(0.026)	(0.019)	(0.031)	(0.025)
Crime*Q3	−0.010	0.002	−0.009	−0.007	−0.005	0.007
	(0.022)	(0.016)	(0.017)	(0.014)	(0.021)	(0.016)
Crime*Q4	−0.070*	−0.060*	−0.080⁺	−0.042	−0.039⁺	−0.031⁺
	(0.030)	(0.024)	(0.044)	(0.036)	(0.021)	(0.016)
Q1	0.274**	0.156**	0.425**	0.211**	0.456**	0.216**
	(0.058)	(0.035)	(0.061)	(0.043)	(0.083)	(0.046)
Q2	0.057	0.019	0.189**	0.108**	0.121**	0.052⁺
	(0.040)	(0.026)	(0.049)	(0.037)	(0.042)	(0.027)
Q3	−0.020	−0.016	0.041	0.037	0.014	−0.006
	(0.043)	(0.028)	(0.043)	(0.034)	(0.034)	(0.022)
Student controls	Y	Y	Y	Y	Y	Y
Lagged test scores	N	Y	N	Y	N	Y
Observations	16,146	16,146	16,146	16,146	16,146	16,146
R^2	0.241	0.463	0.252	0.465	0.245	0.463

Source: Authors' calculations using NYPD complaint data and New York City public schools student-level administrative data, provided to New York University and Syracuse University by the New York City Department of Education.
Note: Standard errors in parentheses (clustered at the school level). Student controls include: black, Asian, Hispanic, free and reduced-price lunch, special education, limited English proficiency, foreign born, home language not English, and over age for grade. All models include grade and year fixed effects, and an indicator for missing lagged test scores. Sample excludes students exposed both before and after the ELA test. Sample includes students in grades six through eight between academic year 2006–2007 and 2009–2010.
⁺$p < .1$; *$p < .05$; **$p < .01$

strong (quartile one) or mixed climates (quartiles two and three).[18]

Subgroup Analyses

Of course, school climate may not matter equally for all students; some students may be more sensitive to the climate of their school. In this section, we explore whether the moderating effect of school climate varies by gender and race-ethnicity. Gender analyses are motivated by the fact that boys and girls may use different coping mechanisms to deal with traumatic events, and may respond differently within these varied school climates (Rasmussen, Aber, and Bhana 2004). As for race-ethnicity, research has shown significant racial differences in sensitivity to violence. In particular, Sharkey and his colleagues find that the school performance of

---

18. We also estimate the probability that a student would pass the ELA test. We find that students in the least safe schools are 5 percentage points less likely to pass the test, and that those in the more disorderly schools are 3 percentage points less likely to pass. Students in schools with a weaker sense of community are also 5 percentage points less likely to pass the ELA test, but this effect is significant at the 10 percent level (see online appendix table B6).

Table 4. Regression Results: ELA, Quartile 4 Schools by Subgroup

DV: z-score ELA	Safety		Disorder		Sense of Community	
	(1)	(2)	(3)	(4)	(5)	(6)
Panel A: Gender						
Crime*female	−0.043	−0.025	−0.064	0.000	−0.044	−0.023
	(0.041)	(0.030)	(0.058)	(0.053)	(0.026)	(0.019)
Crime*male	−0.094*	−0.100**	−0.094	−0.082+	−0.036	−0.041+
	(0.043)	(0.036)	(0.060)	(0.046)	(0.029)	(0.021)
Female	0.062	0.019	0.104	0.040	0.109**	0.060**
	(0.047)	(0.036)	(0.072)	(0.055)	(0.026)	(0.020)
Observations	2,550	2,550	1,013	1,013	6,244	6,244
R^2	0.174	0.448	0.193	0.423	0.190	0.433
Panel B: Race-ethnicity						
Crime*black	−0.066+	−0.054+	−0.047	0.014	−0.037	−0.026
	(0.038)	(0.030)	(0.048)	(0.036)	(0.027)	(0.021)
Crime*Hispanic	−0.081	−0.091+	−0.105	−0.091	−0.037	−0.040
	(0.059)	(0.050)	(0.092)	(0.083)	(0.031)	(0.026)
Black	0.008	−0.025	−0.129	−0.132*	0.027	0.018
	(0.060)	(0.046)	(0.079)	(0.058)	(0.037)	(0.028)
Observations	2,470	2,470	969	969	6,016	6,016
R^2	0.169	0.449	0.183	0.419	0.184	0.431
Student controls	Y	Y	Y	Y	Y	Y
Lagged test scores	N	Y	N	Y	N	Y

Source: Authors' calculations using NYPD complaint data and New York City public schools student-level administrative data, provided to New York University and Syracuse University by the New York City Department of Education.

Note: Standard errors in parentheses (clustered at the school level). Student controls include black, Asian, Hispanic, free or reduced-price lunch, special education, limited English proficiency, foreign born, home language not English, and over age for grade. All models include grade and year fixed effects, and an indicator for missing lagged tests scores. Sample includes students in grades six through eight between academic year 2006–2007 and 2009–2010. Panel B sample excludes students who are Asian or white.

+$p < .1$; *$p < .05$; **$p < .01$

black students is especially sensitive to violent environments, and that exposure to violence has little effect on the academic performance of Hispanic students (2014). It is possible that differences in the school environments experienced by black and Hispanic students (and the concentration of black students in schools with weaker climates) explain these differences. In the analyses that follow, we focus on schools with weak climates (quartile four).[19]

Our results suggest that the negative effect of exposure to neighborhood crime is concentrated among boys attending weak climate schools. As panel A of table 4 shows, boys exposed to violent crime in the week before the ELA exam score approximately 0.10 standard deviations lower when they attend the least safe schools. They score 0.08 standard deviations lower (significant at the 10 percent level) in the most disorderly schools, and 0.04 standard deviations lower in schools with weaker sense of community (also significant at the 10 percent

---

19. Results reported for the weak climate schools in each category only because there are no effects of attendance at a strong or mixed climate school on test scores (tables available from authors on request).

level). There is no observed effect for girls, but these coefficients are not statistically different than those for boys.

Next, we explore differences by race and ethnicity. Due to sample size limitations, these models include only Hispanic and black students.[20] Black students exposed to violent crime before the ELA test attending schools perceived to be the least safe, score 0.05 standard deviations lower on the ELA exam (table 4, panel B). The largest effect, however, is for Hispanic students in the least safe schools. These students score 0.09 standard deviations lower. This finding suggests that stronger school climates might offer some protective effect for Hispanic students. We observe no effect of exposure to violence on test scores among black and Hispanic students who attend more disorderly schools or schools with the weakest sense of community. Note that the samples in the disorder measure get very small, so we may be underpowered to detect an effect. Coefficients for black and Hispanic students are not statistically different from each other and, in general, results in this table are only significant at the 10 percent level.[21]

Robustness and Falsification Tests

The results so far show that school climate may play an important role in moderating the effects of neighborhood violence on student outcomes. However, there may be school-level confounders that bias these results. School climate measures may reflect differences in other factors that are correlated with student perceptions and achievement. To address this issue, we add several additional sources of administrative data to construct time-varying school-level controls. First, we combine our student-level data with the school-based expenditure reports. These data provide detailed information regarding school spending by budget item as well as pupil-teacher ratios. We select spending on classroom instruction, leadership, and relevant instructional support spending categories (counseling services, drug prevention programs, attendance-outreach, and school safety). Second, we add the rate of reported school violent incidents from the violent and disruptive incident reports data. As an additional test, we reestimate our models adding school fixed effects to control for time-invariant characteristics of schools that may be correlated both with school climate and student achievement.

In these models, our results remain largely unchanged (table A3). Students in the least safe schools exposed to violent crime in the week before the ELA test score 0.056 standard deviations lower than those exposed after. As for the other measures, results are not statistically significant, but point estimates are similar as our main specifications (–0.035 for disorder and –0.021 for sense of community). Taken together, these results support our finding that school climate matters for children exposed to violent crime, but we cannot completely rule out that other unobserved school-level factors might still be at play.

If violent crimes are more salient and the key source of stress for students and not simply capturing other things happening in the neighborhood, we should see little change in school performance after exposure to property crimes (for results of this falsification test, see table A4). Indeed, we find no evidence that exposure to property crime affects test scores, or that this effect varies with the climate of the school.

The primary results are estimated on a high poverty sample. To test the robustness of our findings we estimate the school climate specifications on the full sample of students. Overall, our conclusions are unchanged (table A5). Ex-

---

20. When we stratify the sample by school climate quartiles and race-ethnicity we are left with a very small number of observations for white and Asian students: forty for students who are white in quartile four schools in the safety measure, and forty-five for students who are Asian. In the most disorderly schools (quartile four), observations number 105 for students who are white and 134 for students who are Asian. Numbers are even smaller in the schools with a weak sense of community (quartile four): nineteen and twenty-seven for whites and Asians, respectively.

21. We find no statistically significant differences between students exposed to crime before the ELA exam attending schools in quartiles one to three and those exposed after. Tables available from authors.

posure to violent crime before the ELA test lowers test scores of students in schools deemed least safe by 0.04 standard deviations. This coefficient is smaller but within the confidence interval of the estimate for the high poverty sample. We also find that children exposed to neighborhood crime who attend schools that have a weak sense of community score 0.03 standard deviations lower in ELA (all significant at the 10 percent level).

Results by gender and race-ethnicity are also robust to using the full sample of students. Schools that are perceived as unsafe and having a weaker sense of community seem to exacerbate the negative effect of neighborhood crime on boys. Point estimates are smaller (−0.06 and −0.04, respectively) and significant at the 10 percent level only. As for race-ethnicity, results on the full sample are also consistent with the high poverty sample (see table B7 of the online appendix).[22]

Mathematics

So far we have only reported results for the ELA test because research shows the largest effects of community violence on reading and no effects on math (Sharkey et al. 2014; Schwartz et al. 2016). We also estimate our baseline model with math test scores as the outcome. The baseline specification—without stratifying the sample by school climate—shows no significant impact of crime exposure on math performance (table 2). Stratifying the sample by school climate quartile for each of the climate measures also yields no significant differences in test performance between students exposed to violent crime before the math test and students exposed after. That is, school climate does not moderate the effect of neighborhood violence on students' math test scores, providing further evidence that community violence tends to affect performance in reading but not math (table 5).

DISCUSSION

This article investigates the role of school climate on the relationship between exposure to neighborhood violence and academic achievement for middle school students (grades six through eight) in New York City public schools. To do so, we leverage several sources of administrative data that provide advantages for this kind of analysis. Most notably, by using data on the entire city public school system we are able to generate more precise estimates than most of the literature using survey data with much smaller samples. As a result, we are able to focus our attention on very specific windows of time around public school assessments, and to make comparisons among students living in individual blockfaces within the city. By combining multiple administrative datasets, including student records, incident records from the NYPD, and school climate surveys, we are able to make progress in understanding the mechanisms by which violence in the residential environment affects students' performance in school. Merging together multiple datasets that cover the entire city and all of its public schools allows for an analysis that would not be possible with any single source of data.

The results from our analysis provide a more nuanced picture of the impact of violence than shown by previous research. Overall, we find no significant acute effect of exposure to violence for the sample of sixth- to eighth-grade students in high poverty neighborhoods. This finding, however, masks the substantial variation in effects found in schools with different levels of disorder, safety, and sense of community. Schools with strong climates (across all dimensions—safety, disorder, and sense of community) and those with mixed climates (quartiles two and three) may insulate students from the negative effects of exposure to neighborhood violence. It follows that students ex-

---

22. We also test the sensitivity of results reported in the paper to opening the window of exposure. We estimated all baseline and subgroup models on the high poverty sample using a two-week and a one-month window of exposure. These results are also consistent with findings for the one-week window, albeit smaller in magnitude. Specifically, students exposed to violent crime two weeks before the ELA test attending the least safe schools score 0.04 standard deviations lower and those exposed in the month before the test score 0.024 standard deviations lower and 0.022 standard deviations lower in schools with weaker sense of community. Tables available from authors.

Table 5. Regression Results: MATH, Exposure to Neighborhood Violent Crime, and School Climate Quartile

	Safety		Disorder		Sense of Community	
DV: z-score MATH	(1)	(2)	(3)	(4)	(5)	(6)
Crime*Q1	0.005	0.006	−0.040	−0.034	−0.040	−0.037
	(0.055)	(0.049)	(0.046)	(0.042)	(0.078)	(0.069)
Crime*Q2	0.005	0.010	0.003	0.010	−0.026	−0.024
	(0.026)	(0.023)	(0.028)	(0.025)	(0.042)	(0.038)
Crime*Q3	−0.038	−0.017	−0.011	−0.000	0.018	0.032
	(0.024)	(0.022)	(0.022)	(0.022)	(0.023)	(0.022)
Crime*Q4	−0.004	−0.009	−0.027	−0.020	−0.033	−0.023
	(0.043)	(0.037)	(0.041)	(0.037)	(0.025)	(0.023)
Q1	0.349**	0.263**	0.565**	0.407**	0.568**	0.399**
	(0.072)	(0.057)	(0.073)	(0.063)	(0.081)	(0.063)
Q2	0.225**	0.175**	0.235**	0.167**	0.279**	0.226**
	(0.050)	(0.041)	(0.062)	(0.053)	(0.057)	(0.045)
Q3	0.068	0.046	0.056	0.043	0.129**	0.104**
	(0.050)	(0.040)	(0.057)	(0.050)	(0.037)	(0.029)
Student controls	Y	Y	Y	Y	Y	Y
Lagged test scores	N	Y	N	Y	N	Y
Observations	16,676	16,676	16,676	16,676	16,676	16,676
R^2	0.210	0.339	0.226	0.345	0.217	0.342

Source: Authors' calculations using NYPD complaint data and New York City public schools student-level administrative data, provided to New York University and Syracuse University by the New York City Department of Education.

Note: Standard errors in parentheses (clustered at the school level). Student controls include black, Asian, Hispanic, free and reduced-price lunch, special education, limited English proficiency, foreign born, home language not English, and over age for grade. All models include year and grade fixed effects, and an indicator for missing lagged test scores. Sample exclude students exposed both before the math test. Sample includes students in grades six through eight between academic year 2006–2007 and 2009–2010.

†$p < .1$; *$p < .05$; **$p < .01$

periencing decreases in ELA test scores after exposure to neighborhood violence are concentrated in schools with the weakest climates, particularly those perceived as the least safe. Specifically, students exposed to community violence before the test attending the least safe schools score 0.06 standard deviations lower, which amounts to 40 percent of the test score gap between poor and nonpoor students in our sample.[23] For these students, attending a school with a weak climate further increases their academic disadvantage.

The analyses by race-ethnicity and gender uncover that the effect of exposure to violence is particularly salient for boys and Hispanic students in schools deemed the least safe. This last finding is interesting in light of previous research that found no effect of neighborhood crime on the test performance of Hispanic students (Sharkey et al. 2014). Indeed, it seems that although the majority of Hispanic students attend schools with strong climates, those in schools with weak climates see large declines in achievement following exposure to violence.

23. The estimated test score gap between poor and nonpoor students in the full sample is 0.15 standard deviations.

Thus, the null average effect from previous studies obscured the finding that students in schools with weak climates may be particularly affected by neighborhood violent crime.

The magnitudes of the effects are significant. For example, a 0.10 standard deviation decrease in test scores for boys represents a 33 percent decline relative to the mean for boys in the sample. To put these numbers in context, the magnitude of this effect is comparable to the positive gains from school-level interventions such as class sizes (Chingos 2013).

We find no effects on math. This finding, while still puzzling, is not surprising. Previous work in New York City shows effects of neighborhood violence are concentrated on ELA scores (Sharkey et al. 2014; Schwartz et al. 2016). Differing psychological and cognitive processes may be involved in learning reading and math concepts, and these may be differentially affected by acute stress resulting from neighborhood violence. For example, Sharkey and his colleagues find that exposure to homicides is linked with lower attention and impulse control, which is especially important for reading instruction (Sharkey et al. 2012; Liew et al. 2008). Further, the development of language skills is more dependent on home factors, whereas math tends to be more influenced by school-level mechanisms (Bryk and Raudenbusch 1988).

We note a few key limitations in the empirical work. First, the estimation strategy provides strong identification of the acute effect of exposure to violence but does not provide evidence of whether or not this is a testing effect of it has long-term consequences for learning. Further, this article does not speak to the effects of repeated or cumulative exposure to neighborhood violence or how schools might respond. Understanding these longer-term effects may illuminate potential interventions aimed at children experiencing chronic exposure. That said, the acute effects are important, in and of themselves, due in part to the reliance on standardized tests for decisions about retention, high school admissions, or program participation for middle school students. Second, although we find no effect of exposure to violence on test scores for students at schools with strong or mixed climates, this does not imply that exposure to violence has no effect on these students. Exposure to violence may manifest in the lives of children in other ways that are not captured by test scores in the short run. Further work should investigate the effect on other outcomes, such as absenteeism, behavioral problems, or disciplinary referrals, to gain a broader perspective on how neighborhood violence affects students. Examining such outcomes would also provide insight into the mechanisms underlying the decreases in test scores for students in schools with weak climates.

Finally, more work could be done to unpack what is captured by our measures of school climate. For example, we are unable to say anything in this article about teacher quality or teacher experiences in these schools, and how their views and actions might shape school climate. As other articles in this issue suggest, the school environment is complex and factors such as teacher's views on issues like diversity and cultural competencies (Penner et al. 2019) or school organizations such as PTAs (Murray et al. 2019) might be important determinants of school climate. Further, although schools with weaker climates have more reported incidents of violence, school climate is more than a reflection of violence in the school or in the neighborhood. Our climate constructs capture overall perceptions of school climate, but we cannot fully measure what particular factors contribute to a stronger (or weaker) school climate.

In sum, although schools are unable to control the experiences students have beyond their walls, the climate within each school can play a role in helping students cope with external forces. This article provides suggestive evidence that many schools are safe havens for young people who live in dangerous neighborhoods, insulating them from the acute effect of exposure to violence on achievement. More research is needed to understand how schools successfully foster strong climates along multiple dimensions, to identify strategies to improving school climate, and to measure how changes in school climate affect other student outcomes.

Figure A1. Blockface Geography

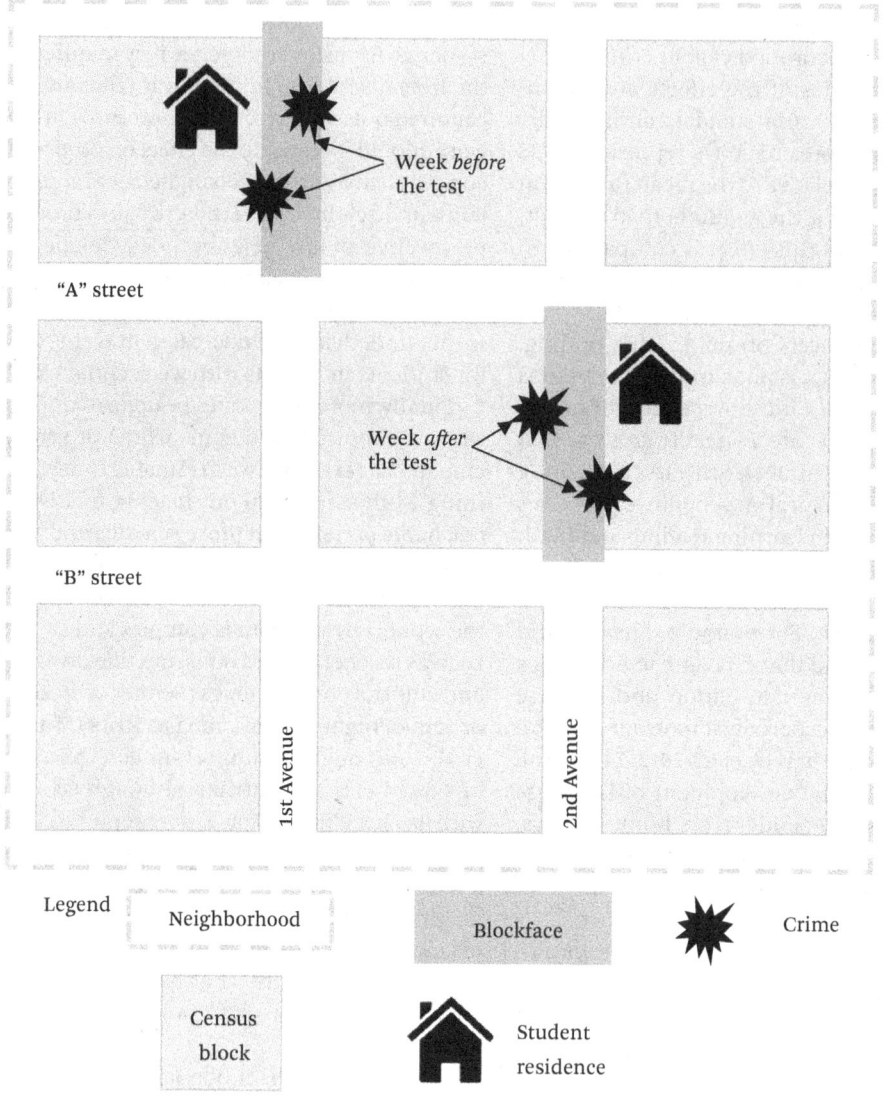

Source: Authors' compilation.
Note: Students living in the shaded parts of adjacent census blocks are as residing on the same blockface and would be coded as exposed to the same crimes.

Table A1. Response Rates, School Climate Questions

Year	Students	Mean
2007	141,897	0.52
2007	186,700	0.81
2009	181,936	0.79
2010	186,463	0.81

Source: Authors' calculations using data from the New York City Learning Environment Survey.
Note: Mean response rate indicates share of students with no missing responses on all seventeen questions used in the school climate scales.

Table A2. Student Characteristics by Exposure to Violent Crime, One-Week Window, High Poverty Sample

	ELA		MATH	
	Before	After	Before	After
Race-ethnicity				
Black	39.3	38.4	38.9	38.7
Hispanic	54.0	52.1	52.0	52.1
Asian	4.4	6.0	6.1	6.2
White	2.2	3.5	3.0	3.0
Gender				
Female	50.3	50.6	51.8	50.4
Poverty status				
Free or reduced-price lunch	94.9	93.9	94.7	94.6
Other demographics				
Foreign born	14.6	16.7	17.6	17.5
Special education	11.7	11.8	11.9	11.1
Limited English proficiency	11.5	11.6	13.3	14.1
Home language not English	43.8	46.0	45.9	46.0
Overage for grade	16.5	15.7	15.8	14.8
Observations	9,071	7,075	7,941	8,735
F-stat	1.40		0.77	
Prob>F	0.17		0.67	

Source: Authors' calculations using NYPD complaint data and New York City public schools student-level administrative data, provided to New York University and Syracuse University by the New York City Department of Education.
Note: Table includes column percentages. Variables included in F-test: black, Hispanic, Asian, female, free and reduced-price lunch participation, foreign born, special education, home language not English, limited English proficiency, overage for grade. Models include borough, grade, and year fixed effects. Standard errors are clustered at the school level. Sample includes students in grades six through eight between academic years 2006–2007 and 2009–2010.

Table A3. Robustness Test: ELA, School Climate Specification with School-Level Controls

	Safety		Disorder		Sense of Community	
DV: z-score ELA	(1)	(2)	(3)	(4)	(5)	(6)
Crime*Q1	−0.026	−0.018	0.009	0.021	−0.024	0.007
	(0.029)	(0.032)	(0.033)	(0.034)	(0.051)	(0.055)
Crime*Q2	0.029	0.025	0.004	−0.007	0.038	0.033
	(0.020)	(0.020)	(0.020)	(0.021)	(0.026)	(0.028)
Crime*Q3	0.004	−0.001	−0.005	−0.007	0.007	−0.009
	(0.016)	(0.018)	(0.014)	(0.016)	(0.016)	(0.018)
Crime*Q4	−0.055*	−0.056*	−0.043	−0.035	−0.026	−0.021
	(0.025)	(0.026)	(0.037)	(0.040)	(0.017)	(0.017)
Q1	0.129**		0.178**		0.165**	
	(0.034)		(0.043)		(0.046)	
Q2	0.011		0.093*		0.022	
	(0.027)		(0.037)		(0.028)	
Q3	−0.010		0.043		−0.018	
	(0.028)		(0.034)		(0.023)	
Student controls	Y	Y	Y	Y	Y	Y
Lagged test scores	Y	Y	Y	Y	Y	Y
School resources	Y	Y	Y	Y	Y	Y
School violence incidents	Y	Y	Y	Y	Y	Y
School FX	N	Y	N	Y	N	Y
Observations	15,032	15,032	15,032	15,032	15,032	15,032
R^2	0.467	0.500	0.467	0.500	0.467	0.500

Source: Authors' calculations using NYPD complaint data and New York City public schools student-level administrative data, provided to New York University and Syracuse University by the New York City Department of Education.

Note: Standard errors in parentheses (clustered at the school level). Student controls include black, Asian, Hispanic, free and reduced-price lunch, special education, limited English proficiency, foreign born, home language not English, and over age for grade. All models include grade and year fixed effects and an indicator for missing lagged test scores. School controls include natural log of per pupil spending in classroom instruction, leadership, attendance/outreach, drug prevention programs, counseling, school safety, and pupil teacher ratio. School violence rate per 1,000 students. All spending variables are inflation adjusted using the 2010 CPI. Sample includes students in grades six through eight, academic years 2006–07 and 2009–10.

†$p < .1$; *$p < .05$; **$p < .01$

Table A4. Falsification Test: ELA, Exposure to Property Crime and School Climate Quartile

DV: z-score ELA	Safety (1)	Disorder (2)	Sense of Community (3)
Crime*Q1	−0.001	−0.014	0.013
	(0.016)	(0.018)	(0.029)
Crime*Q2	−0.000	0.005	−0.002
	(0.008)	(0.008)	(0.011)
Crime*Q3	−0.002	−0.005	−0.007
	(0.009)	(0.008)	(0.009)
Crime*Q4	0.001	0.024	0.003
	(0.012)	(0.015)	(0.008)
Q1	0.185**	0.300**	0.250**
	(0.027)	(0.030)	(0.041)
Q2	0.080**	0.145**	0.104**
	(0.018)	(0.025)	(0.022)
Q3	0.022	0.069**	0.034*
	(0.018)	(0.023)	(0.016)
Student controls	Y	Y	Y
Lagged test scores	Y	Y	Y
Observations	66,626	66,626	66,626
R^2	0.482	0.485	0.483

Source: Authors' calculations using NYPD complaint data and New York City public schools student-level administrative data, provided to New York University and Syracuse University by the New York City Department of Education.

Note: Standard errors in parentheses (clustered at the school level). Student controls include: black, Asian, Hispanic, free and reduced-price lunch, special education, limited English proficiency, foreign born, home language not English, and over age for grade. All models include grade and year fixed effects, and an indicator for missing lagged test scores. Sample excludes students exposed both before and after the ELA test. Sample includes students in grades six through eight between academic years 2006–2007 and 2009–2010.

†$p < .1$; *$p < .05$; **$p < .01$

Table A5. Robustness Test: ELA, Exposure to Neighborhood Violence and School Climate Quartile, Full Sample

DV: z-score ELA	Safety		Disorder		Sense of Community	
	(1)	(2)	(3)	(4)	(5)	(6)
Crime*Q1	-0.053	-0.030	-0.033	0.003	-0.070	-0.032
	(0.038)	(0.028)	(0.039)	(0.030)	(0.056)	(0.048)
Crime*Q2	0.020	0.029	-0.009	0.004	0.011	0.022
	(0.024)	(0.018)	(0.025)	(0.018)	(0.030)	(0.022)
Crime*Q3	-0.013	-0.002	-0.007	-0.009	-0.003	0.011
	(0.022)	(0.016)	(0.017)	(0.013)	(0.021)	(0.016)
Crime*Q4	-0.046	-0.042+	-0.060	-0.020	-0.034+	-0.027+
	(0.029)	(0.022)	(0.039)	(0.031)	(0.020)	(0.015)
Q1	0.285**	0.157**	0.444**	0.229**	0.486**	0.243**
	(0.055)	(0.034)	(0.057)	(0.040)	(0.081)	(0.045)
Q2	0.067+	0.020	0.203**	0.116**	0.128**	0.051*
	(0.037)	(0.024)	(0.045)	(0.032)	(0.041)	(0.025)
Q3	-0.002	-0.010	0.065+	0.053+	0.015	-0.007
	(0.040)	(0.026)	(0.037)	(0.029)	(0.032)	(0.021)
Student controls	Y	Y	Y	Y	Y	Y
Lagged test scores	Y	Y	Y	Y	Y	Y
Observations	18,254	18,254	18,254	18,254	18,254	18,254
R^2	0.252	0.469	0.263	0.471	0.258	0.470

Source: Authors' calculations using NYPD complaint data and New York City public schools student-level administrative data, provided to New York University and Syracuse University by the New York City Department of Education.

Note: Standard errors in parentheses (clustered at the school level). Student controls include black, Asian, Hispanic, free and reduced-price lunch, special education, limited English proficiency, foreign born, home language not English, and over age for grade. All models include grade and year fixed effects, and an indicator for missing lagged test scores. Sample excludes students exposed both before and after the ELA test. Sample includes students in grades six through eight, academic years 2006–2007 and 2009–2010.

+$p < .1$; *$p < .05$; **$p < .01$

REFERENCES

Arcia, Emily. 2006. "Achievement and Enrollment Status of Suspended Students: Outcomes in a Large, Multicultural School District." *Education and Urban Society* 38(3): 359–69.

Arseneault, Louise, Lucy Bowes, and Sania Shakoor. 2010. "Bullying Victimization in Youths and Mental Health Problems: 'Much Ado About Nothing'?" *Psychological Medicine* 40(5): 717–29.

Bhatt, Rachana, and Tomeka Davis. 2016. "The Impact of Random Metal Detector Searches on Contraband Possession, and Feelings of Safety." *Educational Policy* 32(4): 1–29. DOI: 10.1177/0895904816673735.

Bowen, Natasha K., and Gary L Bowen. 1999. "Effects of Crime and Violence in Neighborhoods and Schools on the School Behavior and Performance of Adolescents." *Journal of Adolescent Research* 14(3): 319–42.

Bronfenbrenner, Urie. 2004. "Ecological Models of Human Development." In *Readings on the Development of Children*, 4th ed., edited by Mary Gauvain and Michael Cole. New York: Macmillan.

Bryk, Anthony S., and Stephen W. Raudenbush. 1988. "Toward a More Appropriate Conceptualization of Research on School Effects: A Three-Level Hierarchical Linear Model." *American Journal of Education* 97(1): 65–108.

Burdick-Will, Julia. 2013. "School Violent Crime and Academic Achievement in Chicago." *Sociology of Education* 86(4): 346–61.

Burdick-Will, Julia, Jens Ludwig, Stephen W. Raudenbush, Robert J. Sampson, Lisa Sanbonmatsu, and Patrick Sharkey. 2011. "Converging Evidence for Neighborhood Effects on Children's Test Scores: An Experimental, Quasi-Experimental, and Observational Comparison." In *Whither Opportunity? Rising Inequality, Schools, and Children's Life Chances*, edited by Greg J. Duncan and Richard J. Murnane. New York: Russell Sage Foundation.

Chen, Greg. 2007. "School Disorder and Student Achievement: A Study of New York City Elementary Schools." *Journal of School Violence* 6(1): 27–43.

Chingos, Matthew M. 2013. "Class Size and Student Outcomes: Research and Policy Implications." *Journal of Policy Analysis and Management* 32(2): 411–38.

Eccles, Jacquelynne S., and Robert W. Roeser. 2011. "School as Developmental Contexts During Adolescence." *Journal of Research on Adolescence* 21 (January): 225–241.

Grogger, Jeffrey. 1997. "Local Violence and Educational Attainment." *Journal of Human Resources* 21(4): 659–82.

Harding, David J. 2009. "Collateral Consequences of Violence in Disadvantaged Neighborhoods." *Social Forces* 88(2): 757–84.

Hu, Winnie. 2014. "A Brooklyn School's Curriculum Includes Ambition." *New York Times*, December 12.

Janosz, Michel, Isabelle Archambault, Linda S. Pagani, Sophie Pascal, Alexandre J. S. Morin, and François Bowen. 2008. "Are There Detrimental Effects of Witnessing School Violence in Early Adolescence?" *Journal of Adolescent Health* 43(6): 600–608.

Juvonen, Jaana, Yueyan Wang, and Guadalupe Espinoza. 2011. "Bullying Experiences and Compromised Academic Performance Across Middle School Grades." *Journal of Early Adolescence* 31(1): 152–73.

Kirk, David S. 2009. "Unraveling the Contextual Effects on Student Suspension and Juvenile Arrest: The Independent and Interdependent Influences of School, Neighborhood, and Family Social Controls." *Criminology* 47(2): 479–520.

Kraft, Matthew A., William H. Marinell, and Darrick Shen-Wei Yee. 2016. "School Organizational Contexts, Teacher Turnover, and Student Achievement: Evidence from Panel Data." *American Educational Research Journal* 53(5): 1411–49.

Lacoe, Johanna. 2015. "Unequally Safe: The Race Gap in School Safety." *Youth Violence and Juvenile Justice* 13(2): 143–68.

———. 2016. "Too Scared to Learn? The Academic Consequences of Feeling Unsafe at School." *Urban Education*. First published online, October 24, 2016. DOI: 10.1177/0042085916674059.

Lacoe, Johanna, and Mathew P. Steinberg. 2018. "Do Suspensions Affect Student Outcomes?" *Educational Evaluation and Policy Analysis*. First published online, August 17, 2018. DOI: 10.3102/0162373718794897.

Liew, Jeffrey, Erin M. McTigue, Lisa Barrois, and Jan N. Hughes. 2008. "Adaptive and Effortful Control and Academic Self-Efficacy Beliefs on Achievement: A Longitudinal Study of 1st Through 3rd Graders." *Early Childhood Research Quarterly* 23(4): 515–26.

Mateu-Gelabert, Pedro, and Howard Lune. 2003.

"School Violence: The Bidirectional Conflict Flow between Neighborhood and School." *City & Community* 2(4): 353–69.

Murray, Brittany, Thurston Domina, Linda Renzulli, and Rebecca Boylan. 2019. "Civil Society Goes to School: Parent-Teacher Associations and the Equality of Educational Opportunity." *RSF: The Russell Sage Foundation Journal of the Social Sciences* 5(3): 41–64. DOI: 10.7758/RSF.2019.5.3.03.

Patton, Desmond Upton, Michael E. Woolley, and Jun Sung Hong. 2012. "Exposure to Violence, Student Fear, and Low Academic Achievement: African American Males in the Critical Transition to High School." *Children and Youth Services Review* 34(2): 388–95.

Penner, Emily K., Jane Rochmes, Jing Liu, Sabrina Solanki, and Susanna Loeb. 2019. "Differing Views of Equity: How Prospective Educators Perceive Their Role in Closing Achievement Gaps." *RSF: The Russell Sage Foundation Journal of the Social Sciences* 5(3): 103–27. DOI: 10.7758/RSF.2019.5.3.06.

Rasmussen, Andrew, Mark S. Aber, and Arvinkumar Bhana. 2004. "Adolescent Coping and Neighborhood Violence: Perceptions, Exposure, and Urban Youth's Efforts to Deal with Danger." *American Journal of Community Psychology* 33(1–2): 61–75.

Rausch, M. Karega, and Russell Skiba. 2004. "Unplanned Outcomes: Suspensions and Expulsions in Indiana." *Education Policy Briefs* 2(2): 1–7.

Rendón, Maria G. 2014. "Caught Up": How Urban Violence and Peer Ties Contribute to High School Noncompletion." *Social Problems* 61(1): 61–82.

Schwartz, Amy Ellen, Agustina Laurito, Johanna Lacoe, Patrick Sharkey, and Ingrid Gould Ellen. 2016. "The Academic Effects of Chronic Exposure to Neighborhood Violence." Maxwell School working paper no. 195. Syracuse, N.Y.: Syracuse University, Center for Policy Research.

Sharkey, Patrick. 2010. "The Acute Effect of Local Homicides on Children's Cognitive Performance." *Proceedings of the National Academy of Sciences*, 107(26): 11733–38

Sharkey, Patrick, Amy Ellen Schwartz, Ingrid Gould Ellen, and Johanna Lacoe. 2014. "High Stakes in the Classroom, High Stakes on the Street: The Effects of Community Violence on Students' Standardized Test Performance." *Sociological Science* 1(14): 199–220.

Sharkey, Patrick, Nicole Tirado-Strayer, Andrew V. Papachristos, and C. Cybele Raver. 2012. "The Effect of Local Violence on Children's Attention and Impulse Control." *American Journal of Public Health* 102(12): 2287–93.

Thapa, Amrit, Jonathan Cohen, Shawn Guffey, and Ann Higgins-D'Alessandro. 2013. "A Review of School Climate Research." *Review of Educational Research* 83(3): 357–85.

Theriot, Matthew T. 2009. "School Resource Officers and the Criminalization of Student Behavior." *Journal of Criminal Justice* 37(3): 280–87.

Wang, Ming-Te, and Rebecca Holcombe. 2010. "Adolescents' Perceptions of School Environment, Engagement, and Academic Achievement in Middle School." *American Educational Research Journal* 47(3): 633–62.